dedicated to my beloved parents
dr. b.v. raman
smt. rajeswari raman
who have made me what I am today

CONTENTS

Preface

This book is an inspired collection of writings that exposes the fraud of "scientific temper" in its attacks on Astrology. Astrology has always had its critics— criticism is indeed healthy for the growth and proper understanding of any science. But unfair, unjust criticism made up of distortions, lies and bias must be forcefully met and nipped in the bud. Otherwise, it can be a dangerous enemy of all honest intellectual inquiry and examination. This volume is an attempt at meeting unfair criticism.

I thank all the thinkers from various sources from whom I have drawn my ideas and inspiration. I thank Mr. Anand R. Kundaji of the Indian Institute of World Culture, Bangalore who has been extremely helpful in securing me some vital information found in this book and also my brother Mr. B. Niranjan Babu but for whose dedicated and whole-hearted help the production of this volume would not have been so competently executed.

Bangalore **GAYATRI DEVI VASUDEV**

24.12.1989

INTRODUCTION

Today the age of science is full upon us. Apart from the benefits conferred on mankind to make material life more comfortable, science is collaborating in massacres and today, in this age of scientific thought we stand on the brink of scientific destruction. Social ill-health that we see in our country - alcoholism, violent, crimes, accidents, suicide, terrorism and disregard for ethical principles even in the highest quarters - is the product of the age of science.

The tentacles of science threaten us as it claims truth is its monopoly and it fosters materialism! Over-reliance on the method of science as the sole font of valid knowledge has blinded a certain section of educated persons to the possible alternatives employed in ancient India to discover disciplines like Astrology, Yoga, Vedanta etc.

Today, the term science is being abused by some so-called 'men of science'. What they need to be told is that science needs Astrology to improve and harmonize the life of man. Science has been measuring the speed of falling stones and peering through lenses, Yet it has no explanation for gravity. The scientist does not know the meaning of gravity as such although he will rush to identify its manifestations. The trouble is some men of certain so-called recognised sciences have taken upon themselves the role of social reformers depending upon the official recognition and state patronage their discipline currently enjoys. They hasten at every opportunity to denigrate Astrology. Their so-called scientific approach is nothing but a subterfuge, meant to confuse and mislead the common man. Their prejudice against Astrology rests more on a misconception of what science is than on a true understanding of the basics of Astrology. What they have not realized is that the techniques of objectivity that distinguish science are already in trouble in the areas of relativity and particle physics. It is now being discovered, to the chagrin of the rigid orthodox scientist, that the universe is non-material and non-rational. The first step for these self-styled men of scientific temper is to free themselves from a misconception of Astrology and to be clear about the definition of science, of the methods of science.

We commend to the attention of our pseudo-scientists who denigrate Astrology, what the famous Australian neurologist and Nobel Laureate Sir Eccles says viz., "This is an age more beset by superstition than any other age and the worst superstition is that materialistic science can explain all things. The materialists have had their long innings of arrogance. Their beliefs are worn out. They land nowhere. Materialism gives you a hopeless empty life, one without values."

The aim of science is truth, not running down branches of knowledge like Astrology. Prejudice is no sign, however, of a true scientific mind and prejudice is what sticks out in attacks against Astrology.

Criticism against Astrology has always been from a standpoint of ignorance. A careful review of some of the most vociferous critics and their antics will reveal a frightening mixture of both lack of a knowledge of what science is and what Astrology is. How else can one describe critics who tear a handful of predictions out of context and brand them as failures and proceed to say, that Astrology therefore is not a science? How else can one explain the obstinate refusal of critics to look at hundreds of correct predictions, some of them, for instance so remarkably accurate as of the 1975 Emergency made months before in the pages of THE ASTROLOGICAL MAGAZINE, and their mischievous libel that it had not been predicted at all. Show us one discipline where there is not 100 percent success as critics of Astrology demand, but even a mere 50 percent success. Incidentally Astrology can boast of 65 to 70 percent success in the hands of qualified men and women. For some of the western scientists who claim to have tested Astrology, Astrology means only the Sun-sign and the Sun-sign forecasts published in the media. They equate the entire subject of Astrology with the Sun-sign readings and betray colossal ignorance of this systematized knowledge, namely, Jyotisha developed in ancient India thousands of years ago.

What is distressingly unfortunate is that some of our scientists and media persons imitate western thinking in the name of modernism, impervious to and ignoring their own great heritage.

The so called men of 'scientific temper' irresponsibly play with young people's minds and lead them away from the spirit of scientific enquiry by peddling neo-superstition as scientific truth before them. The consequences of such intellectual dishonesty can only be disastrous on young minds in their formative age.

These pseudo-scientists indulge in nit-picking all the time. They have developed the knack of quoting, out of context, one or two isolated predictions that may have gone slightly off the mark and rushing to the press to proclaim Astrology is therefore not science.

Proclamations, even if endorsed by the highest authority of the land, do not make up science. If the yardstick of hundred percent accuracy is applied to other disciplines, then SROSS-I and its miserable end (24-3-1987) and the fate of ASLV-D2 (13-7-1988) can only be described as the greatest science hoax of the century. In fact these failures of science have only confirmed astrological axioms. Space science and meteorological failures costing crores of rupees are indulgently overlooked by the same critics which proves they have no sense of science or fairplay. They dare not criticise such colossal failures, because if they do, they must pay the price of forfeiting their official positions. With Astrology, it is not that way. Astrology has no godfather in the governmental patronage which these other 'sciences' enjoy.

The material provided in these pages is from different sources. Some of it embodies my own painful experience with so-called men of science and the highly confused 'rationalists'. Some of it is from genuine men of science. Part of it is from some of the greatest thinkers we have had in our country in the past. But all of it is fact. No concocted fiction like some of the rationlists have done in their own books and Sunday supplement-articles decrying Astrology.

The loudest critics of Astrology in our own country have, as far as I have known, not shown any trace of the spirit of science in their obsessive attacks against Astrology. Their "facts" have been cooked up; and their language undignified. This has not hurt Astrology one wee bit. But the nuisance has to be checked. And these critics must be reminded of an Arab proverb which says "You can fool some people for all time, you can fool all people for some time, but you can't fool all people for all time".

I only hope that after reading these pages you realise what a big fraud the critics of Astrology are indulging in by their antics. I also hope you will appreciate the ancient heritage we have in Astrology and learn to question the lies critics try to spread against it. The best way we can combat these lies is to understand Astrology properly starting from its basics. Astrology is a *Vedanga* and therefore *Sat*. It will always remain for ***Truth is***. It has survived worse attacks in the past and wherever there are true men of science who respect truth, Astrology will always be respected.

In the opinion of the famous psycho-analyst Carl Jung "Western civilisation by ignoring Astrology gains little and may be losing much" by what he calls "the contemptible treatment and defamation of an ancient art which defied a reasonable explanation and after 200 years of intensive scientific progress we can risk testing them in the light of modern truths."

Gayatri Devi Vasudev B.Sc., LL.B.

Bangalore

24-12-1989

NEHRU WANTED RAJIV'S HOROSCOPE

When Rajiv Gandhi was born, grandpa Jawaharlal Nehru wrote to Indira Gandhi asking her to get a "proper horoscope made by a competent" person.

Writing to his sister Vijayalaxmi Pandit on August 29, 1944, Nehru said: "In my letter to Indira, I suggested to her to ask you to get a proper horoscope made by a competent person. Such permanent records as the date and time of birth are desirable. As for the time, I suppose the proper time should be mentioned and not the artificial time which is being used now. War time is at least an hour ahead of the normal time."

When astrologers speculated about Mr. Nehru's birth time, his private secretary wrote on June 19, 1962 to the editor of THE ASTROLOGICAL MAGAZINE, Bangalore, stating:

"The Prime Minister has asked me to write to you that, so far as he knows, the time of his birth was 11.30 p.m. on November, 1889."

Astrologers have been speculating about the birth time of Mr. Rajiv Gandhi in the columns of THE ASTROLOGICAL MAGAZINE since his entry into politics. - UNI

CHAPTER ONE

WHY SINGLE OUT ASTROLOGY—I

Gayatri Devi Vasudev

Computer software has ushered in a revolution in the intellectual world. Medical diagnosis, legal information, accounts and auditing, business management and a variety of other uses have been ascribed to the computer with considerable success. Astrological charts, known as horoscopes, have also been possible in a matter of minutes using computers. There is hardly any area of intellectual activity that has not been explored by computer technology.

Horoscope casting (provided the chart is cast in its entirety which includes Rasi, Navamsa, Shadvargas and/or Shodasavargas, Dasa-balance as well as Ashtakavarga charts) done manually is a tedious job but done by a competent person is always accurate. What the computer does is to practically eliminate the labour involved and save on time. This is about all that a computer can do in the field of Astrology. Its role is limited only to the calculational or computational part. To the conscientious astrologer, the utility of the computer stops here.

What then does one have to say on computer forecasts? Simply this. Exit the astrologer and enter the mercenary, enter the peddler, enter the businessman. Computer forecasts are absolutely unreliable. The blame here must not unfairly be laid at the door of Astrology or the astrologer but at the doorstep of the tribe of men who will exploit human weaknesses.

This tribe is active not only in Astrology but also among educationalists (otherwise why would marks-cards' scandals erupt periodically or question papers leak out), medical fraternity (trade in human spare-parts is reported all the time), engineering, legal and every other field of professional activity.

So, the next time someone advertises a computer forecast we can surely conclude it is a fraud as in the case of education, medicine etc., where too, unscrupulous elements exist in larger numbers but under the more dangerous cloak offered by official recognition and state patronage.

Patients die under medical care and some even worse, get incapacitated for life due to indifferent and negligent medical treatment. Brilliant students find their academic future jeopardised and even destroyed by avaricious dons who indulge not only in favouritism but also sell success in examinations for monetary and other considerations. Such things happen in every profession and to single out Astrology only as fraud is to display an obsessive prejudice against it.

When two people marry, sometimes the doctors are approached and if the blood groups are not agreeable, the match may be set aside. Similarly young men and women with serious cardiac conditions are advised against marriage.

Does one therefore say that marriages are destroyed thereby and hell created for the young people. Most certainly not. The same logic applies to horoscope matching. When the disparities between two charts are high the match is not recommended. Here the role of Astrology is preventive. Future unhappiness is avoided. Likewise where a chart is said to have *kuja dosha*, it means chances of strife in marriage are more. But by pairing such a horoscope with one containing counter-balancing features marital harmony can be achieved. Astrology was formulated by the ancient Rishis of India and with the specific purpose of ensuring Loka Kalyana or the welfare of the largest number. Only a short-sighted view and an inability to understand men and matters can conclude that Astrology is fraud. No one who has had enough experience of life, of inter-relationships between members of a family, of human limitations and the weaknesses of the mind will ever condemn Astrology.

Some critics class Astrology with the evils of dowry. This is the ultimate in infantile logistics and to be strongly condemned. The motive in dowry is greed. The intention of horoscopic matching is the total welfare of all concerned. One who cannot distinguish this simple difference between the two is quite incapable of appreciating the nuances of Astrology.

Astrology is a preventive measure and the very anti-thesis of the adage 'ignorance is bliss'. Do schools and IITs admit mentally retarded pupils on their rolls? If they do not, can you describe it as injustice and of labelling the mentally retarded as misfits. Here it is only a perception of the fact of the intellectual abilities of the individual that is being made and not discrimination. So also in Astrology, when a chart is described as having some blemish, all that is being done is cautioning the parents that certain precautions must be taken while matching so that the girl or boy may be happy. Otherwise, it would be like justifying a heart patient's eating cholesterol rich foods and arguing that if he is not given fat-rich foods he is being discriminated against. How unreasonable prejudice can make one is evident from this comparison?

The favourite argument of some critics of Astrology is that a negative forecast to someone led him to commit suicide. Incidentally this was due to a computer forecast. A computer is a mechanical thing and with no ability to judge human nature. That is why a computer forecast is not reliable. But no competent human astrologer would have made this kind of forecast. So why blame Astrology for this. Blame the man peddling such software.

It is common knowledge that indiscreet medical diagnosis often has had far reaching dangerous consequences. As a result couples have divorced, young men and women told by doctors they have terminal illnesses have killed themselves, wrong SD tests have led women to abort foetuses prematurely and so on. The list of tragedies due to such diagnoses is endless.

Now take the legal profession. Instead of counselling warring couples to reorganise their marriages, lawyers have prompted their trusting clients to file divorce-suits and destroyed thereby, innumerable marriages. Not only that, children of such legally invalidated marriages have been shuffled from parent to parent thereby damaging forever their growing minds with the idea that adjustment between family members is impossible. Later when such children grow up, the first solution they seek when emotionally low is in the courts perpetuating thereby a death blow to the very foundations of the institution of marriage. Or, where differences erupt between collaterals, lawyers are the first to advise partition of not only property but also of human feeling. Does no critic of Astrology have the guts to point this out?

I know of whole families, generations of them, living in hate simply because of ill-advised litigation relating to joint families. In one case a young man wrote to me saying his wife had left him following some tension. She had taken away their 6-month child with her. The young man wanted to know if his marriage would get re-sorted. After a look at the 2 charts I told him, his wife was basically a nice person, an extrovert and fond of friends. The marriage itself was safe and after a few months, he would be reunited with her. He then told me he had consulted his lawyer friends and one of them had said he could divorce his wife on the ground of adultery by carefully using the fact she was an extrovert. I told him this was unfair and her own chart showed she was a faithful wife and a little persuasion from a common friend would help. About 6 months later, he wrote to say they were now living together and he had set aside the lawyer's advice and gone by astrological counselling.

Can one therefore call jurisprudence a fraud?

You can go on and on in this refrain taking every single profession under the sun and you will be shocked by the negative side that every profession has to it. But the point here is, I repeat, why single out Astrology? The arguments against Astrology speak of an obsession, may be because of some personal experience, but that is no valid argument against Astrology.

The attacks on Astrology are both ill-conceived and highly biased. The critics show by their arguments not only their utter ignorance of the basics of the science of Astrology but also an absence of an open mind which is the hallmark of a true thinker and intellectual.

Astrology In Moscow

By Bill Keller

Astrology is not taboo in Soviet Russia. Sophisticated Muscovites swap astrological signs at parties. Horoscopes are a hot item in the weekly public market. Young engineers devote their free time for running astrological computer programmes.

In a one-room clinic a few paces from Moscow's most popular pedestrian mall, Dzhuna Davitashvili, celebrity psychic healer, gesticulates over the head of a deaf and blind man, as if pulling invisible weeds from his cranium.

The criticism against Astrology by so-called rationalists (which term includes some officially designated scientists as well) proceeds from a point of ignorance. In the first place, it is due to an absence of knowledge of even the fundamentals of the science. The second, and this is more serious, is a mistaken belief that anything that is beyond the known laws of science is not science at all. *What such critics forget is science, at any point of time, is both incomplete and inconsistent.* Where a fact or a phenomena keeps occurring but there is no explanation, only a fool would dismiss the fact itself. A true scientist, in contrast, would try to expand the frontiers of science by hard work and study, investigating into the heart of the phenomena.

No sane man with even an inkling of scientific temper will shut his eyes off to phenomena which he cannot explain. Newton, talking of gravitation, said "Action at a distance can only be described; it cannot be explained." Gravitation

> Watched by a rapt crowd, she works unself-consciously, chattering about the hundreds of people, high and low, who flock to her for a sample of the healing touch she calls Effect D, for Dzhuna.
>
> In the United States, land of all faiths, people laugh at Nancy Reagan for consulting an astrologer. But in the Soviet Union, land of scientific materialism, Dzhuna Davitashvili has a state business license, an honored spot on the Soviet Peace Committee and a coterie of friends that includes scientists, artists, journalists and intellectuals.
>
> Horoscopes, folk medicine, psychic healing and all manner of mysticism occupy a prominent place in Soviet society.

and its laws are known to everyone but no one knows why gravity exists, why celestial bodies with mass have the property of gravitation. Anyone who says that there is no way to explain the role of planets in human destiny and thinks that this is a valid argument against Astrology is fooling no one but himself. In science, facts precede theories. Apples fall to the ground; so do material objects and unsupported bodies. Taking this fact into account Newton began his investigations and came up with the law of gravitation. He attributed gravitation to the forces of mutual attraction between material objects. Later, when Einstein came on the scene he explained the same phenomenon as due to the curvature of space in the neighborhood of the material object. Both were great scientists. Yet each had his own theory which the respective contemporary scientific community accepted. How can the same phenomena have two divergent scientific explanations? Both may be wrong, or, one may be right.

"It is our secret silliness", said the wife of a government official, who nonetheless noted that as soon as Mikhail S. Gorbachev became the Soviet leader, she looked up his sign. He is a Pisces.

"Leave Nancy Reagan alone," the woman admonished.

Except in the unlikely event that some Kremlin counterpart of Donald T.Regan writes a tell-all book, it may never be known whether astral omens guide Soviet affairs of state. Mr. Regan, the former White House Chief of staff, says that has sometimes been the case in the Regan family.

Dzhuna Davitashvili, who prefers to go by the personal name she gave herself because "Yevgenia" seemed inadequate to her gift, reputedly was summoned to the bedside of

Only time and another more brilliant explanation from another scientist can tell. But the facts which these theories seek to explain are beyond doubt. If they had not existed, no one would have bothered to find out why they happened at all. This brings us to the crucial truth that the function of science is not to ask hypothetical questions but to explain admitted facts. **Do those who question Astrology accept the facts put forth by the astrologer?** If not, they have no business to waste his time with their idle questions. As a scientist in his own right, he has every right to reject the idle queries of the prejudiced critic.

Swami Abhedananda, a fire-brand brother-monk of Swami Vivekananda, would, talking of Astrology, tell his talented American audiences "So the study of this science is beneficial to mankind and for that reason I thought that I would give you an idea and open your views and your minds to the universal laws and the highest

Leonid I. Brezhnev when he was slipping beyond the help of conventional medicine. Dzhuna carefully does not deny this report.

Whatever Mr. Gorbachev and his wife, Raisa, make of the occult sciences, his constituents seem to feel that such arcana explain at least as much about life as Marx and Lenin ever did. Sophisticated Muscovites swap astrological signs at dinner parties, horoscopes are a hot item at the weekly public market in Izmailovo Park, and at one Moscow scientific institute a young engineer says he and his friends spend most of their free time running astrological computer programs for themselves and friends.

spiritual truths which are hidden behind the surface of the phenomenal world... After studying this you may become more superstitious and you may feel you are like a slave to the physical conditions of this planetary influence, but Vedanta teaches the will of the human-beings is all powerful, and if you hold the thought and bring out the soul's power, you will be able to overcome all these natural influences... That is also taught in our country (in India). If an astrologer would cast your horoscope, he would tell you, 'these are the conditions but there is the way out of it, and you can overcome these conditions by performing the spiritual practices or observing the spiritual laws."

Swami Abhedananda would go on "In this age of skepticism and agnosticism we may laugh at the claims of the science of true astronomy, but it is certainly a study of the power fascination which it has extended over the greatest men through 7000 to 8000 years, and a vast number

> A Moscow based New Yorker was astonished recently when a renowned physicist who had received permission to emigrate to the United States asked, as a parting favour, advice on where to get his horoscope done in New York.
>
> Oleg, 49, an astrology buff encountered Thursday on the Arbat mall around the corner from Dzhuna's studio professed to have retired a few years ago after winning about $1,50,000 in the state lottery using a system dictated by the stars and planets. He said he was delighted to hear on a Voice of America radio broadcast that Mrs. Reagan shared his interest....

of authenticated fulfilment of prophecies by astrologers which have been handed down through generations will prove that there is some underlying truth at the bottom of its claims."

In fact, it is childish for an adult to rave and rant about a subject about which he knows nothing. Most of these rationalists are obscurantists who will refuse to see anything that is beyond their individual power of comprehension. This is very tragic indeed for science cannot be structured to fit into the limited brain-corridors of a handful of confused individuals. However, we must, when relating to such men remember they are very much human and when their passions are excited, they may go off at a tangent and believe their personal prejudices define the ultimate boundaries of science.

Although astrology is officially frowned upon in the Soviet Encyclopedia as a "false science", scholarly works have been devoted to such subjects as the healing properties of mumiyo, a tar-like resin collected from the places wounded animals go to die.

Parapsychology is accorded serious discussion in the Soviet Academy of Sciences. When Soviet newspapers or television feature practitioners such as Dzhuna, as the hip late-night program "Vzglyad" did recently, there is nary a hint of smugness . . .

Her forecast is bright: "Just see what kind of friendship will blossom between Reagan and Gorbachev. They will be like brothers. That's what the stars show me".
NYTS

*Courtesy : **NagpurTimes** (29.5.88)*

CHAPTER TWO

WHY SINGLE OUT ASTROLOGY—II

Gayatri Devi Vasudev

Simple Truths about Astrology are being confirmed by recent findings by scientists in the West.

In Astrology, the Moon is said to rule the mind and described as *manahkaraka.* Afflictions to the Moon give rise to various kinds of mental characteristics. The Moon with Venus makes one pleasant, friendly, fond of ease. The Moon with Mars gives an aggressive nature, restless and sometimes, dictatorial. It also makes one intolerant of others' views. Instead of Mars if we substitute Jupiter we have a benign, tolerant, expansive personality, balanced in outlook. The Moon and Saturn together make one rigid in outlook, over-cautious and pessimistic.

Scientists in the West have now confirmed the role of the Moon in defining mental states. And they offer an explanation as well.

The earth is made up of about 80 percent water and 20 percent inorganic matter. When the Sun and the Moon exert their combined pull on the earth there are high tides. When the combined pull of the Sun and the Moon is low, there are low tides. The joint pull of the Sun and the Moon is maximum when they are moving towards a conjunction (0^0). When the two are 90° apart, the combined influence of their gravitational fields is lowest and this acting on the watery surfaces of the ocean leads to low tides. In astrological language the 180° position of the Sun and the Moon is called *Pournami* and the 0° position of the two is called *Amavasya.* Like-wise when the distance between the two is 90°, astrologically it is called *Ashtami,* and like the watery surfaces the fluids in the human body are also in a state of relative rest. That is why during Ashtami medication is advised by the ancients as per the dictum *Ashtami vyadhinasini.* During the conjunction and opposition of the Sun and the Moon the oceanic surfaces are subjected to a mighty pull and so, rise up in high tides. The composition of the human body is similiar to the earth - 80 percent fluid. About these periods, the brain fluid encased in a tough case, the skull, is also subjected to the combined gravitational pull of the luminaries. As a result it is thrown into turbulence within the walls of the skull leading to tension and impaired judgment. That is why about these two periods there is an increased incidence of family tensions, accidents, crime.

Jyotisha Sastra which is loosely translated as Astrology is a study of the correlations of the planetary positions and terrestrial phenomena. The word planet is a misfit and the right word would be *graha.* Like *Dharma, graha,* has no proper English equivalent.

There are 9 *grahas* of importance and the mutual juxtapositions of these planets at birth carry the blue-print of an individual's future.

The ancients knew that there were countless celestial bodies in the heavens but they pitched on to only 9, known as Navagrahas, as influencing life on earth. They addressed God or the Cosmic Being as *Akhilanda Koti Brahmanda Nayaka* meaning 'Lord or Master of infinite crores of *Brahmandas* or Cosmic Eggs'. This expression alone is evidence of the fact that the ancients knew of the existence of *grahas*, other than the Navagrahas, but which they did not deem necessary for analysing birth-charts.

A *graha* may be described as not only a material body with a field of force of its own but also as a geometric point with a field of force. In this respect, not only Mars, Venus, Jupiter, Saturn, Mercury but also the Sun and the Moon are *grahas*. Rahu and Ketu, the points of intersection of the ecliptic and the Moon's orbit round the earth are also included in the Navagrahas.

A question often asked is why not include the now discovered trans-saturnine planets— Pluto, Neptune and Uranus in the scheme of Jyotisha. As I have said earlier only 9 *grahas* were considered important and others rejected for astrological purposes. Therefore, the question itself is redundant. The mere fact that they were discovered recently cannot imply they were not known to our ancients. Only our ancients did not consider them important enough.

Recent findings now tell us how these trans-saturnine planets are dissimilar from the *grahas* recognised in Jyotisha. A zodiac is defined as a belt extending to 9 degrees on either side of the ecliptic over which the planets *(grahas)* are said to move. This belt therefore has a latitudinal limit of about 10 degrees, north or south. Pluto's orbit is inclined 17° to the ecliptic. Therefore, how can anyone include Pluto in the Navagrahas (confined to a belt of 9° on either side of the ecliptic) when Pluto is orbiting outside the zodiac. The latitude of none of the Navagrahas exceeds 7 degrees. Perhaps this could be why Pluto was not included amongst the Navagrahas. It is also believed by modern astronomers that taking into account Pluto's high orbital inclination and eccentricity, its small mass and other properties that it may not be a planet at all but only an escaped satellite of Neptune. It is possible, in future, astronomers will come up with facts justifying the exclusion of Neputne and Uranus from the Navagraha scheme. But until then let us bear in mind that **absence of evidence is not evidence of absence (of proof).** A Russian scientist Prof. A.L. Chizevskiy (1892-1964) found there was a correlation between sunspot activity and human affairs. As a result he founded "heliobiology", which in our language is Jyotisha.

The Soviet scientist V. Desyatov relates suicides and automobile accidents to solar flares. Every time there is a peak in solar flares, suicides go up by a factor of four on the following day.

Solar activity occurs in 11 years cycles with a maxima and minima every 5 1/2 years. The geocentric period of Jupiter is also a 11-year cycle. This way a correlation between Jupiter and mundane events can also be established.

There are hundreds of astrological dicta that work in actual practice. Anyone can verify for himself these astrological dicta. ,Now, where are these dicta to be found?

The oldest known work and which is popularly relied upon is *Brihat Parasara Hora*, dating back to the *Pre-Mahabharata* period. Dicta found in this work are astrological dicta and anyone keen on investigating into the truth of Astrology must experiment on these.

Some critics of Astrology very naively advance the argument that all buses which start in Rahukalam do not meet with accidents and therefore Astrology is nonsense. Whoever said this belief has an astrological background? Let those critics give us the reference of the work that carries this pseudo-astrological enunciation. This is not an astrological dictum at all and is as true or false as the belief that all men who were Gandhi topies are all honest or plain rogues.

More important, anyone who is keen on testing astrological laws must know the laws in the first place. Without knowing that if one goes on making up something and then proves it wrong, what has that to do with Astrology? It proves nothing against Astrology. All that it proves is the ignorance of the one airing these non-existent rules. **And some 'scientists' and rationalists are doing just that.**

Certain stars such as Jyeshta, Moola etc. are classified as not good and many critics pounce on this to attack Astrology. In order to understand this classification we have to start at the very beginning. This classification is of relevance only at the time of matching charts for marriage. And the part played by this classification in the total process of matching is a mere 2 to 4 percent. Further, the blemish does not extend to the entire Nakshatra. A constellation is 13^0 20' of arc and is divided into 4 equal parts, each of 3^0 20' duration. Each arc of 3^0 20' is called a *pada*. Only certain *padas* of certain Nakshatras are said to be blemished. The following *padas* of the following Nakshatras come under this rule:

Moola (1st *pada*) : Aslesha (1st *pada*)

Jyeshta (1st *pada*) : Visakha (4th *pada*)

And the blemish is not absolute. Where the other party's chart has neutralizing influences, it loses its sting. This is the purpose of matching charts.

Kuta agreement also comes in for attack. Many people mistakenly believe that if Kuta agreement is lacking and a count of less than 18 against 36.5 is obtained, the match is best dropped. This test of Kuta agreement is only one of 8 factors considered while matching for marriages. Not all these factors are of equal importance. Dosha Samya or balancing of afflictions in the 2 charts is second only to an approximate estimate of longevity in the 2 charts. The Kuta test is only about 10 to 12 percent of the total matching process. Most critics of astrological matching of charts are blissfully unaware of these facts.

While testing horoscopes for marriage, an overall assessment of health is also important. In the chart of an energetic young man brought to me by my friend for his daughter, I found material prosperity was good. But Venus, who has an important say in matters relating to marriage, had two malefics in the 7th from it. This meant, unless there were countering features in the girl's chart, conjugal life would be adversely afflicted and perhaps, even denied. I found no such features in the girl's chart. However, my friend was swayed by other considerations and went ahead with the marriage. Ten days after the marriage he came running to me saying that the girl had found the boy incapable of conjugal life. This is the kind of tragedy astrological counselling can avert.

If horoscopes are matched only on the basis of *gunas* by some astrologers, then there is nothing to defend except to say they are doing disser-

Financial Astrology Popular in Tokyo

Tokyo: Ask some Tokyo currency dealers what the US dollar is going to do next and they will reply with conviction: Heaven knows.

Faced with the task of a second-guessing the financial markets, some dealers in Tokyo are turning increasingly to the stars to guide their decisions on when to buy and sell.

A Japanese bank specialist on economic fundamentals analysis for foreign exchange rates said his department used financial Astrology to predict currency fluctuation.

vice to Astrology. But every profession has its quota of misfits and incompetents and for this reason can we dismiss the discipline itself as nonsense? If this tendency is more apparent amongst astrologers, it is only because the media plays it up. Otherwise let people investigate into the tragedies wrought by medical and legal men as well as educationalists and they will be appalled at the high incidence in these areas.

A horoscope is a guide to abilities and drawbacks. Irrespective of whether one is male or female, the picture that a horoscope paints is the true picture of an individual. Unfortunately during the post-1950's, the chauvinist male found the horoscope often showed his own drawbacks as well as highlighting the plus points of his wife. This was something domineering brutish husbands did not relish and so, they set about trying to run down Astrology to serve their own selfish ends. This was how the rumblings against Astrology first began and still continue in certain sections of men. This was fanned by the western

"It is a part of our bank's strategy for predicting the dollar's outlook" , the specialist said.

The manager of a major Japanese bank's treasury section said he also uses Astrology in trading.

"You know, J.P. Morgan, founder of Morgan Guaranty Trust Company, said that a millionaire does not believe in financial Astrology, but a billionaire does," he said.

Like other star-struck dealers , he declined to allow the publication of his name, presumably concerned that clients might not be universally impressed.

education many men received in our country. While they themselves led highly westernised lives, they wanted their wives to remain in a permanent state of ignorance so that their male tyranny could go unchecked. It was precisely to perpetuate a state of permanent feminine subjugation and male domination that many such so-called educated men starting crying hoarse against horoscopes and matching of horoscopes. Many a time, an honest astrologer would reject the boy's chart as being of a womaniser, debauchee, or suffering from impotence or of being extremely cruel in nature or avaricious for dowry. Naturally greedy men resented the role of Astrology which frustrated their plans to grab money under the excuse of marriage. Women's organisations must fight not only social evils such as dowry but also the more subtle and insidious plans of such men who know that by dispensing with horoscope- matching, they can fool the parents of the brides.

"We can predict direction of exchange rates, stock and bond prices from planetary aspects," the manager at a Japanese Bank said.

"For example, you can predict the turning point for the dollar/yen rate from relationships between Earth, Mercury and Uranus," he added.

The dollar is supposed to change direction when the angle between Mercury and Uranus is at 30, 45, 60, 90, 120, 135,150 and 180 degrees, which happens once or twice every month he said..

In another case of horoscope matching brought to me, the father was eager to get his daughter married to a rich man's son. He said his priest had said the *kuta* agreement was good between the two charts and showed harmony. There are many factors, other than *kuta*, that need to be studied while judging horoscopes for marriage. One of them is the psyche of the individual. The chart in question, indeed, had its plus points but a study of the 4th house and the boy's Moon joining Mars, Saturn and Rahu in the 7th left me little doubt of the boy's avaricious and heartless mental disposition. It also showed promiscuous personal habits. So I hinted to the girl's father the drawbacks of the chart and rejected it. The father of the girl, however was carried away by pictures of his daughter living like a queen with this rich boy. So the marriage was performed at great expense. The girl soon found that her husband had affairs with just about everyone who was willing and whom he met in his work-a-day life. When she protested,

> The theory is that planets radiate various magnetic waves which are believed to affect everything on the earth including human beings and financial markets, the manager said.
>
> Mars is a symbol of fierceness in mythology, but to astrologically-minded dealers it implies "restrained monetary policy," a bearish factor for the financial markets.
>
> Capricorn is also deeply related to monetary policy, while Uranus indicates sudden changes in exchange rates, bonds, stocks and other financial markets.

he began beating her with his belt. Not satisfied, he even tried to get some business deals through by trying to use her. This was the last straw and the poor girl came back to her now totally disillusioned parents. Many girls, thanks to the scrutiny of horoscopes before marriage, have escaped such tragedies. Many greedy men, on the other hand, resent horoscope matching under the garb of scientific temper. A horoscope reveals all and men shy away from it because it can reveal much more than they would like their future inlaws and brides to know. Women's organisations in the country must insist on a horoscopic study of the groom to ensure their fellow-women do not suffer at the hands of greedy brutes. Women's activist groups must ensure horoscopes are matched so that their sisters everywhere are protected from dangerous man and in-laws.

Mercury and Uranus being in parallel is bearish for the dollar, and on December 10 last year, when they were so aligned the dollar began to fall sharply from 132 yen towards its post war low of 120.45 yen reached in early January, the manager said.

But the crystal ball is sometimes just as fallible as economic analysis.

The manager at the US securities house said he had been studying the principles of financial astrology for 10 years.

The uses of horoscope-analysis are infinite. The wise man will sift the rice from the chaff and not throw out the baby with the bath water as many ill-informed critics of the science are trying to advocate.

"The use of Astrology for trading is getting popular among Tokyo dealers, but the problem is that it takes many years for dealers to be able to use the Astrology, properly because it is very complicated, he said. - ***Reuter***

CHAPTER THREE

PROOF OF THE PUDDING

K.N.Rao, I.A.A.S.

Dr. B.V. Raman's Amazing Achievements in Forecasting World Events

(Son of late Mr. K. Rama Rao, the well-known founder and editor of *National Herald*; was in a responsible position in the Delhi Corporation; keenly interested in our ancient culture).

I met Dr. B.V. Raman for the first time and introduced myself to him on December 26, 1982, in Delhi. But I have read his writing so closely for so many years that I was absolutely amazed that so brilliant a person with so amazing a record, instead of being honoured with Bharat Ratna in this country should have been attacked by the pseudo-intellectuals in the Indo-Anglican lineage of the English press in India. The explanation for this, of course, flows from a rather inherent slavish mentality of persons who have privately depended upon Astrology but have publicly denounced it.

Without knowing Dr. Raman personally, and after critically appraising his achievements for the last 10 years, I once wrote a long article 'Is Astrology a Hoax' for the *Search-light*, Patna, and not, in THE ASTROLOGICAL MAGAZINE. The October 1974 issue of THE ASTROLOGICAL MAGAZINE reproduced my article when a professor of Patna University sent it to the Magazine. What I want to clarify here is that I neither wrote for the THE ASTROLOGICAL MAGAZINE nor personally knew Dr.Raman, till I had made my own absolutely honest assessment about his greatness.

What is my assessment? He is in the history of the world of at least the last four hundred years, the greatest among successful astrologers; the greatest among the successful teachers of Astrology, particularly applied Astrology, through his books and writings in THE ASTROLOGICAL MAGAZINE; and the greatest promoter of the cause of Astrology through the encouragement he has given to others.

To explain why I had to make this assessment I have to talk about the critics of Astrology and astrologers. They fall into the following categories:

(A) Well-meaning critics: Some, like my father, late Mr. K. Rama Rao, founder-editor of the *National Herald,* and later, editor of *Search-light,* Patna also, and many other papers, attacked Astrology because they found astrologers driving Indians into fatal inaction. My father did not see many good astrologers and had no benefit of seeing the evidence of great mundane astrological predictions. The late Mr. C Rajagopalachari who led a Rishi-like life, was, perhaps, prompted by the desire to save Indians from fatal inaction when he attacked astrologers.

After I learnt Astrology and gave many successful predictions myself, I discovered that many of the professional astrologers, unlike a non-professional like me, commercially exploited the fear of the unknown of persons who consulted them. I personally, heartily, endorse even today the attack on astrologers as was done by my late father and the late Mr. C Rajagopalachari but I do not accept their attack on the great supra-science of Astrology. In so doing, I have the advantage of seeing in my mother, an extraordinarily successful astrologer but, her area being non-mundane, she herself could not assess the greatness of Dr. B.V. Raman with whom she sometimes exchanged letters. It was my Jyotish Guru, Yogi Bhaskaranandji of Ahmedabad who told me that Dr. Raman was the greatest astrologer of the world.

(B) Indo-Anglican critics : The Indo-Anglican streaks of the colonial days survive strongly in the Indian character, particularly among English knowing Indians. They have attacked Astrology irrationally. The astrologers can always silence them in at least 60 out of 100 cases through correct predictions.

(C) Modern critics: To preserve a modern image men like Pandit Nehru privately consulted astrologers directly or through men like Mr. Gulzari Lal Nanda, but publicly attacked it. In view of this, many people in this country felt that Pandit Nehru did not believe in Astrology. An extract of the letter written by Pandit Nehru on

29.8.1944 to his sister, Mrs. Krishna Hutheesing, is given here. It is self-explanatory.

Letter No. 74

From : Jawaharlal Nehru - Ahmednagar Fort

To : Krishna Hutheesing-20, Carmichael Road, Bombay. 29.8.44

"In my letter to Indu I suggested to her to ask you to get a proper horoscope made by a competent person. Such permanent records of the date and time of birth are desirable. As for the time, I suppose the proper solar time should be mentioned and not the artificial time which is being used outside now. War time is at least an hour ahead of the normal time."

(***Nehru's Letters to His Sister*** - edited with an introduction by Krishna Nehru Hutheesing- Faber and Faber 24 Russel Square, London.)

Surprisingly this portion has been omitted by the editor of the letters of Pandit Nehru published by the Publications Division, Government of India, perhaps, in his over-anxiety to preserve the "secular image of Pandit Nehru". The editor exercised his selective judgement in a way as will distort some facts of the personality of Nehru.

(D) "Scientific " Critics: Irrational attacks have been made on Astrology by scientists and astronomers. The scientists, with their tremendous limitations, have no capacity to understand how supra-physical laws and pure scientific methodology get combined in Astrology. It is these scientists that men like me will keep on challenging day in and day out, and, other

astrologers must join me by exhibiting their successes on the predictive side with scientific explanation. Basically, failures of the western Astrologers on the predictive side have been responsible for attacks on Astrology. If the western astrologers had properly learnt the principles of Hindu Jyotisha and developed enough predictive powers such an attack could never have been made.

(E) Astronomer-critic: I reserve astronomers as a special category of men who, having learnt so much already about planets, must have found themselves lacking in higher intellectual faculties and gifts for astrological predictions.

2. Limitations: Constraints: In discussing Dr. Raman, let me first mention the limitations and constraints within which an astrologer has to work. This must be appreciated, *intelligently,* in assessing the merit of an astrologer.

(A) Birth-time: The correct time of the birth of an individual, a political party, independence of a nation, signing of an agreement etc. is rarely

out of such an awkward situation by giving predictions on the basis of the Moon, as he did, in the case of Vietnam as early as 1946 and predicted continuous violence, blood-stained history which would not be over till 1975. It was only in 1976 that there was a reunification of

"crimes against humanity" were committed. But in making predictions on the basis of the Moon alone, and the rising sign, Dr. Raman partly succeeded and partly failed in some prediction he made about political parties of India. Since people in India were interested in the political future of their own country, part- failures of Dr. Raman have been overemphasized and his much greater and more outstanding successes have not been discussed. This was an unscientific appraisal and to rectify the imbalane, I decided to tabulate his great predictions, not without mentioning causes for his failed predictions without which such an appraisal would become one sided.

Dr. Raman got the wrong time of Nixon when he predicted victory for Him in 1960. Fortunately this was corrected by U.S. astrologers after which Dr. Raman made his world famous predictions about Mr. Nixon winning his re-election in 1972 but not completing his term. Yet Dr. Raman's failures teach valuable lessons in Astrology because he still imparts Astrological knowledge when he discusses a horoscope - a wrong horoscope, to risk his reputation, to justify his sense of adventure, to justify the aspect of Mars on his own birth Ascendant.

(B) Birth details: In many cases, the birth details, the day, month and year of important men of the world are not available. To make predictions about them on the basis only of the national horoscope is not the safest course always, through Dr. Raman has made many such brilliant predictions about the destiny of "the men of destiny".

(C) Supplementary researches: There is no one else in the country or in the world whose researches in mundane Astrology could help Dr. Raman. Small men like me, who have also given some successful predictions, have borrowed from him, even "stolen his predictions and passed them on as ours". We have been intellectually dishonest. If we had done our own researches and passed them to Dr. Raman for publication in his famous THE ASTROLOGICAL MAGAZINE it would have served the larger and nobler cause of Hindu Jyotisha.

(D) Margin for failure: All scientists particularly doctors have areas of failure for which we provide a percentage. Why do we want an astrologer to give hundred percent correct predictions only? Dr. Raman's failure to predict in 1971 and again in 1980, the return of Mrs. Indira Gandhi to power with a thumping majority is an instance which will show that we have not helped Dr. Raman with our researches based on dependable data. Falling back upon his own great researches, he was utilising wrong data of political parties and even wrong horoscopes of political rivals of Mrs. Indira Gandhi sometimes. In other words, for a full assessment of political fortunes full details about individual horoscopes and political parties have never been available to Dr. Raman or, for that matter, to any astrologer.

3. I have discussed the failures of Dr. Raman which have been actually very few. But I am more interested in projecting his successes which

must have been perhaps above 80% if his career average is taken.

4. *Aims:* The specific aims of my assessment of Dr. Raman's are as follows:

(a) Eclipses: The impression created by physical scientists and astronomers that eclipses have no effect on the destiny of nations and men of destiny will get exploded after actual instances of such predictions made are seen in the tabulated summary.

(b) Astrologer-adviser: Hindu Sastras laid emphasis on a king having the benefit of objective astrological assessment of the future for shaping state policies. Looking at the instance given in both tables, the value of the advice given in Hindu Sastras will be appreciated.

(c) Superior intelligence : **With so many intelligence agencies in so many countries functioning all over the world with all their man-power and researches, their failures should be compared with the failure of one individual, Dr.Raman, who, in his discussion of global trends and tensions, year after year since 1937, has predicted what intelligence agencies could not foresee. It may appear enigmatic to the physical-science-afflicted-intellect of an average educated man anywhere in the world today that an Indian astrologer, sitting in Bangalore, casting horoscopes, is able to collect more intelligence from planetary indications, and more successfully, in most of the cases.**

(d) Supra-scientific tradition: And the purpose also is to show that the Hindu tradition based on Sastras is supra-scientific: Hindu Jyotisha proves it; through this proof, the supra- scientific validity of the Hindu tradition stands vindicated, with brilliance, through the predictions of Dr. Raman.

(e) Benefit to humanity: The benefit that flows to humanity from the acceptance of a supra-science is obvious. To serve the larger interests of mankind, and, at the same time wherever necessary, to attack the manifold superstitions prevalent in modern society through excessive influence of physical scientists and astronomers, who have attacked Astrology. I am giving two Tables here.

Table I: Table I is a bird's eye view of some of his great predictions among thousands. I have chosen such predictions as linger in public memory. The small instances given are of recent years, particularly Indian, so that readers will be able to verify them immediately.

Table II: The difference between astrological foresight and historical hindsight cannot be understood and appreciated by the modern man, totally blind and cynical in his materialistic pursuits, in the technology-corrupted age of ours unless he knows that in Astrology there is a method, a discussion, a manner of drawing conclusions before actual prediction is given, and that even if 60% of such predictions come out correct, this achievement is much greater than the achievement of others who employ vaster resources in terms of men, power and money-and achieve a much lower percentage of success.

How does this amazingly great astrologer make his predictions? What is the method? Let that be described briefly.

(A) Classical Basis: *(a)* He adopts Hindu Lunar Saka year for his predictions of all the countries of the world. It is amazing that the basis of the Hindu New Year should apply so accurately to predictions given about all the countries of the world - Hindu, Buddhist, Muslim, Christian, Jew etc. Instances have been given in Table I.

(b) The beginning of the Hindu-Birth Year is converted into local meantime for the capital of the country about which predictions are given.

(c) The Navamsas for all these are also cast.

(d) The Hindu system of planetary cabinet for the year is mentioned and the broad general indications and promises for the New Year delineated.

(B) Traditional Methods: Along with the classical Hindu methods Dr. Raman uses the time-tested traditional methods given, among others, by the great Varahamihira thus:

(a) The transits of planets, particularly major planets like Saturn, Jupiter and Rahu, in different Rasis give their unfailing results in the zodiacal areas concerned.

(b) The transit of planets into Nakshatras is also pointed out wherever and whenever necessary as given by Varahamihira.

(c) The effect of eclipses as given by Varaha Mihira has been used very brilliantly by Dr. Raman in some of his most sensational predictions like fall of Bhutto, fall of Morarji; earthquakes in Iran and China.

(C) Neo-classical basis: Dr. Raman is the greatest researcher in Mundane Astrology in the last 400 years of human history. He never makes any departure from the classical frame of the text- books. But within this classical frame, he introduces innovative style, tests them vigorously and gives his results. The features of his neo-classicism are as follows:

(a) He takes into consideration the changed boundaries of India; therefore, departing from Varahamihira, he would give to Goa Satabhisha Nakshatra and Aquarius Rasi; to West Bengal Mrigasira (3), Gemini Rasi, and on this basis, after testing it with historical incidents begins to give predictions about future which come out correct brilliantly.

(D) Additional material: To all these, he adds additional astrological data like the following:

(a) The formation of a state in India like, say, Andhra, or the emergence of a country like, say, India or Pakistan on the attainment of their independence.

(b) The oath-taking ceremony of a cabinet newly formed or of an important dignitary; for instance, on the basis of the oath-taking ceremony of Mr. Sanjiva Reddy, the former President of India, he predicted about his ailment for which

he had to go to U.S.A. for a major surgical operation.

(c) Through experimentation again Dr. Raman has reduced the Vimshottari Mahadasa of 120 years into five years proportionately, it being the period of the life of a new Government under Indian Parliamentary System; and on the basis, perhaps, he predicted brilliantly when the late Mr. Lal Bahadur Shastri assumed the office of the Prime Minister that his cabinet was not likely to last more than one year.

How by applying these methods he discusses the finer points of Astrology and not merely foresees the coming events but takes along with him Astrology-knowing readers is illustrated in Table II.

In his long, now nearly 50 years of astrological career, he must have written at least 400 editorials on mundane matters affecting the history of the world.

Five examples have only been chosen here to give to readers only an idea of the depth, range, brilliance and pre-visions, which Hindu Jyotisha gives without the use of Pluto, Neptune and Uranus. The first example shows how astrological foresight is more dependable; second why the astrological vision is superior to the foresight of statesmen; the third, how an astrologer can sift from a complex combination of planets the predictable events and allay the panic created by alarmist-astrologers and astronomers; the fourth how research in Astrology is done and applied;

and the fifth how ancient astrological formulae are eternally modern, and so brilliant.

Inferences that flow from both Tables will very clearly establish the following:

(A) Eclipses: The effects of eclipses on destiny of man and nation in causing rise and the fall of important men, earthquakes, railway accidents and railways' strikes. Out of the 110 instances given in the Table, I have endeavoured to collect different bases for the predictions given to show the extraordinarily brilliant range of Hindu Jyotisha and the varieties of approaches that can be made to arrive at results. For instance, the various methods through which the predictions have been made by Dr. Raman would fall into three broad categories:

(a) The pure classical category when he quotes from the Sastras and applies them in a practical way thus:

(i) The Vimshottari Mahadasa as applied to different vargas: see predictions about the deaths of Hitler and Pandit Jawaharlal Nehru and the fall from power of Malenkov and Khruschev.

(ii) Use of sensitive points as given in ancient Hindu classical texts (see in Table II the instances of such formula being applied to predict the death of Indian National Congress of 1885 in the period between 1963-1970).

(iii) The effect of yogas-raja, arishta, maraka- in all types of horoscopes.

(b) Researchers : Dr. Raman has given to his readers the benefits of his researches time and

again, See for instance, his research on 'Planetary Combinations' for the breaking out of a war and the analysis of the Ashtagraha (eight-planet combination of February 1962) and the death of Pandit Jawaharlal Nehru.

(c) Synthesis : A skillful use of the Mahadasa (Vimshottari) and transit of planets applied to different vargas and synthesised with the planetary indications in the horoscopes of concerned individuals is the most scientific method for predictions, which is why Dr. Raman has maintained such a high average of successful predictions. [See his prediction about the short-life of the space-craft Bhaskara. (*A.M.*, August 1979).] More important is the fact that even when his predictions have failed, he has taught his readers a scientific method of arriving at a prediction which makes it possible for some of his readers to arrive at results different from his, sometimes, even better. That is how a great teacher imparts training.

As Mrs. Rukmini Arundale rescued Bharat Natyam from the houses of *devadasis* and Vishnu Digamber Pulaskar and V.M. Bhakthande rescued Hindustani classical music from the houses of Muslim *gharanas*, so has Dr. Raman rescued Astrology from the houses of persons, who were slowly getting out of tune, with the ancient intellectual tradition of the Rishis, and were unable to apply those principles to modern complex life.

Dr. Raman's achievement is greater than that of any other Indian. His revival of Hindu supra-scientific tradition very clearly proves that the word "revivalism" is not an act of resurrecting what is historically archaic but the act of explaining what is eternally valid which, being non-physical, is less understood, therefore, less appreciated in this age of physical science and technology when human I.Q. functions at lower, physical, sex money-sleep level only.

Table I

Some Instances of Dr. B.V. Raman's Predictions

1. These are all documented predictions answering the rigidest tests of historical scrutiny.
2. Linked to the Hindu theory of cycle of births, a horoscope is the sum–total of *karmas* of past, allotted for the present incarnation of the native. Astrology is of Indian origin, as it could not have originated, in any culture which does not believe in re-birth. Its roots lie in the Vedas, the world's oldest books.
3. How planets influence human affairs is discussed in Dr. B.V. Raman's *Planetary Influences on Human Affairs*. From his own writings some intances have been given here.

Genl. Sl. No. 1	Refer to the issue of *The Astrological Magazine* 2	Specific Sl. No. 3	Prediction 4	Fullfilment (Persons) 5	When Predicted 6	Basis of Prediction 7	Remarks 8
1.	April 1947	2.	*Gandhiji's assassination* "...point to loss by assassination as violent Mars is with Saturn in the 12th, of a respected mass leader of the country".	3. **India** 30-1-1948 Gandhiji was assasinated.	One year before	"Sade-sati third and maraka-dasa	Gandhiji's name was not mentioned.
2.	July 1962	2.	*Pt Nehru's death approaching* 1-8-1963 to 16-5-1964 critical	Died on 27-5-1964	More than two years before	Mahadasa of Rahu-Ketu	Referred specifically as Prime Minister

1	2	3	4	5	6	7	8
3.	Jan, 1964	3.	*National mourning*	—do—	—do—	Hindu New year's horoscope	
4.	June 1964 (read by us in May : written in March 1964)	4.	"All these are not favourable for his continuing in office"	—do—	Two months before	His natal horoscope	"My life is not going to end so very soon Pt.Nehru had said in a Press Conference on 22-5-1964. Five days after, he died.
5.	August 1964	5.	Lal Bahudur Shastri's Cabinet–Longevity about one year–Shortlived	Died on 11-1-1966	One year and seven months before	Oath taking Ceremony of the Cabinet ; its inauspicious time and day 11-20 a.m. 9-6-1964 Oath	Held back discussion of his horsocope. Revealed it indirectly Muhuhrta

1	2	3	4	5	6	7	8
6.	March 1966	6.	The prediction given to VVIPS was made public	—do—	—do—	Birth horoscope 12-30 ghatis 9-10-1904	2nd October is not his birthday
7.	July 1967	7.	*President Zakir Hussain* "...may not be able to complete full term"	Died on 4-5-1968	One year before	Time when the Oath was taken	Importance of Muhurta like item No.5

8.	March 1977	8.	Dasa of Saturn; Bhukti of Maraka; Saturn aspecting, as the 7th and the 8th lord, the 10th house; transit of Saturn in Lagna and Mars in the 8th dramatic reversal	On 23-3-1977 Mrs. Indira Gandhi lost elections	Two months before	Astrologers only can recognise that it applied to Mrs. Indira Gandhi's horoscope	Veiled prediction again like Nos. 1 and 5. He does so in national interests
9.	Jan. 1979	9.	*Fall of Morarji Desai.* Eclipse falling on his natal Moon in August 1979	Fell in July-August 1979	Ten months before	Eclipse	Horoscope analysis avoided like No. 5

1	2	3	4	5	6	7	8
10.	Issues of 1964, 1965, 1966, 1967, 1968, 1969	1.	Death of Indian National Congress (1885)	*Parties Political.* The great organisation spilit in 1969. In 1967 many north Indian States had non-Congress Govts.	Repeated year after year	The birth horoscope of the Indian National Congress of 1885. Dec.	Importance of birthtime of a political party
11.	June 1978	2.	Split up of Janata Party	Split in July 1979	One year and two months before	On the basis of the Moon in a horoscope whose Lagna was doubtful	In 1971, Dr. Raman had made predictions on the basis of wrong horoscope of political parties. When accused of wrong predic-

							error of judgement gracefully.
12.	Jan. 1954	1.	War in 1962 only, not before with China	*Wars (Indian)* in 1962 India-China War broke out	More than eight years	An extraordinary piece of research Hindu New Year	An absolutely dazzling chain of predictions followed which no statesman of the world could visualise or foresee
13.	August 1964	2.	War with Pakistan (1965)	War broke out in September 1965	One year three months before	Oath taking ceremony time of Lal Bahadur Shastri's Cabinet	Gave hints of many impending disasters

1	2	3	4	5	6	7	8
14.	May 1971	3.	War with Pakistan (1971) "Celestial warnings"	December 3 1971	Seven months before	Pianetary transits	—do—
15.	Jan 1966	1.	Devaluation of Indian currency : "Drastic economic measures"	*Mixed (Indian)* Sometime in the middle of 1966 Indian rupee was devalued	Few months before	Hindu New Year	How planets affect economy

16.	April 1969	2.	Mr. Jyoti Basu's Cabinet of 1969 : West Bengal. Fairly long term – not less than four years	Lasted for more than four years Mr. Siddhartha Sankar Ray (Congress) formed Govt. after 1973	Five years before	Time of Oath of the Cabinet	Muhurta (election) is so important
17.	Jan. 1958	3.	Train Accident	Ambala Train Accident of 1-1-1958	Two months before	Saturn-Mars in Scorpio, the 3rd from Virgo, India's Lagna	How planets cause accidents is illustrated

1	2	3	4	5	6	7	8
18.	April 1973	4.	Railway strike after Mars moves into eclipse- point on 10-4-1974	A terrible strike during Mr. L.N.Misra's time took place in 1974 April, May, June	Thirteen months before	A great piece of research on eclipses	Mars causing a railway strike–Eclipse
19.	March 1966	5.	Exit of Mr. T.T.Krishnamachari from the Central Cabinet	T.T.K. had to leave at the end of the year	Few months before	Oath - taking ceremony	Importance of Muhurta

Recent Events

20.	Dec. 1974	1.	Growth of totalitarianism in Indian Democracy	Emergency of 1975 June	Acutally many years before. Here eight months before he predicted it	A great piece of re-search, Jupiter in Pisces and Saturn in Cancer in the past—battles of Panipat and 1857 Mutiny	An astrologer foresees for-ces that shape history

1	2	3	4	5	6	7	8
21.	Oct. 1977	2.	President Sanjiva Reddy's ailment. "Saturnine movement not easy to identify his ailment"	Dr. R.K. Caroli, then President's physician, detected a shadow on Mr. Reddy's lungs. Operation was in USA	Few months before	Oath	Importance of Muthurta
22.	July 1979	3.	Mr. Jaya Prakash Narayan is also exposed to effect of Eclipse	J.P. died on 6-10-1979	Six months before	Eclipse	Importance of Eclipse

23.	A speech in *A.M.* 2-4-1981	4.	Mrs. Gandhi should be careful about her safety	A plane (Makalu) in which she was to fly was sabotaged 27-4-1981	Few days before	Perhaps Mrs. Indira Gandhi's horoscope
24.	—do—	5.	Communal Riots in Bihar	In May 1981 communal riots took place in Bihar	—do—	National horoscope possibly
25.	Jan. 1982	6.	Partisan decisions by the Supreme Court	No comments	No comments	Hindu New Year
26.	Jan. 1983	7.	Supreme Court will reverse earlier dicision	Guess	—do—	Hindu New Year

1	2	3	4	5	6	7	8
27.	Jan. 1982	8.	"A minority leader will pass away"	Sheikh Abdullah died some months after	Some months before		
28.	Jan. 1982	9.	Punjab Problem	Remains unsolved	Brillant prediction based on deep research. Two years before	Saturn represents west and Libra north. So trouble in Punjab, also Kashmir Hindu New Year	See how planets and Rasis represent directions
29.	Jan. 1983	10.	Punjab Problem	—do—	—do—	—do—	—do—
30.	Jan. 1982	11.	Islamic Fundamentalism in Kashmir	No comments	No comments	With some special research on Kashmir	

						added New Year	
31.	Jan. 1982	12.	Restrictions on Press	Dr. Jaganath Misra passed the Bihar Press Bill which created a national controversy	Many months before	Hindu New Year 3rd house	Well-known area of Mundane Astrology
32.	Jan. 1982	13.	Re-shuffle of the Central Cabinet	Mr. Kedar Pandey, Mr. Sitaram Kesri and Mr. V.C.Shukia were dropped. A sensation was created	Many months before	Hindu New Year	Research

1	2	3	4	5	6	7	8
33.	Jan. 1983	14. Increase in Postal Rates		In the Budget of March 1983 Increased	—do—	—do—	Fantastic Research
34.	Jan. 1983	15.	Bank Scandals will be detected	Syndicate Bank, Indian Overseas Bank, New Bank of India, Punjab and Sind Bank are in news and under CBI investigation	—do—	—do—	—do—

35.	Jan. 1983	16.	Business Scandal will be detected	Inquity. Beef Tallow Scandal of Jains has tormented Hindus. Swaraj Paul's case is still very hot	—do—	Hindu New Year	Fantastic Research
36.	Jan. 1983	17.	There will be devastating fires in Delhi, Bombay around June eclipse	Gopala Towers and Indane Gas fires in Delhi in May, June shook Delhi, On June 6, fire broke out in 26 places in India	A great research on Eclipse, Zodiacal allocation of regions in India	—do—	This prediction is far greater than Lily's about London fire

1	2	3	4	5	6	7	8
37.	Jan. 1983.	18.	At least one more South Indian State will opt for non-Congress rule	Mr. N.T.Rama Rao in Andhra and Mr. R.K.Hegde in Karnataka have formed non Congress Govts. after Jan. 1983 elections.	Zodical allocation for Andhra Revati (Pisces Rasi). Two months before	Special researches of Dr.Raman Hindu New Year	No other astrologer has done so many new researches

38.	Jan. 1983	19.	Performance of Congress may not be that bad	Won elections in Delhi in many municipal elections in MP and Assam State elections	At least three months to five months before	Hindu New Year	Newspapers totally failed to assess this

Pakistan

39.	Dec. 1947	1.	Re-union with India a certainity	Watch it	Birth horoscope of Pakistan 13/14 August 1947 midnight Karachi and 14/15 for India	Birth horoscope	This method yields best results

1	2	3	4	5	6	7	8
40.	June 1949	2.	Democracy will be a farce, totalitairiain tendencies visible in the horoscope	Judge your-self	Thirty four years ago	—do—	Afflicted Moon
41.	Jan. 1953	3.	Significant change—loss or resignation	Kwaja Niza muddin was dis-missed in July 1953	Nine months before	Hindu New Year	Fantastic Re-search
42.	Jan. 1955	4.	Mr. Mohd. Ali will be thrown out	Was thrown out in August 1955	Ten months before	Hindu New Year	—do—
43.	May 1956	5.	Ayub's Islamic Republic will collapse Balarista	Collapsed in less than three years	Three years before	Birth horo-scope of Is-lamic Republic	Time is the crux of Muhurtha

44.	May 1956	6.	Economy will improve- Massive aid from USA	US aid flowed into Pakistan massively during Ayub's regime	Two months before	Position of Mercury representing USA	How planets and Rasis represent countries
45.	August 1964 May 1971	7.	Indo-Pak Wars	See under India			
46.	June 1969	8.	Upsurge in East Pakistan-bloodshed	Two years before Bangladesh was formed	Two years and some months	It was an old prediction based on Pakistan's birth horoscope	Dr. Raman's consistent astrological prevision is revealed
47.	July 1969	9.	Significant change	Ayub goes, Yahya becomes Pakistan's dictator	A few months before	Transitting planets	Great Research

1	2	3	4	5	6	7	8
48.	Jan. 1977	10.	Solar eclipse of Pakistan's Ascendant; significant change	On 5th July, 1977 Bhutto was displaced and Gen. Zia became Martial Law Administrator. Bhutto was later hanged	About ten months before	Hindu New Year eclipse	A very great prediction
			Bangla Desh				
49.	Jan 1975	1.	Unexpected developments-crucial for BanglaDesh	August 1975 Mujib was killed	About ten montiis before	Hindu New Year	Late Mr. Y.Keshav Menon had also predicted

50.	April 1975	2.	'Violent movement to unseat Mujib'	—do—	—do—	Saturn's entry in Cancer and aspect of Mars	—do—
51.	Jan. 1982	3.	"The President of Bangla Desh will be overthrown"	Was overthrown on 25-3-1982	Five months before	Hindu New Year	A piece of research

World Problems

52.	World prospects 1937–1938	1.	World war II will begin in Europe following Eclipses	War broke out as predicted (1959)	One year before	Eclipse	Dr. Raman's grandfather late Prof. B. Suryanarain Rao had predicted about the 1st World War. Dr. Raman at the age of 25 predicted the

1	2	3	4	5	6	7	8
							Second World War when most of the Western astrologers had ruled out such possibilities.
53.	August 1940	2.	Russo German Pact will be dead (German-Soviet Non-Aggression Pact concluded on 23/24 August 1939) (Molotov-Ribhen trap)	Died after 1942 when Stafford Cripps made trip to Moscow	At least three years before	The time of signing of the Pact transit of planets	If Stalin and Hitler had joined, world would have been enslaved. But only Dr. Raman knew that the Pact would collapse. Europe was nervous

54.	July 1940	3.	Italy would enter war and get ruined	Mussolini's Italy had become Hitler's liability. Italy was ruined	Two years and five months before	Transit of planets	It was not a certainty at one stage
55.	Jan. 1941	4.	Fascist dictatorships will collapse in four years	Collapsed in 1945 (see 56 and 57 below)	Four years before	Transit of Saturn in Taurus and Jupiter in Cancer	Astrological foresight; no one else, statesman or political scientist, could have been so confident

1	2	3	4	5	6	7	8
56.	Sept. 1944	5.	Hitler will have a violent end	30-4-1945 committed suicide	One year (see 4) before	Dr. Raman had made a very deep study of the horoscope of world figures - see his *Notable Horoscopes* and *Studies in Jaimini Astrology*	Hitler figures in the calculation of longevity in Dr. Raman's book on Jaimini
57.	Nov. 1943	6.	Mussolini will have a violent end	Was shot dead on 29-7-1945	See(4) above also Two years before	—do—	Deep study of individual horoscopes, transits of planets in Italy's Hindu New Year

							horoscope is Dr. Raman's technique
58.	Jan 1982	7.	"Global shortage of energy"	The problem has become terrible. On Sept. 19, 1983, Global Energy Meet in New Delhi	One year before	Hindu New Year's horoscope	A great piece of research

Russia

59.	June 1950	1.	Stalin's death approaching Dasa Chidra of Mars (ending in 1952-53)	Stalin died on 5-3-1953	More than three years before	Stalin's birth details 21-12-1879 at 3-5 p.m. Gori (Georgia)	Dr. Raman rectifies Lagna in a very extraordinary manner with fantastically

1	2	3	4	5	6	7	8
							high percentage of success.
60.	Jan. 1953	2.	Critical for Russia... Stalin's own position	Stalin died on 5-3-1953	Five months before	Hindu New Year converted into LMT of Moscow	Lunar Saka Hindu New Year is the most dependable scientific basis for mundane predictions. Dr. Raman has used it for over four decades

[illegible]	March 1954	3.	Malenkov's fall : troubles begin from May, June, 1954. Will be overthrown and not shot dead like Beria	Nikolai Bulganin replaced him sometime in 1955	A horoscopic analysis thus. 'The Moon' lord of 8th is in Ketu's nakshatra and Ketu is aspected by Mars and Mars in his turn is not subject to any affliction but only aspects the 8th. Consequently Malenkov's fall by being overthrown One Year before	See the previous column. The further discussion was : in Rahu Dasa when Rahu transits the nakshatra held by Mars Malenkov will be on his way out	Planets are God's agencies of control. Marxists are not spared. Planets do not discriminate betwen capitalists and communists. Marxist opposition to Astrology is proof of how Marxism has become a mind-deadening opiate

1	2	3	4	5	6	7	8
62.	March 1962	4.	Khruschev : What is the future? At the moment the ruling sub-period is that of Rahu. Here Saturn is in the constellation of Mars, a *maraka*. Rahu whose sub-period lasts till Oct, 1963... will be the exit of this great personage	Khruschev was overthrown on 6-10-1964 by Brezhnev	Two years and ten months before	Birth on 17-4-1894 Kalinorka (Kurk). Dr. Raman rectified Lagna and gave Vargottama Libra Lagna in keeping with Khruschev's liberal, balanced post-Stalin policies	During his Indian visit Khruschev had asked where is God? Hindu Astrology, and Dr. Raman's prediction would have given him adequate answer

63.	Jan. 1979	5.	Brezhnev's health will be affected at time of Solar eclipse of February 1979	World came to know about it much later	How many years or months before cannot be known	Hindu New Year converted into L.M.T. of Moscow and the effect of eclipse is first studied. Then transit of Mars to the point of eclipse affecting Russian political power-structure analysed	Physical scientists and astronomers are still nursing the belief that eclipses have no effect on human destiny. Primitive men who knew this were wiser than modern scientists

1	2	3	4	5	6	7	8
64.	Jan. 1982	6.	Dramatic changes in Kremlin. A leading Soviet Statesman will pass away	Brezhnev died on 12-11-1982	One year before	18 of Cancer rises. Mars aspects the 10th house and the 8th lord Saturn is assoicated with Mars. Hindu New Year	Dr. B.V. Raman predicted it one year ago yet an Indo Anglican of the English Press in India wrote that no Indian predicted it while a Russian woman had.
65.	Jan. 1980	7.	A considerable shake-up in the Soviet Government is expected about the middle of the year	Kosygin was removed in April 1980	Six months before	With Libra as Lagna in the Hindu New Year horoscope and the Moon	See remarks, Indo-Anglican should be educated properly by

						the 10th lord in the 6th withthe Sun but aspected by Saturn and retrograde Mars power struggle is indicated	Hindu astrologers
GC.	Jan. 1979	8.	The Soviet influence in Afghanistan will rise dramatically and cause serious concern among its neighbours.	Details not known, But December last week 1979 Russia moved into Afghanistan	Ten months before	Afghanistan is Krittika (Aries)	Most sensational foresight

1	2	3	4	5	6	7	8
67.	Jan. 1980	9.	Jupiter lord of the 3rd or the house of neighbours is associated with Mars and Rahu...planetary disposition is indicative of the Soviet Union getting bogged down in Afghanistan's war	In December 1979 it happened	One month before	—do—	Only an astrologer could have foreseen it
			U.S.A.				
68.	World prospects 1940	1.	Re-election of President Roosevelt	Was elected	About one year before	Jupiter and Saturn transiting their radi-	

						cal positions	
69.	Sept. 1940	2.	Death of President Roosevelt	Died in 12-4-1945	Four years before	Transit of major planets	Dr. Raman's prediction was given much earlier than perhaps by a lady clairvoyant of U.S.A.
70.	World prospects 1948-49	3.	Election of Truman "Stars are not in a frowning mood in regard to Mr.Truman ...consequently there are chances of his re-election to the Presidential chair"	Truman was re-elected	About one year before	Truman's horoscope	We have quite a number of astrological journals in this country. Except one or two, the others have reduced Astrology to a farce. Most of our

1	2	3	4	5	6	7	8
							astrologers and prophets predicted that Truman would never succeed this time—New York John Jeffries, *(A.M. 1949 Jan. p.110)*
71.	Nov. 1968	4.	Mr.Nixon would be elected as President of U.S.A.	Mr.Nixon was elected	Few months before	Mr. Nixon's horoscope	In 1960 Dr. Raman had wrong birth-time of Mr. Nixon when he went wrong. Importance of birth time

72.	Dec. 1972	5.	Mr. Nixon would be re-elected	Mr. Nixon was re-elected	Few months before	Mr. Nixon's horoscope	In 1960 Dr. Raman had wrong birth time of Mr. Nixon when he went wrong. Importance of birth time.
73.	Dec. 1972	6.	But will he complete the term? Disquieting features for the second term.	Mr. Nixon resigned on 9-8-1974 after the Watergate affair	Two years nine months before	—do—	Dr. Raman has hundreds of more brilliant predictions but USA remembers this as one of his great predictions.

1	2	3	4	5	6	7	8
74.	In 1972 in addressing U.S. Astrologers	7.	This prediction about repeated	US papers reminded their readers about the great prediction about Mr. Nixon	—do—	—do—	—do—
				China			
75.	Jan. 1949	1.	Fall of Chiang Kai Sheik by September 1949	Fled in October 1949	About eleven months before	Saturn's transit on the cusp of the 10th house of Chiang Kai	Series of predictions followed
76.	March 1950	2.	Chinese revolution will remain Chinese	Remains so	Thirty-three years ago	Chinese Republican horoscope 3-15 p.m. 1-10-1949	Mao had accused Russia of even 'distortions'

77.	March 1950	3.	Sino Russian relations will be strained in Mars Dasa (1958-1965)	See Table II. In 1960, ten years after the prediction and within the predicted time it happened	Ten years before	Chinese Republican horoscope	No statesman of the world could foresee or say this
78.	March 1950	4.	Will be a world power in Rahu Mahadasa (1965-1983)	China is a nuclear power	Nearly twenty years before	Planetary yogas and position in the Republican horoscope	Surprisingly in spite of bad Sino-Soviet relations
79.	Jan. 1976	5.	Chou-en-Lai will fade away	Died on 8th January 1976	Three months before	Hindu New Year's horoscope	Who expected this?

1	2	3	4	5	6	7	8
80.	Jan. 1976	6.	Mao-Tse-Tung will fade away	Died on September 9th 1976	Eleven months	Hindu New Year	Note how scientific his Hindu New Year basis is
81.	Jan. 1981	7.	Earthquake following penumbral eclipse of the Moon on 20th January 1981	On 26-1-1981 South China sustained a major earth quake, Many were killed.	Three months before	Hindu New Year	Let physical scientists, seismologists note this
			Egypt				
82.	Feb. 1952	1.	Drastic political changes... the king must... careful about personal safety	On 23rd July 1952 King Farouk was deposed	Nine months before	King's horoscope	Which is better- political guess or astrological foresight?

83.	Nov. 1952	2.	Dictatorship not democracy	Nasser used Naguib as a figure head in a controlled democracy and replaced him as Egypt's dicatator by 1954	One year before	Planetary position of revolution	Planets decide the form of Government.
84.	Jan. 1981	3.	Coup against Sadat	Sadat was shot dead on 6-10-1981	Eleven months before	Hindu New Year	Again see how Hindu New Year basis becomes applicable

1	2	3	4	5	6	7	8
			Yugoslavia				
85.	Jan. 1977	1.	Mars-Jupiter conjunction may see flags half mast in Yugoslavia	Prime Minister Dzemal Bijidie died in a plane crash	Seven months before	Hindu New Year	Again see how Hindu New Year basis becomes applicable
			Pope				
86.	Jan. 1982	1.	Year critical for Pope	On August 8, 1982 Pope survived assassination attempt but was seriously injured	Ten months before	Hindu New Year	Could anyone know beforehand

Israel

87.	Jan. 1967	1.	War between Israel and Egypt	June 1967 war broke out	Ten months before	Hindu New Year	Hindu New Year for Jews also as basis
88.	Jan. 1973	2.	West Asia on the brink of war	Oct. 6, 1973—War broke out between Israel and Egypt	Ten months before	Hindu New Year	Hindu New Year for Jews also as basis
89.	Jan. 1982	3.	Armed confrontation with Arabs	June 1982 war broke out	Eight months before	—do—	All wars predicted successfully
90.	Jan. 1983	4.	Begin Govt, may not last whole year	Begin quit in Sept. 1983	Ten months before	—do—	Letters of appreciation received for these predictions are many

1	2	3	4	5	6	7	8
				Iran			
91.	Jan. 1953	1.	Maussadiques fall	Fell in Nov. 1953	One year before	Hindu New Year	Hindu New Year applied to Iran
92.	Nov. 1978	2.	Fall of the Shah; abdication or misfortune	Jan. 1979 Shah fled	Four months	Shah's horoscope	Accurate horoscope helped giving of accurate prediction
93.	Jan. 1978	3.	Total lunar eclipse on 16-9-1978 causes Earthquake	Teheran was rocked on 16-9-1978 Thousands killed	Eleven months before	Hindu New Year Eclipse	Yet scientists and Kovoors will not appreciate

			Saturn conjunction of 20-7-1981 Iran may be rocked by Earthquake	1981 Iran was rocked by earthquake and thousands killed	months before	tion of major planets	tists say planets do not affect us

King Faisal

95.	Jan. 1975	1.	One Arab dictator will be victim of violence	King Faisal was shot dead by his own nephew in April 1975	Six months before	Hindu New Year	—do—

England

96.	Nov. 1951	1.	Victory for Conservatives	Conservatives won	Few months before	Horoscope of the Conservative Party	Importance of a party horoscope

1	2	3	4	5	6	7	8
97.	Jan. 1952	2.	Death of King George VI	The King died on 6-5-1952	Seven months before	Hindu New Year	Perhaps also the horoscope of the King
98.	June 1955	3.	Victory of Anthony Eden	In 1975 Anthony Eden became British P.M.	Few months before	Horoscope of England according to Zodiacal sign and Eden's horoscope	Fortunes of a party too are predictable
				Ghana			
99.	Jan. 1966	1.	Not favourable for continuance of Nkrumah	Was overthrown on 22nd Feb. 1966 on his way to Hanoi while at Peking Airport	Few months before	Hindu New Year	A fantastic prediction

South Africa

100.	May 1960	1.	South Africa will quit com-mon-wealth	Quit on 31-5-1961	One year and two months before	Horoscope of South Africa	A piece of re-search

Fall of Idi Amin

101.	Jan. 1977	1.	Fall of Amin	Fell in May 1977	Seven months before	Hindu New Year	A fantastic prediction

Thailand

102.	Jan. 1981	1.	Coup in Thailand	May 1981 there was a coup	Six months before	Hindu New Year	Astrology has no limitations; astrologer may have

1	2	3	4	5	6	7	8
				France			
103.	April 1982	1.	Fall of French Govt.	22-5-1981 French Parliament was dissolved	Seven months before	Horoscope of France	Planets affect Parliament also
				Indonesia			
104.	Jan. 1966	1.	Exit of Sukarno	Exit in 1966	Few months before	Hindu New Year	Could also be Indonesian horoscope of independence

Vietnam

105.	March 1947	1.	The above chart has a lot of explosive elements. Enemy France	The French continued their battle for eight long years till they lost in Dien Bien Phu	Seven years it continued	Birth time not known. The Moon offers the basis for prognostication	One of Dr. Raman's extraordinary method of depending upon the Moon only when birth time is not known
106.	March 1947	2.	...combined influences of Saturn, Mars, Rahu in the 10th–therefore, full of complications	USA got involved first indirectly and later directly when Red China came into power	Seven years it continued	Birth time not known. The Moon offers the basis for prognostication	One of Dr. Raman's extraordinary methods of depending upon the Moon only when birth time is not known

1	2	3	4	5	6	7	8
107.	Sept. 1954	3.	*Geneva Agreement* ...relations worsened ... death, disaster, in connection with the army and the navy ... dangers of war... Mars dominates	The blood-stained history is well-known	Continued for years	Geneva Agreement's horoscope 21-7-1954	Importance of the time of Agreement
108.	June 1968	3.	*17th Parallel* No bright shades. Rahu Dasa lasts till 1975. Only after Saturn enters Gemini— prospects of peace	After 1975 re-unification of Vietnam took place in 1976 when Rahu Dasa was over	Eight years before	Republic of Vietnam 26-10-1955 was the basis	The only person who timed the return of peace not before 1975

109.	Jan. 1979	4.	Chinese intensions towards its neighbours could be deceptively dangerous in view of conjunction of Saturn and Rahu in the 3rd house..... Vietnam will continue to be a sore spot	China launched a large-scale offensive against Vietnam on 17-2-1979	Four years before	Hindu New Year, Saturn-Rahu conjunction. Rahu Dasa in Chinese horoscope	Military experts may profit from such an example
110.	April 1979	5.	*Sino-Vietnamese War 1979* Obviously Vietnamese are not badly placed. Because Jupiter aspects Mars the Dasa lord, the conflict may not lost long	Vietnamese fought valiantly. The war was over soon (No definite date could be ascertained)	Some weeks before	Horoscope of China and Vietnam and Mahadasa in both	Comparative study of combatants from the war horoscope is a brilliant research of Dr. Raman

TABLE II
Astrologer Versus Statesman

The difference between Astrology and all other subjects of the world—political, social, economic together with the intelligence report of the Intelligence Agencies of the different countries is vast. In this part gets illustrated the difference between astrological foresight and historical hindsight.

Astrological Foresight *Dr. B.V. Raman* *Goa*	*Historical Hindsight* *Pt. Nehru* *Goa : Pt. Nehru's Speeches*
According to Avakahada Chakra Goa falls under Satabhisha or Kumbha Rasi...But after Rahu enters Scorpio and Saturn quits Libra their movements will have reference to the tenth house from Kumbha...Therefore it occurs to us the end of Portuguese rule is in sight within the next two years. Sani Bhukti in Rahu Dasa is in operation now. Saturn is in a *maraka* place while the major lord Rahu occupying the 9th or house of fortune, and aspected by the *maraka* Saturn clearly indicates "the death of the native" (the end or Portuguese rule)	"What are the basic elements of our policy in regard to Goa? First, there must be peaceful methods. This is essential unless we give up the whole roots of all our policies and our behaviour. There is nothing I can argue with any person who thinks that the methods employed in regard to Goa must be other than peaceful, because we rule out our non-peaceful methods completely."

In view of the incendiary nature of Saturn—Rahu conjunction, the Portuguese authorities will not gracefully withdraw. The problem of "peaceful negotiation" cannot work in the case of Goa, in view of the strong disposition of malefics in the 7th, 8th and 9th houses...Therefore, a grave situation is likely to develop by about October 1956 (Saturn—Rahu conjunction)...before Rahu leaves Scorpio, the Goa problem will have been satisfactorily (but not entirely non-violent) solved and Portuguese authority terminated, (*A.M.*, August, 1955)

(Pt. Nehru's speech in Lok Sabha, September 17, 1955)

(Dr. Raman's editorial written earlier clearly stated what Pt. Nehru could not foresee.

Later when military action was taken what Pt. Nehru said is :

Background of Liberation of Goa

"The whole operation there took about 26 hours. It would have taken half that time but for the fact that roads were mined and vehicles could not move."

Vol. IV, p. 36 of Jawahar Lal Nehru's Speeches)

Hindu Jyotisha and Statesmen's Wisdom

(2)

01. Hindu Shastras refer to Astrology as a Science of Wisdom for the management of day-to-day affairs which the King must make use of, it being an infallible peep into the future.

02. Instead of respecting the astrological wisdom of Rishis, it has been looked down upon. True what is inevitable, could not have been prevented, but could have been foreseen and minimised.

03. All foreign offices of the countries of the world have their own China specialists. In the years referred to below, we had our China specialist in late K.M. Pannikar, V.K.N. Menon, K.P.S. Menon and a vast team of officers.

04. Given below is a contrasting study between what Dr. Raman said in March 1950 and December 1954, the same year in which Pandit Nehru concluded an agreement with China which was signed in Peking. Two points worth noting below are what Dr. Raman says about relations between China and Russia on the one hand and China and India on the other.

Dr. Raman, March 1950

01."The period of Mars in the Chinese Republic Horoscope will be of far-reaching consequences. While the Soviets will be despaired of their Chinese friends, the Chinese themselves will follow in Asia a policy more or less on the pattern of the policy followed by the Soviets in Europe after the II World War.

Pt. Nehru and others

01."As we know how, the CCP delegates did not attend as meek followers of Moscow-dictated policies. Until 1960 China was willing for the sake of block unity to issue harmonious sounding communiques, but from that year onwards they displayed an increased willingness to challenge Moscow openly. And at the four Congresses in late 1962, and one in early 1963 the Sino-Soviet dispute was on the table for all to see. It is no accident that Peking had attended only block Congresses in Rumania and Albania since that time." (Management of Foreign Affairs in China in the book *China: Management of a Revolutionary Society* (p 335) George Allen and Unwin Ltd.)

December 1954.

02 Chinese expansionism will be aimed at the destruction of the capitalist system and the establishment of communism. It occurs to us therefore that the adage 'trust begets trust', referred to by our Prime Minister in his recent Calcutta speech, will not hold good in regard to our Chinese friends in view of the dominant position of Mars. We beg to differ from the Prime Minister's view that "nobody can foresee what will happen in the future. The future can be foreseen with appreciable accuracy and the future indication in the horoscope of China does not warrant the optimism that China will scrupulously adhere to the terms of recent joint-statement issued by the Prime Ministers of India and China... China will continue to follow a policy of expansion until the end of Mars Dasa. India should beware of this. Otherwise the true interests of India will be in jeopardy... A firm grasp of the basic issues involved is essential on the part of our leaders, it policies adequate to meet the communist menace are to be eventually evolved.

(A.M., December 1954)

02 " A few days ago, an agreement between India and China was signed in Peking.. The agreement is based on the principles of mutual respect for each other's territorial integrity and sovereignty, mutual non-aggression, mutual non-interference in each other's internal affairs, equality and mutual benefits, and peaceful co-existence ...If these principles were recognised in the mutual relations of all countries, then indeed there would hardly be any conflict and certainly no war. This agreement not only settles some outstanding points between the great countries of India and China and establishes their relationship firmly on a peaceful basis, but I think it will help in the maintenance of peace in Asia."

(p.253 Broadcast from Colombo, May 2, 1954)
Jawahar Lal Nehru's Speeches, Volume three, The Publications Division.

Ashtagraha of 1962-An Instance of Astrological Peep into Future

(3)

Editorial of November 1960, THE ASTROLOGICAL MAGAZINE

Even today there are lots of critics of Astrology who cite the instances of the panic created about the possible results of the Ashtagraha Combination of February 1962, and refer to it as a glaring instance of failure of Astrology. It is therefore, necessary to know what exactly Dr. B.V.Raman said about the Ashtagraha combination in the month of November 1960, editorially, i.e., 16 months before the event.

Dr. Raman's Prediction

Hindu Attitude

01 It is not necessary to suggest that our interpretation of the combination is in the light of Hindu Astrology supplemented of course by our humble experience. Hindu methods of approach differ to a certain extent from those employed by European and American astrologers. One should not go by mere precedents.

Comments :

01 Dr. Raman's own researches have led him to discard the Western Astrological method of pronouncing judgement merely on the basis of precedents. There are so many other factors taken into consideration as is obvious.

02 Varahamihira recognises five types of combinations, viz., Sammoha (tarnishing), Samaja (meeting), Kosa (Fellowship), Sannipatha (encounter) and then Samagama (general conjunction) when four or five planets meet together in a sign Samavarta. If Rahu or Ketu should join then it is Sammoha. The combination in question takes the character of Kosa also because Jupiter and Saturn meet. Sammoha and Kosa are considered to be dangerous to people.

02. The factors to be taken into consideration are the five types of combinations referred to by Varahamihira. Western astrologers should learn from these finer naunces of different results. It is particularly necessary because it is western astrologers who through their stupendous follies have brought down the level of Astrology, as a predictive science. *The Jupiter Effect*, a book sold in enormous numbers all over the world, had predicted almost the end of the world in July, 1982, and Dr. Raman had assured his readers that no such impending catastrophe would take place. Therefore, going back to Hindu Shastras and acknowledging it, would help western astrologers more than their plagiarising like Alan Leo, who lifted bodily the principles of Jyotisha of India without acknowledging, and, also lifted the tatva-theory- =Agni, Prithvi, Vayu, Jal, Akash, in his esoteric Astrology. The recent glaring instance of astrological piracy is that the British astrologers who have adopted the Shadvargas of India, and without acknowledging it, they call it "harmonics".

03.In Mr. Nehru's chart. the planets conjoin in a maraka place. These are not happy dispositions. Lessons of history should not be ignored. We must beware of China.

04.Declaration of some sort of a national emergency cannot be ruled out... The threat from China will be real and no effort should be spared to meet this threat.

,03 Ashtagraha combination in Capricorn Rasi was a clear indicator of the coming events. Anyone,who knows elementary Astrology, could have seen that Pandit Nehru who made fun of Ashtagraha himself was to be affected by it and Dr.Raman very clearly points out that the planets are conjoining in the Maraka place in Nehru's chart.

04.More remarkable still, it was in 1962 October when the Sino- Indian war broke out that the first external emergency was declared in the country. Dr.Raman had already predicted about this emergency. He had predicted again in 1974 December, the internal emergency of 1975.

05.There is also another important thing to consider. In 1962, there will be two solar eclipses one on the 5th February and the other on 31st July. Moreover the lunar fortnight between 19th June and 1st July has got only 13 days which is said to be a rare phenomenon. It is said that in the year in which the lunar fortnight is only 13 days war is likely. In the 1962 combination Mars is dominant. He is exalted and in close conjunction with Saturn.

There is also a powerful Kalasara Yoga, i.e., all planets being hemmed in between Nodes. Hindu astrological works use for such a disposition, such terms as"certain death of Kings", great political revolutions and immense suffering for the people in the northern hemisphere.

06.Capricorn being a movable sign the conflict, if it breaks out, is not likely to be a long drawn affair.

07.In view of the favorable directions operating in the horoscopes of both America and Russia, we do not think either of them will start the war.

05.A tremendously valid principle of Hindu Shastras is that if eclipses fall within a ludar fortnight of 13 days, a war breaks out. Dr.Raman's extra-ordinary research of eclipses will restore the faith of the world back in super-scientific tradition of Hindu Astrology.

06.The war between China and India was of short duration only as was clearly predicted.

07.Pandit Nehru had delivered a very pessimistic speech when Khruschev was sending a Russian ship loaded with nuclear missile and President Kennedy gave to Russia 24 hours ultimatum. It appeared that the Third World War would break out but it was Dr.Raman who had already stated in 1960 November that there would be no war between USA and Russia. So in spite of the Bay of Pigs disaster no such war broke out. But on the other hand, war between India and China as repeatedly predicted by Dr.Raman did break out, that was the beginning of the end of Pandit Nehru who next year had a stroke of paralysis. A smart photographer of US *Newsweek* took a photo of Pandit Nehru bending sideways, and dangling his arms in a helpless posture. A Bombay weekly reprinted that and created a sensation in India; one year after 1963, Pandit JawaharLal Nehru thought that he had made partial recovery and his era was not over. In a press conference in Bombay sometime in February and later in a press conference in Delhi on 22nd May 1964, he clearly stated, "I am not going to die so early", But five days after 22nd May, he died.

Foreseeing Future History (War)

(4)

01. When in introducing Dr.Raman I remarked that an astrologer foresaw forces that shape history which the historian chronicles after the events have happened some academicians thought that it was to big a claim. Please read the following.

02. In India very few men, particularly in the North, know both English and Astrology.

03. Most of them do not know how Dr.Raman has been making predictions in advance, many years in advance, when others strutting on the world's stage, least expected the events, that happened to happen.

Dr.B.V.Raman.

THE ASTROLOGICAL MAGAZINE

July 1954

01 Wars–especially involving great nations can break out only under certain definite planetary patterns when Saturn, Rahu, Mars are either in kendras or trikonas and signs and constellations involved are of particularly sensitive nature such as Mrigasira, Aswini, Satabhisha, etc.

Comments

01.It is planets only that decide when a war would take place. Men are instruments of planetary decisions and through them, Hitlers and Mussolinis, wars break out. But for a war to break out planets, malefic in nature moving in malefic places, must occupy certain strategic positions from each other. These are the three conditions to be fulfilled.

02.Planetary movements during 1957 do not warrant the outbreak of hostilities between USA and Russia.

03.If we just study' the movements of planets in 1959, we find that by the end of August Saturn, Mars and Rahu will have occupied kendra positions ... These influences favour increased tension between world powers.

04.But the real crisis can come only in 1962 when Saturn, Mars, Ketu and Jupiter will be in Capricorn and Rahu in Cancer the disposition having reference to the 8th from Gemini ruling USA and the 12th from Aquarius ruling Russia.

02.Panic is created periodically by war-monger, western astrologers, western astronomers, now futurologists (who get wide publicity and get good commercial profits from books like *Jupiter Effect)* by giving alarming predictions about war. Dr.Raman deprecates such fears for 1957.

03.Out of the three conditions mentioned one condition will be fulfilled in 1959. So there will be tension between and among world powers. (Tensions had increased then between India and China ; between China and Russia and between USA and Russia.)

04.All the three conditions will be fulfilled in 1962. Russia will be in difficult situation caught in two minds whether to wage a war or not.

Please note

Dr.Raman predicted very clearly in a series of editorials.

(a) US-Russia will not be involved in a war (Bay of Pigs a war nearly broke out).

(b) India-China war would break out. War broke out in 1962.

(c) It was in 1954 that he forewarned about war in 1962. That is how an astrologer foresees future history.

Predicting the Death of a Political Party (THE ASTROLOGICAL MAGAZINE,October 1963) Supra-Technical Discussion in Hindu Jyotisha (From Dr.Raman's editorial)

(5)

For Astrologers

01."According to Jaimini, the Congress has a full term of life. The disposition of lords of Lagna and the 8th gives the length of life as above 83 years".

For Non-Astrologers

01.Length of life of 83 years added to the birth year of the Congress 1885 + 83 = (1968) brings to us the year of death of the old Congress party in 1969, when this great organisation split.

(Please remember that it was written when Pt.Nehru was alive and six years before the death of I.N.C.)

02."It is also suggested by ancient writers that a Bhava suffers destruction when Saturn transits the Rasi and Navamsa held by the lord of the 8th or the 12th from the concerned Bhava. Saturn's transit of trinal places from these two houses can also destroy the Bhava...Saturn's transit of Scorpio, Pisces or Cancer should cause destruction to the 8th house.

03.The sum-total of the longitudes of Saturn, Jupiter, the Sun and the Moon (here it is Capricorn 28°) is a point of death (Mrityubhaga)
In the case of a full term life, Saturn's transit of this point in the 3rd cycle can prove fatal.

04.The longitude of Mandi less that of Saturn indicates another death-dealing point. Saturn's transit of which can prove fatal. In the Congress horoscope this point happens to be (44° 22'- 73° 50') Pisces 18

02.Here the principle of timing is given. The timing according to Lahiri's ephemeris would be

8-4-1966 to 2-11-1966
19-12-1966 to 16-6-1968 } For Pisces
28-9-1968 to 6—1969

03.Pt.Nehru came out with his Kamraj Plan in August, 1963, when this point of death got activated. Many old Congress stalwarts had to resign from his cabinet. After Pt.Nehru's death some of the old stalwarts claimed that they were the original Congressmen of the original party, and in later years, they formed an alliance with Swatantra Party formed by the oldest surviving Congressman, Raja-Gopalachari.

04.The timing arrived at is again as in paragraph 2 for Pisces. But the fine timing will be Pisces 18.

05.Multiply by 9 the longitudes of Mandi and Saturn. Add the products. The transit of this point (here it is Pisces 16°) by Saturn would give extremely evil results.

06.The sign representing the Navamsa occupied by the lord of the Ascendant is Taurus. This is second from Aries.

In the Congress Chart such a sign again happens to be Pisces.

When Saturn transits the sign as far removed from the sign occupied by the lord of the 8th death is likely.

07.It is clear therefore that Saturn's transit of Aquarius and Pisces should be extremely significant and crucial in future history of the Congress Party.

05.Again Pisces. First the longevity was fixed as 83 years ; Saturn's transit of three sensitive areas located now out of the three Pisces as the sensitive area for the death of the Congress is established. Then it is seen that Saturn will be in this area as death's agent at the age of 83 years of the Congress Party.

06.Again Pisces.

07.Symptoms of death will appear

Saturn enters Pisces in March 1966 and stays there until June 1968.

08.Mercury's Dasa ends in 1970. It will be during the remaining seven years that the Congress organisation would have to completely disintegrate.

08.Now the scheme of three-fold timing of death is complete.

(a) Longevity of 83 years - 1968.

(b) Saturn's transit - 1968.

(c) According to the Moon at birth before 1970.

The great organisation died before 1970, and the quarrelsome children partitioned paternal property which between 1970 and 1980 was fragmented three times more.

CHAPTER FOUR

AIR CRASHES RELATED TO ASTRONOMIC EVENTS

V. Zakharko

No one knows the exact number of sea accidents and plane crashes in the area of the Atlantic, lying between the Bermuda Islands, Florida and Puerto Rico, but it is known that there have been very many accidents there.

But that is not the only place marked by accidents of inexplicable origin. In the area between Japan, Guam and the Philippines so many ships and planes have been reported missing that the Japanese Government has officially declared it a dangerous zone.

An opinion is in currency that there exists no mystery of "triangles" and that accidents in them result from the inexperience and errors of navigators and pilots, rather than the action of certain natural forces. But this point of view has not been substantially proved.

There now comes an interesting hypothesis on the "triangle" problem, recently put forward by A. Yelkin who holds a chair at the Moscow Civil Engineering Institute.

"I do not want," he says, "to advocate any of the views on the 'triangles'; is there a scientific problem here or not? What I did was simply to assume that the problem existed and try to find out whether there was any regularity in those accidents.

"After collecting statistics on planes, I saw that the moments at which they had disappeared—as distinct from ships, these are established with a precision of one—had something definitely regular about them, related to astronomic phenomena, or, more precisely, to the position in regard to each other of the Earth, the Moon and the Sun.

"It is known that the Sun and the Moon do not always exert the same influence on the Earth.

"Since the Earth is compressed at the poles, the Sun and the Moon more strongly pull the part of it at the equator that is nearer to them. There arise the so-called forces of precession straining to turn the axis of rotation of the Earth.

A Case for Astrology

ASTROLOGY has fascinated mankind for centuries and a belief in it is spread over many nations. In this country we have always paid it its due respect and do not allow the avowed disbelief of a few to interfere with our faith in it. Astrology does forecast definite trends in an individual's life and that it is not always able to foretell all events in detail certainly does not mean that it is incapable of fulfilling its objectives. There are those who argue that considering how a person's life runs according to preordained trends, there is no point in consulting an astrologer at all and that it may often be better not to know what the future has in store for us. But it is important to realise that Astrology has other

"These forces can become most important in December and June, with a zero influence in March and September. Revolving around the Earth along an elliptical orbit, the Moon now comes nearer to us, now moves away. When it is the nearest to the Earth (in perigee), its tide-forming power is 40 per cent greater than in apogee.

"Knowing from the statistics when the planes had disappeared, I established what coordinates the Sun and the Moon had held in those days. Without going into the subtleties of this question now, I would like to say the most important thing: it turned out that there was a definite regularity in the moments at which the air accidents had taken place—they coincided with new moons and full moons and the Moon's position near perigee, as well as with the moments of the greatest magnitudes of precession forces.

aspects which may be studied with profit. In his inaugural address to the All- Kerala Astrological Association, Prof. B.V.Raman has stressed this factor. He said that Astrology could also be studied "with advantage to help medicine, agriculture, meteorology and psychology". He has argued, too, that as Astrology has shown that foreknowledge of events is possible, science must find a place for it in its purview of the Universe. There are many enthusiastic scholars both here and in the high-advanced Western countries who carry on constant research in Astrology. In this country, with its ancient traditions, every facility should be afforded to the scholarly astrologers to improve their knowledge through study of and research into ancient texts and pass on the resultant benefits to the people. We

"The discovered regularity suggests that at such moments in the Bermuda and other triangles lunar-solar tides may cause a movement of ionized magma beneath the ocean floor which gives rise to magnetic anomalies. These may affect the functioning of common and gyroscopic compasses, clocks and electric and electronic devices, which happened on the planes and ships. This could be one of the causes of the accidents."

A hypothesis is not yet a theory, but there is no scientific theory which has not been preceded by hypotheses. If it turns out that A. Yelkin's hypothesis does identify not an accidental (which the author himself thinks is possible) regularity in the moments of accidents but a real law of nature, this can have not a "purely" scientific but an enormous practical significance.

may even venture to say that centers of knowledge like our Universities should afford facilities to its study. These are days, for instance, in which we hear of the good effect of sound waves in promoting the growth of vegetable life. It has been pointed out that certain mantras have a beneficial effect in the case of afflicted persons, and these mantras are resorted to on the advice of competent astrologers. The analogy with the effect of sound waves on the growth of plants should immediately strike the dispassionate observer who does not look down upon Astrology merely because it is fashionable to do so today. Unfortunately, most people resort to astrologers (and there are many quacks among them, as there are in any other profession) to ask for detailed information about most trivial affairs. There is also

For almost all the "triangles" are areas of very intense sea and air traffic. And how important it would be to know when they can be entered without any risk and when the risk is great.

According to this hypothesis, the nearest time of a "line-up" of the Earth, the Moon and the Sun which causes dangerous situations in the "triangles" will come on January 18, 1977.

It is possible, believes A. Yelkin, that linked with the nature of the formation of the fields of force in the "triangles" also is the mechanism of the long-term development of situations leading to earth- and sea-quakes in certain areas of deep-water depressions.

Such a mechanism may cause destructive earth tremors approximately on December 20-25 and January 5-8 and 18-22 next year in the following areas: Turkey (in the Taurus Mountains zone), New Zealand and Japan (with the ap-

the human tendency among some astrologers to try to play down unpleasant expectations and to tell those who come to them with their horoscopes only what they would like to hear. A reputation as a good astrologer is built upon long study and diligent practice. In this country there is no use pretending that Astrology is not popular. By and large, we believe in it; and the suggestions of men like Dr.B.V.Raman deserve to be studied with due consideration. That there is much in our traditional corpus of knowledge, the result of the experience of generations, is becoming more widely

pearance of a tsunami), South America (from 20 to 35 degrees of the southern latitude) and California, USA.

I have only to add that back in the summer A. Yelkin in conversation with me said he thought that a violent earthquake in Turkey could be expected at the end of November. As is known, the earthquake occurred. "It may be that this coincidence is also accidental," says the scientist.

Courtesy : Deccan Herald (Supplement)

recognised. In this context much can be done by our study of Astrology by the setting up of separate "chairs" devoted to the development of this hoary science.

- Courtesy: THE HINDU 18-9-1958

The Predictions of Tycho Brahe

BETTER known even than Cardan, the Tycho Brahe, some of whose predictions were remarkable. In 1577 he declared that "in the North, in Finland, there should be born a prince who would lay waste Germany and Vanish in 1632", and he went on to give the grisly details. His predictions came true to the letter for Gustavus Adolphus of Sweden was born in Finland. In 1630 he landed in Pomerania and made a treaty with the French statesman Cardinal Richelieu, granting him subsidies. He invaded the German states and won brilliant victories, among them the capture and sack of Magdeburg where 30,000 civilians perished. But, as he foretold, he led the Swedes to victory in the Battle of Lutzen, in which he was killed.

In an article on Tycho Brahe the *Encyclopedia Britannica* says:"The fulfillment of the details of this prophecy suggests that Tycho Brahe had had some basis of reason for his prediction." (!)

Among the famous who studied Astrology even if they did not practise it, were: Copernicus, Galileo, Kepler, Huygens, Flammarion, Roger Bacon, Napier of Merchistoun (the inventor of logarithms), Sir Christopher Heydon and Elias

Ashmole, founder of the Ashmolean Museum in Oxford.

*Courtesy: **Seeing into the Future** by Harvey Day*

Benjamin Franklin and Astrology

ONE of the firmest believers in astrology was Benjamin Franklin, scientist, philosopher, diplomat, and the most outstanding American of his time. He believed nothing he could not test for himself and prove to be true. While at college he drew up the horoscope of a fellow student named Titan Leeds and calculated that he would die at 3-20 p.m. on 7th October 1733 at the instant of the conjugation of the Sun and Mercury. Leeds died at the time predicted....

Astrology was then a respectable art in America and many of the Fathers of the Revolution, among them Jefferson, Washington and Robert Campbell, author of *Our Flag*, practised it. Campbell says that the national flag was designed to express the symbolism of the flag and the nation in terms of the zodiac.

*Courtesy: **Seeing into the Future** by Harvey Day*

CHAPTER FIVE

THE HOAX OF "SCIENTIFIC TEMPER"

A. The Narlikar Episode

Gayatri Devi Vasudev

A science degree tagging a name does not automatically imbibe one with a scientific temper. At a time, in our country, when chaos rules and merit has been stomped upon and trampled to death, it is not unusual for men with doctorates to claim omniscience and play to the galleries. Such men are small fry and best left to clamour amongst themselves. But what is tragic and objectionable and must be viewed with serious concern is the ease with which men in responsible positions spread canards against Astrology.

I attended a discussion meeting led by Prof. Narlikar on "Astronomy and the Scientific Outlook" held on 3-12-1985 at the Indian Institute of World Culture, Bangalore, under the auspices of the Centre for the History and Philosophy of Science. Prof. Narlikar chose to tread on areas he had not investigated and therefore, if he could claim to be one of genuine scientific temper, had no right to trespass into.

* Incidentally, no scientist, official or otherwise, has tested even a single astrological principle found in Sanskrit classics on Astrology and which principles form the basis of the most amazing predictions of Indian astrologers.

One of the topics he chose for discussion was something about beliefs that had their origins in astronomy. He took up Astrology as one such belief and said it was not a science. His argument was that according to the Greeks, the word planet meant "wanderer". The Greeks called a planet by this name because it did not seem to have a fixed path as it moved backwards and forwards in its path round the Sun (probably the astrophysicist was referring to a planet's retrograde and direct motion although he did not make use of these terms). Since it moved in this manner, the Greeks, he said, thought planets had a will of their own. This will, they believed, planets exercised on man and this was the origin of Astrology as a belief. Since planets had no will really Astrology was not a science.

I was surprised that he should be so ill-informed and that he should also subscribe to the theory of the Greek origin of Astrology. When the

Scientific Dogma

Rigid and intolerant ideas, ideas which assert in effect that "I am in possession of the truth, the whole truth, every bit of the truth,and nobody outside the pale has it", narrow men's minds, shutting the door against a tolerant and objective approach, where men not only look up at the heavens without fear but are also prepared to look down into the pit of hell without fear. It seems to me that people in the Buddha's time were more advanced in tolerance and compassion than we are, although they were not so advanced in technology and science....

question hour came I told him that Astrology was Hindu in its origin, being a Vedanga. It was based on the theory that a correlation exists between celestial phenomena and terrestrial events. It was not a cause and effect relationship between man and the universe. Since he was mistaken in the definition of Astrology, he could not dismiss it as of no consequence and as a mere belief with no locus standi. What did he have to say now about Astrology? The astrophysicist gave no answer.

While dismissing Astrology, he further said that astrologers had charged scientists with coming to a conclusion that Astrology was not scientific without ever having made a study of it. He asserted he had details of investigations made on Astrology. He said even allowing for a wide margin of error, none of the astrological dicta had been proved by scientific studies. When I asked him where the studies had been conducted and

The scientist is supposed to be an objective seeker after truth. Science has grown because in a large measure the great scientists have sought truth in that way. But I suppose no man today, not even a scientist, can live in a world of his own, in some kind of ivory tower, cut off from what is happening. Therefore, science today has perhaps begun to cross the borders of morals and ethics. If it gets divorced completely from the realm of morality and ethics then the power it possesses may be used for evil purposes. But above all, if it ties itself to the gospel of hatred and violence, then undoubtedly it will have taken a wrong direction which will bring much peril to the world. I plead with the scientists here and elsewhere to remember that the scientific spirit is essentially one of tolerance, one of

when, whether the results of such studies had been published and who were those who had made such studies and what were the astrological laws tested, he said nothing again, although he had initially claimed he had the references with him. I think a man of his stature should be more responsible and closer to truth. Lesser folk such as displaced educationists and rationalists can get emotional, hysterical and talk a lot of nonsense. But it is a serious matter when it comes from an officially designated scientist from a prestigious institution.

Another statement this astrophysicist made was Sanskrit was suited for literature, not science. Grandoisely he conceded that a *sloka* by Aryabhata (he did not quote which or from where it was) had said that the earth moved round the Sun, yet the Sun appeared to rise and set just as a man in a boat sailing in a river saw the tree on the bank moving. He said this was true and cor-

humility, one of realization that somebody else may also have a bit of the truth. Scientists should note that they do not have a monopoly of the truth; that nobody has a monopoly, no country, no people, no book. Truth is too vast to be contained in the minds of human beings, or in books, however sacred.

Jawaharlal Nehru in his Speech at the Science Cong ess, Calcutta, January 14, 1957.

India And Western Science

"Science has dominated the Western world and everyone pays tribute to it and yet the West is still far from having developed the real temper of Science. It has still to

rect but Sanskrit was such a versatile language that it could be interpreted in any way. Not one in the audience, which was supposed to be distinguished for its intellectual stature, said a word in protest but nodded sheepishly. I wonder how many Sanskrit scholars will agree with the astrophysicist on this kind of versatility of this beautiful language. No other language can be as precise in sound and sense as Sanskrit. The latest findings of scientists is that Sanskrit is the most suitable language for computer-use.

There were many contradictions in what Mr. Narlikar said. When questioned about Newton's and Tycho Brahe's respect for Astrology, notwithstanding their scientific eminence, he said: "Perhaps Newton did not let the other aspects of his life interfere when he was in the laboratory". What did he mean exactly? Was he hinting, as pointed out by Prof. Ramachandra Sharma, a noted psychologist of Bangalore who was also

bring the spirit and flesh into creative harmony. In India, in many obvious ways, we have a greater distance to travel and yet there may be fewer major obstructions in our way for the essential basis of Indian thought for ages past, though not its later manifestations, fits in with the scientific temper and approach, as well as with internationalism. It is based on a fearless search for truth, on the solidarity of man, even on the divinity of everything living, and on the free and co-operative development of the individual and the species, ever to higher freedom and higher stages of human growth." *(Discovery of India.)*

— Jawaharlal Nehru

present at the meeting, that Newton was a schizophrenic, a split, two different beings, rational and irrational at the same time? But there was one point he made when he said scientists were not necessarily scientific-minded!

(Reproduced from THE ASTROLOGICAL MAGAZINE
February 1986)

B. Suppressing Truth

(Another favorite weapon some pseudo-intellectuals try to use against Astrology is a statement said to have been signed by 186 scientists (including some Nobel prize-winners * condemning Astrology that appeared in *Humanist*. This statement was issued in 1975. The matter did not stop there. 186+1 = 187 people with academic degrees issued another statement contradicting the *Humanist* statement. Now read on for the facts and how a real scientist rates the unscientific statement flaunted by critics of Astrology].

Closed and Open Minds **

There is no bar to knowledge greater than contempt prior to examination.

Herbert Spencer.

---

* Incidentally Dr. S. Chandrasekhar whose name is included in the list of Nobel Laureates who signed the statement in 1975 won the Nobel prize only in 1983. This proves those who quote this statement have no respect for truth and are unfit to investigate Truth. In 1983, Dr.Subrahmanyam Chandrasekhar says in an article published in Readers' Digest: "Scientists seem to develop a certain arrogance towards nature. They imagine their success in one area means they have a special way of looking at science that must therefore be right. But it has been shown over and over that the kinds of truth which underlie nature transcend even the most powerful minds."

** *Courtesy*: **Astrology: Science or Superstition?** by H.J. Eysenck and D.K.B.Nias.

There is no doubt about the popularity of astrology. According to various opinion polls roughly a third of the population of Western countries believes in it and another third is interested enough to read astrological predictions, at least occasionally. The last third remains unconcerned or sceptical....

In reaction to this surge of credulity, other people hurry in to denounce everything to do with astrology as an absurd fraud, and among these opponents a number of scientists have been prominent. *The American Humanist* (a magazine devoted to discussions of social problems and irrationatity) in its September 1975 issue, carried the following statement, entitled 'Objections to Astrology'. It was endorsed by 186 leading scientists, including 18 Nobel Prize winners.

Scientists in a variety of fields have become concerned about the increased acceptance of Astrology in many parts of the world. We, the undersigned-astronomers, astrophysicists, and scientists in other fields—wish to caution the public against the unquestioning acceptance of the predictions and advice given privately and publicly by astrologers. (Those who wish to believe in Astrology should realise that there is no scientific foundation for its tenets).

In ancient times people believed in the predictions and advice of astrologers because Astrology was part and parcel of their magical world view. They looked upon celestial objects as abodes or omens of the Gods and, thus, intimately connected with events here on earth; they had no concept of the vast distances from the earth to the planets and stars. Now that these distances can and have been calculated, we can see how infinitesimally small are the gravitational and other effects produced by the distant planets and the far more distant stars. It is simply a mistake to imagine that the forces exerted by stars and planets at the moment of birth can in any way shape our futures. Neither is it true that the positions of distant heavenly bodies make certain days or periods more favourable to particular kinds of action, or that the sign under which one was born determines one's compatibility or incompatibility with other people.

Why do we believe in astrology? In these uncertain times many long for the comfort of having guidance in making decisions. They would like to believe in a destiny predetermined by astral forces beyond their control. However, we must all face the world, and we must realise that our futures lie in ourselves, and not in the stars.

One would imagine, in this day of widespread enlightenment and education, that it would be unnecessary to debunk beliefs based on magic and superstition. Yet, acceptance of astrology pervades modern society. We are especially disturbed by the continued uncritical dissemination of astrological charts, forecasts, and horoscopes by the media and by otherwise reputable newspapers, magazines, and book publishers. This can only contribute to the growth of irrationalism and obscurantism. We believe that the time has come to challenge directly, and forcefully, the pretentious claims of astrological charlatans.

It should be apparent that those individuals who continue to have faith in Astrology do so in spite of the fact that there is no verified scientific basis for their beliefs, and indeed that there is strong evidence to the contrary.

In the editorial it was explained that both the American Ethical Union and the American Humanist Association - the co-publishers of *The Humanist* - had long been opposed to cults of unreason and irrationalism (under which they also classify religion, of course). The editor went on to ask: "What better way to demonstrate this in this anniversary issue than by a major critique of Astrology?" Professor Bart J. Bok, a former president of the American Astronomical Society, was invited to draft a brief statement listing some scientific objections to Astrology. This was subsequently revised and expanded to the statement quoted above and then sent to a selected list of distinguished members of the American Astronomical Society and the National Academy of Sciences for endorsement.

The signed statement was subsequently sent to thousands of newspaper editors in the United States and abroad, with the suggestion that they print it, especially if they carried a daily or weekly horoscope column. The intention, of course, was to counter the ever-increasing trend for Astrology to be foisted on an unsuspecting public which is rarely exposed to scientific criticisms of it. This was an honourable intention, but **as we shall show it is questionable whether the statement is true. It is also unscientific in its approach**. This point was well made by Carl Sagan, a scientist who declined to sign, in the following letter to *The Humanist*.

I find myself unable to endorse the 'Objections to Astrology' statement (September/October, 1975) - not because I feel that Astrology has any validity whatever, but because I felt and still feel that the tone of the statement is authoritarian. The fundamental point is not that the origins of Astrology are shrouded in superstition. This is true as well for chemistry, medicine, and astronomy, to mention only three. To discuss the psychological motivations of those who believe in Astrology seems to be quite peripheral to the issue of its validity. That we can think of no mechanism for Astrology is relevant but unconvincing. No mechanism was known, for example, for continental drift when it was proposed by Wegener. Nevertheless, we see that Wegener was right and those who objected on the grounds of unavailable mechanism were wrong.

Statements contradicting borderline, folk, or pseudo-science that appear to have an authoritarian tone can do more danger than good. They never convince those who are flirting with pseudo- science but merely seem to confirm their impression that scientists are rigid and close-minded....

What I would have signed is a statement describing and refuting the principal tenets of astrological belief. My belief is that such a statement would have been far more persuasive and would have produced vastly less controversy than the one that was actually circulated.

Authority or evidence?

The scientists who signed *The Humanist* statement agreed that Astrology was folkore and superstition and that there was no scientific basis for it. Unfortunately, they do not seem to have investigated any evidence that would have supported or disproved their claim, and so their response seems to have been largely emotional. Rather than appealing to their authority, it would have been better if they had simply presented evidence. This point was well made by Einstein in response to criticisms of his work. In 1920, a racist German group tried to refute the theory of relativity by holding an emotional meeting in the Berlin Philharmonic Hall, and then by persuading a hundred professors to condemn Einstein's theory in a book. Einstein commented: Were I wrong, one professor would have been quite enough.

In addition to the 'appeal to authority' other weaknesses occur in the statement. Feyerabend (1978) points out that the 186 scientists made the mistake of criticising the basic assumptions of Astrology rather than the way in which it is practised. He observed that it is interesting to see how closely both parties approach each other in ignorance, conceit and the wish for easy power over minds. He also notes that, following the statement, **many of the scientists declined interviews because they had not studied Astrology. It appears they had signed merely on the basis of a 'religiously' felt conviction***(bold ours)*

Feyerabend claims that the conviction led the astronomers to overlook even evidence they were familiar with. For example, in an article accompanying the statement, Bok (1975) had stated that because of their distance from us, the planets could not influence human affairs; he similarly assumed that the walls of the delivery room would shield the new-born child from radiation emitted by the planets. He made these statements even though, as an astronomer, he should have known that the planets might influence solar activity which in turn has various effects on us; it is also known that certain types of radiation can penetrate very thick walls to which a delivery room would not be an exception.

The scientists' statement prompted a contrary statement published in 1976 by the astrological journal *Aquarian Agent*. This statement claimed that Astrology is at least a valid area of research, and that it is important to distinguish 'Sun sign frauds' from genuine astrologers, who take far more factors into account than the sign of the zodiac under which one is born. Signatures for this statement were obtained from 187 (!) people with academic degrees. This, while also appearing in authority, does seem to take a less prejudiced view. Of course, simply to state that you are in favour of further research is to say little more than being against sin and for motherhood, but even this is an advance on the simple, prejudiced refusal to examine the evidence.

It is of course possible that there is no truth in any part of Astrology. The point is that the 186 scientists have not *demonstrated* this. To do so would involve systematically examining all the available evidence in favour of Astrology and then showing how it is invalid ....

It is against this background of undisguised hostility, rather than of receptiveness to new ideas and experiments, that open- minded scientists have had to fight in their attempts to establish whether or not there is any truth in Astrology. They have even had to defend their right to do research in this field. As a result, established scientists have often found it best to say nothing, rather than incur derision; only a few have had the courage to admit that 'there might be something in it'.

Prejudice

Prejudice means literally pre-judgment, the rejection of a contention out of hand, before examining the evidence. Prejudice is the result of powerful emotions, not of sound reasoning. If we wish to find out the truth of a matter we must approach the questions with as nearly open a mind as we can, and with a deep awareness of our own limitations and predispositions. On the other hand, if after carefully and openly examining the evidence, we reject the proposition, that is not prejudice . It might be called "postjudice". It is certainly a prerequisite for knowledge.

Critical and skeptical examination is the method used in everyday practical matters as well as in science. When buying a new or used car we think it prudent to insist on written warranties test drives and checks of particular parts. We are very careful about car dealers who are evasive on these points. ...Where skeptical observation and discussion are suppressed, the trut i hidden.

– **Carl Sagan.**

C. Rejoinders to The *Humanist* Statement

1. Astrology And Unscientific Prejudices

B.A.Kumar Babu, B.E., M.S.

There have been appearing in recent times critical and cheap attacks on Astrology. Because of the wide publicity they received, of particular interest is a statement published in *The Humanist* and signed by some physicists and astronomers. Though clothed in scientific jargon the statement published is nothing more than a hastily pieced together, ill-conceived and unscientific criticism of Astrology and astrologers.

What distinguishes the 20th century from the dark ages is the fact that people have realised that a scientist in any field is not omniscient and that all he knows is just an extremely tiny fraction of the sum-total of human knowledge. It might very well be said that because of his concentration on a very small item he gets a totally distorted view of everything else. If you have any doubts about this fact try looking at your door with your eyes about a millimetre from it and see how it appears. Thus it is that a Nobel prize in any field does not count for much except in the extremely narrow and specialised field of research that the Nobel laureate is involved in. The statement published in *The Humanist* bristles with inconsistencies and it is interesting to examine it in detail.

(1) "Those who wish to believe in Astrology

should reaslise that there is no scientific foundation for its tenets."

This presupposes that the signatories of the statement are very conversant with the tenets of Astrology. It would be interesting to see if even ten percent of these people know how to cast a horoscope, let alone how to interpret it. As far as scientific foundations are concerned, it has to be realised that there is a difference between "known scientific foundations" and the relatively longer expanse of the unknown and unexplained scientific phenomena. Science knows that light is an electromagnetic wave. But has it ever really been able to explain why it is so? If you go to the root of any scientific principle you will find that at some stage it begins in a hypothesis.

(2) The statement says that the ancients had "no concept of the vast distances from the earth to the planets".

It is surprising that a group of such specialists as those who issued a statement in *The Humanist* have made remarks that border on the ridiculous. Obviously the signatories (who include astronomers) do not reaslise that without a concept of such distances it would have been impossible to cast a horoscope which in its simplest form is a chart showing the longitudes of some celestial bodies with respect to a reference point.

It might be a comfortable thought to imagine that our futures lie in ourselves. But life is such that in any major thing we do we are held down, influenced and many times thwarted from doing what we want to do by social, religious, family, economic and other compulsions that it is but natural to speculate whether such compulsions which bog us down are in any way indicated by extra- terrestrial phenomena. Until proved otherwise we may well suppose that it is the order of nature that there is a correlation between the movements of planets and the direction of man.

In Lawrence E. Jerome's article in *The Humanist* there is a caption which says that the author has done extensive research on Astrology. Jerome and *The Humanist* must be having their own unique definition of " extensive research". He displays considerable ignorance in tracing the history of Astrology. Nowhere does he mention Astrology in India - and Astrology has existed in India for thousands of years. Astrology was propounded in India not by charlatans and magicians but by the same sages who enunciated the highest philosophical truths which are unmatched in their content by any philosopher or scientist of today - Eastern or Western.

Lawrence Jerome talks about the principle of correspondences as the basis of all Astrology. Little does he realise that the entire gamut of physical sciences is developed on the same basis.

The whole problem with people who make irrelevant attacks on Astrology is that they start on a wrong scientific premise. They accept that Astrology is all wrong and then go about trying to prove it. As such their vision gets blurred and coloured so much so that important facts are brushed aside as of no consequence because they are inconvenient. Under such "unscientific conditions" how can truth be arrived at? Though Jerome goes about trying to make a statistical case against Astrology he himself concedes that statistics can be easily manipulated (consciously or unconsciously) to yield the desired results.

In the same issue of *The Humanist* is an article by Bart J. Bok, an astronomer. He starts off his tirade against Astrology by calling it a pseudo-science. If at all there is a branch of knowledge which has made little or no progress in a thousand years it is astronomy. Except for some very basic facts regarding our solar system astronomers have done nothing but indulge in theoretical speculation which is a scientific word for 'useless work'. Why should so much public money be squandered on a subject so unsure of itself? Whether it is the age of the earth or of the Universe, the origin of life or something else astronomers just do not seem to agree on anything. Everyone of them comes out with weird ideas which look logical enough on paper but are essentially self-contradictory. Astronomers spend years and years wasting public money and do no useful service. It is time the public took a critical look at the work of astronomers. It is not a co-incidence that the majority of the signatories are astronomers - it is because they feel insecure about the irrelevance of whatever they are doing that they have to bring out cudgels against another branch of knowledge.

In the same article Bok talks about the Moon and other planets having similar physical properties. In the first place irrespective of what properties planets possess let us concede that we are talking about correspondence of phenomenon and not a cause and effect relationship. The fact that we do not know why a certain phenomenon happens does not imply that the existence of that phenomenon itself is in doubt. It only means that the frontiers of science have still a long way to go. If I did not know why light has to be an electromagnetic radiation and not something else, does it mean that the existence of light is itself unscientific.

There is ample proof to show that Astrology can be used as a very valuable aid in studying the psycho-physical characteristics of a person. There is proof to show that it is valuable in long term weather forecasting. There are proofs to show that it is an extremely valuable and powerful tool in the hands of man to help him lead a more sane existence.

It is time conventional scientists stretched their mental horizons to include branches of knowledge they do not comprehend. When Edison was asked to define electricity he said: "Why define? It exists. Use it." Why not we use Astrology in the same way?

There might come a time in future when advances made in other branches of knowledge would solve the mystery of why terrestrial happenings are in synchronism with planetary movements but till then let us not waste time arguing whether Astrology is scientific or not - but let us use it.

(Reproduced from **The Astrological Magazine** April 1976.)

ii). About Astrology

Buell D. Huggins

But if the humanists have doubts and fears about the United Nations, in this issue they had more about the stars, which to them are just inanimate bodies so far away that none of them, not even the Sun, could possibly give light and warmth to inhabitants of the earth, much less affect their physical appearance, personality, or terrestrial destiny.

It is astonishing how the humanists uphold psychologists, most of whom - Skinner, Watson, Freud and others - have been firm believers in determinism, but when it comes to Astrology Lawrence Jerome concludes his article "Astrology: Magic or Science" with the statement that to believe in Astrology is "to abandon free will". Evidently, Jerome does not know that most astrologers accept free will, and that it is the scientists and psychologists who reject it. Just eight months earlier (January - February 1975 issue), *The Humanist* editor Paul Kurtz, in a diatribe against religion, wrote as follows:

"The religious believer insists that he is free for he is created in God's image. But the problem of evil turns this eternal drama into a divine comedy. God entrusted me with the power and freedom of choice, yet he will punish me if I stray from Him. Why did he not program me during the act of creation, so that I could not avoid knowing Him and following His guidelines? Since it is He who created me, why does He condemn me for satisfying my natural inclinations, which He implanted in me? Why does He permit suffering and pain, torment and tragedy, disease, strife, war and plunder, conflict and chaos?"

Is it not plain that Kurtz does not believe in free will?

Jerome further claims that humanists believe in rationality, or rationalism. Yet this hardly seems possible. When rationalism was the 17th century philosophy of Rene Descartes, Gottfried Leibniz and Baruch Spinoza, who believed not only in rationality, or reason, but also intuition and *apriori* knowledge. Kurtz and his fellow humanists belong to the camp of the empiricists and pragmatists who came along later—David Hume, Gerbert Spencer, John Dewey, Bertrand Russell.

Jerome's linking of Astrology with magic is another blunder. Magic is a ritual performance involving slight-of-hand tricks and other ingenious acts which children and the uneducated are prone to link with the mystical or supernatural. Astrology, on the other hand, is based upon the powers and laws of nature and upon the electromagnetic, gravitational and radiative effects of those powers - the planets and luminaries.

Nor is Astrology a mode of fortune-telling. Of the 30 types of fortune-telling listed in *Collier's Encylopaedia*, Astrology is not mentioned, though dreams, the Bible, tea leaves, animal livers, the crystal ball, the Tarot and other cards are listed. While there may be some connection between magic and fortune- telling, there is none between magic and Astrology. And the horary branch of Astrology, the least favoured and practised of all branches, is the only one which has any resemblance to fortune-telling, divination and omens.

Jerome's complaint about the "daily horoscopes" in the newspapers does, we admit, have some validity. But did he ever stop to figure out why the "daily horoscopes" are there? They are there simply because there is a demand for them—just as there is a demand for the comic strips, the recipes, sports section, the crossword puzzle, and the women's section. In recent years, the newspaper publishers have discovered that certain readers are interested in Astrology. Most of the publishers know nothing about it and care nothing about it, but to supply the demand of certain readers and increase , on the one hand (and to appease the rest by publishing simple transits or "daily horoscopes" on the other) they publish these non- sensical columns based upon the tropical Sun-sign alone. If a competent astrologer were to offer them the true horoscope of George Washington, they would turn it down.

Jerome finds fault with astrologers using statistics. Prof. Skinner, the psychologist, does not like statistics, either, stating in one of his books that psychologists should use the laboratory. Does Jerome want Prof. Skinner to put him in a laboratory for several months for an experiment, along with the pigeons and mice? Astronomers cannot use the laboratory, either, being unable to capture the planets and put them there; so, like astrologers, they use mathematics.

Bart J.Bok, in his article "A Critical Look of Astrology" wonders why astrologers do not use the time of conception, instead of the time of birth, for casting the horoscope. If Bok can give us a foolproof method of arriving at the moment of conception, we will be glad to use it. The ancient Hindu astrologer, Satyacharya, said the time of conception might be preferable, but that it could not be discovered. We will let the scientists discover it. However, Bok should know that if a conception horoscope were used, it would become the object of the severest criticism and ridicule, since the humanists and scientists, who favour abortion, do not consider even the foetus an "entity", let alone the moment of conception, and the courts do not consider the foetus a "person". So the moment of conception, before the foetus formed, would be too much like "magic" or an accident for the humanists and scientists. And if the walls of a room shield a baby from the radiative effects of the planets, as Bok contends, does he not think there would be much more shielding inside the uterus?

Bok, Jerome and Kurtz all spoke of the bad psychological effects that predictions could have on one. Jerome feared the Gemini native might conclude he had a "split nature" and become schizophrenic. Yet he furnished no proof that the majority of schizophrenics are Geminis.

According to radio and television news commentators, buyers of securities in the stock market are very strongly influenced by "psychological factors". We are for ever being told that it was a very bad day at the stock exchange because of a report that some city is bankrupt, or the oil producing countries have raised their prices, or the steel workers went on strike, or the President was hospitalized, or a dictator seized power in some foreign country. How people intelligent enough and rich enough to buy expensive stocks could be so psychologically immature is not understood. They certainly lack Jerome's "rationality". But then may be they are all Gemini people. A "scientific survey" of all schizophrenics and stock purchasers should be made immediately.

The Humanist statement blasting Astrology was shipped to thousands of news editors in the United States and abroad. *Science News* magazine (September 13, 1975 issue) noted that the *Washington, D.C. Star* editor called it "the most futile broadside of recent memory." *Science News* then concluded: "Whether any minds have been changed remains to be seen." If Astrology could survive persecution by the medieval Church, it is likely to outlive another scholarly blast". With this the astrological savant agrees.

(Reproduced from THE ASTROLOGICAL MAGAZINE February 1976.)

The Evils of Specialisation

We must return to the study of the whole man. Increasing specialisation in practice has led to increased compartmentalism, departmentalism and fragmentation in teaching, with all the evils that follow. The doctor must never forget that man is more than the sum of his parts. Basic medical teaching must aim at presenting a 'synoptic' view of man, in health and in disease. Unless this be achieved, then the training will be misdirected in aim, in structure and in balance. The student will lack the necessary guiding principles when confronted with the novel situations which rear daily in front of him in typical practice.

— Margery Blake.

Astrology is Astronomy brought to earth and applied to the affairs of man

— Emerson.

D. Rationalist Plays to the Galleries

Gayatri Devi Vasudev

In the mid-seventies, Prof. N.K. Narasimha Murthy, retired Professor of Mathematics, Mysore University, wrote a small book entitled *Manavanamele Grahangala Prabhava Unte* (Do Planets Influence Man) in Kannada. It was written for and under the inspiration and guidance of a local rationalist Mr.Narasimhiah, an erstwhile Vice-Chancellor of Bangalore University. This book was a hastily written affair, full of contradictions. It contained some cheap gibes against Astrology.

At the book-releasing function held at the Senate Hall in the Central College Grounds, Bangalore, the erstwhile Vice-Chancellor chuckled into the mike that since the Sun, the Moon, Rahu and Ketu were not planets Astrology was proved baseless and not science. It was simply the rationalist's concept of Astrology and of definitions used in this science and had absolutely no relation to the proper definitions used in the science. Amused by such peurile and infantile criticism, I walked upto the man and asked him if he had studied Astrology. In order to pronounce judgement on a subject, one must know not only its basics such as definitions but a lot more of it. Criticism, from a point of ignorance, is both invalid and untenable. The rationalist's answer only exposed his hypocrisy and bias against the subject.

"Where do I have the time to study it?" he said. The next moment he realized the cat was out of the bag and hastily scampered into his waiting car and drove away refusing to answer my questions. It is exactly such bias that Carl Sagan refers to when he says "Prejudice means literally pre-judgement, the rejection of a contention out of hand, before examining the evidence. Prejudice is the result of powerful emotions, not of sound reasoning. If we wish to find out the truth of the matter we must approach the question with as nearly open a mind as we can, and with a deep awareness of our own limitations and predispositions. On the other hand, if after carefully and openly examining the evidence, we reject the proposition, that is not pre-judice. It is certainly a prerequisite for knowledge...."

Mr.Narasimhaih's is a case in point. He only displayed his ignorance of Astrology by his criticism. What has that to do with Astrology being a science?

A great scientist Dr.Richard Garnette sums up such attitudes lucidly when he says"....the study of facts and the observation of nature must always be stronger than any abstract reasoning; and the investigation of the arguments brought against Astrology will disclose a great reluctance on the part of the objector to resort to the testimony of facts, and a thoroughly unscientific habit of mind".

Another firsthand experience was of Mr. Narasimha Murthy confiding in my father

Dr. Raman that he had anticipated his mother's death to the particular day on the basis of the Moon crossing the *Vipat-tara* from her birth star. This damning confession from Mr. Murthy understandably created a stir amongst the don's group and led us to believe he had been coerced into lending his name to the book already mentioned implying he did not really endorse its contents. This confession came at the All India Radio Station, Bangalore, after a discussion on Astrology between Dr. B. V. Raman and Mr. Murthy had been recorded with Mr. Justice Tukol as the moderator. The discussion was initially to be between Dr.Raman and Mr.Narasimhiah, but like every time in the past, the latter stayed away sending his deputy.

Search for Truth

By investigation, experiment and reason. Every human being should be allowed to investigate to the extent of his desire-his ability. The literature of the world should be open to him-nothing prohibited, sealed or hidden. No subject can be too sacred to be understood. Each peron should be allowed to reach his own conclusions and to speak his honest thought.

He who threatens the investigator with punishment here, or hereafter, is an enemy of the human race. And he who trie to bribe the investigator with the promise of eternal joy is a traitor to his fellow-men.

There is no real investigation without freedom, freedom from the fear of Gods and men.

So, all investigation—all experiment—should be pursued in the light of reason.

– Robert Green Ingersoll

Validity of Astrology—A Radio Discussion

Justice Tukol : I welcome today Dr.B.V.Raman, who is a well-known student and an expert in Astrology. I welcome also Mr.Narasimha Murthy who had been a Professor of Mathematics in the Central College of the former Mysore University. Today we have met to discuss about the validity of Astrology or Astrology as a science. So, in view of the discussion, Prof. Raman may kindly define what is Astrology in the scientific sense.

Dr.Raman : Astrology is a science of correlation of the movements of celestial bodies and terrestial affairs which means natural phenomena physical phenomena and human psychological phenomena. In other words, Astrology is a science which deals with man's responses to planetary stimuli.

And what are the objections of Mr.Narasimha Murthy to doubt the validity of Astrology?

Mr.Murthy : We are discussing now about the validity of Astrology. That is the subject—matter. You have defined Astrology. I understand.

[The discussion reproduced above was broadcast by the All-India Radio, Bangalore, on 1st December 1976 at 9-30 p.m. The participants were Dr.B.V. Raman, Editor, THE ASTROLOGICAL MAGAZINE, Justice T.K. Tukol, former Vice-Chancellor of Bangalore University and Mr. N.K. Narasimha Murthy, Retired Professor of Mathematics, Mysore University. Justice Tukol acted as moderator. The discussion was carried on extempore by the participants.]

We cannot consider Astrology as a valid science I emphasise science–because it is not a science, for, it has no definite units of measurements like length, mass and time which are there for all other sciences of modern times. Next, it is not based on the methods of experimentation, observation and deduction as is done in other sciences. Statistical methods like the mean, the mode, the standard deviation, etc., are not employed in analysing the predictions of Astrology. I say it is not valid because its foundation itself is unsound in my opinion.

Dr.Raman : I think the objection raised by Mr. Narasimha Murthy cannot hold good in the light of the fact that all sciences cannot be reduced to occular demonstration. There are sciences like Psychology, Biology, Statistics which are not amenable to the methods of experimentation, etc., which acording to Mr. Narasimha Muthy should form the basis of such validity. If by science you mean, reducing everything to occular demonstration, then Astrology is not a science, Medicine is not a science, Psychology is not a science, Statistics is not a science. If by science you mean systematised knowledge, then Astrology is a science. Astrology is so vast and comprehensive in its scope that it embraces all phenomena in nature; for instance, weather forecasting, diseases, psychological aspects of human nature, events in human life. So Astrology is amenable to experimentation in respect to say, weather forecasting or prediction of natural events. Astrology has quite a good deal of statistics and quite a good deal of astrological facts to show that it is a science. For instance, History depicts the character of Shivaji and Aurangzeb. But it is not possible to find out the character of Shivaji or the fact that Shivaji lived on the basis of science. I mean, Western science. By historical facts, we can establish that Shivaji lived or Aurangzeb lived. Similarly, we can adduce any amount of astrological facts to show that a correlation exists betweeen certain groupings of planets and certain events on earth.

Justice Tukol : You mean to say that you can explain certain events of Shivaji's life or Aurangzeb's life by the planetary systems that existed in their horoscope?

Dr. Raman : What I suggested was just as for demonstrating the truth of history we have to use histroical facts, similarly for demonstrating the truth of Astrology, we have to use astrological facts. Supposing in hundred horoscopes, Mars is in the second house....

Justice Tukol : That is exactly what I mean by saying....

Dr. Raman : Mars is in the second house and there is some trouble with the eyes. So I am justified in providing these statistics to show that in the 101st horoscope, a similar situation of Mars might indicate a similar result. That is why we are going to astrological facts.

Mr. Murthy : Have such sttistical methods been employed or is there any indication to show that they had been employed by ancient Indian Astrologers as a method?

Dr. Raman : Yes. The sages of yore might have discovered all these phenomena not merely by observation but also by intuition. In fact according to one of the great scientists. Dr .Hans Eysenik, Professor of Psychology, General Medicine Hospital, London, "The only conclusion the unbiased observer can come to, must be, that there does exist a small number of people who obtain knowledge existing in other peoples' minds or in the outer world by means, as yet unknown to Science." Therefore, unknown to modern science does not mean that it can be unknown to sages also. They might have made a series of observations. They might have conceived that such groupings of planets may give rise to some such events and in the statistical studies that have been carried out subsequently, it has been clearly established that by a certain juxtaposition of planets, a certain event has happened. Much research in this line has not taken place in India, I must confess. But much research has taken place in Western countries because in the West, the scientists of the recent generation are open-minded. They have not made up their minds, whereas our scientists still seem to feel that they must get the inspiration from the Westerners.

Justice Tukol : If I have understood Mr. Narasimha Murthy, what he wants to say is whether there has been a study, by way of verification of what is predicted by astrologers and if it is of certain old individuals or ancient people.

Mr. Murthy : Have the practising astrologers kept registers showing their clients' cases and the way in which they have predicted and subsequently testifying whether they have succeeded in their predictions or failed. Whether it is in India or elsehwere, I would like to know if there is any regular documentation of such things in sufficient numbers to warrant a statement that there is a statistical method and if such things have been published in magazines available to many people and if such things are not published there, are they published in India? I think many statistical persons, even individuals can publish such things. We are not telling of only this one, I am talking of ancient India of course, ancient India had no such statistics that I would like to know, they had no such terms, methods and other things, statistical methods such as means, mode and moderation and all those things. I do not think there were sciences like statistics formerly.

Dr. Raman : We are not bothered about the want of statistics in ancient India. We are now concerned with the proposition—Validity of Astrology, and not the validity of Astrology as devleoped by the ancients. So what they have given as principles have been applied in a number of cases and we find that they work in actual practice.

Mr. Murthy : That I want to know. I would like to know statistics for the application of the ancient science of Astrology within the statistical frame work.

Dr. Raman : Statistics has been applied and those principles that have not been found to be quite valid, they have not been accepted, they have been rejected. In this aspect, you must always allow some margin for the deprecations of the professional astrologers. So whether they have preserved an account of their predictions and fulfilments I do not know. But I am not a professional Astrologer. So as a research scholar in Astrology, I have plenty of horoscopes which we have classified: we have found out which are the combinations for short life, so he has lived for so many years and these are the combinations for fall from political power. For instance, we went on making researches as to the significance of Saturn in the tenth house. So this idea came to my mind at the time of the second World War when the British Government wanted to know about their future. Then I collected the horoscopes of all these monarchs in Europe during whose times such world wars occurred. For instance, Georges III, V, VI, Queen Elizabeth's, Spanish Armada—nobody expected that England would win but one chance storm destroyed the Armada. But astrologically we found that Phillip II, King of Spain, had Saturn in the tenth house, whereas Elizabeth had Jupiter in the tenth house. That is repeated in the horoscopes of George III and Napoleon;

George V and Kaiser and George VI and Hitler. So we came to the conclusion that Hitler would fall. This way, there is plenty of statistics which we were making available from time to time in the pages of THE ASTROLOGICAL MAGAZINE. This is so far as India is concerned. But so far as the West is concerned, many of the scientists have found out not only the theoretical basis of Astrology—they are not quite successful—but they have made experiments to find out how for instance there would be change in the chemical composition of certain fluids at the time of eclipses, how a certain position of planets in the meridian and the horizon—they have ignored all the technical aspects of Astrology but the have confined only to the astronomical constants—the position of Mars in the meridian and horizon predispose one to becoming an athlete or a military man, etc. So if you want, we can produce all that statistics to show that these principles hold good.

Mr. Murthy : Astrology naturally arose out of the data supplied by Astronomy. Therefore ancient Indian Astrology was based on ancient Indian astronomy. Indian astronomy was imperfect and defective. Astronomers after astronomers—Aryabhata, Varahamihira, Brahmagupta, Bhaskara, Ganesha and Ketkar have declared previous Acharyas as ignorant and their results as inaccurate.

Dr. Raman : The proposition is reduced to this that the knowledge of Astronomy was not well developed and that Astrology has been developed on the basis of that knowledge of Astronomy. First I will come to this knowledge of Astronomy. Somehow, it has been our ill-luck that we have been treated to a distorted image of our ancient Indian achievements. Most of these astronomical books were written by Western scholars who had a certain sense of prejudice and their blind Indian admirers.

Mr. Murthy : One minute Sir, I have not quoted any Western astronomer so far, I have quoted only Indian texts and I am quoting Indian astronomers. Astronomer after astronomer has criticized the previous astronomer and there has been no definite science like Astronomy and it has been inaccurate throughout. That is why I say it has been inaccurate. It has been corrected again and again by the application of what is called as Beeja, and one of the last is Ganesha Daivagna who lived in the sixteenth century.

कथमपि यदिदम्

स्वाद्भूरिकाले श्लयं चेत्

Even this will become inaccurate in course of time.

मुहुरपि परिलक्ष्मेन्दुग्रहाद्दक्ष योगात्

Then the intelligent people will observe the Moon, the eclipses of the Moon, the planets in combination with the stars and all that.

सदमलगुरुलब्धप्राप्त बोधप्रकाशैः
कतिथ दृपपत्या शुद्धिकेन्द्रे प्रचाल्ये ।

With the help of the knowledge, they will find out the correct positions and put the planets into correct orbits. This is what Ganesha Daivagna has said. What I have now been saying is that Astrology which is based on Indian Astronomy, but Indian Astronomy was not static. It has been improved from time to time while correct corresponding improvements and corrections have not been noticed in Astrology.

Justice Tukol : Would I be right if I say that all of them recognised that the Indian Astronomy was at a stage of evolution from one generation or from one person to the other and making gradual strides of progress from time to time?

Dr. Raman : You have quoted the Siddhantas, the astronomical works relating to the Siddhanta period. There you see, our knowledge of Astronomy had already become decading by the time of the Siddhantas. What about the knowledge of Astronomy during the period of the Vedas?

Mr. Murthy : Is it improved by the period of Vedas?

वेदाहि यज्ञार्थमभिप्रवृत्ताः ।
कालानुपूर्वा विहितश्च यज्ञाः ।
तस्मादिदं कालविधान शस्त्रम् ।
यो जौतिषम् वेद स वेद यज्ञम् ॥

This is Vedanga Jyotisha—Lagadha—3rd or 4th century B.C.

Dr. Raman : My submission is, even regarding the Vedic Astronomy what we have tried to understand is only from the Vedanga Jyotisha. But there is an aspect of Astronomy which is to be found in the Atharvana Veda. For instance in the appendix to the Atharvana Veda, which consists of 16 formulae and which have been made public by the Sankaracharya of Puri in a book called **Vedic Mathematics.** For instance in the 16 *sutras*, beginning from एकाधिकेन पूर्णेन and ending with गुणगण गुणक समुच्चय simple formulae for world's mathematical, problems have been laid down. Dr.V.P. Dalial of the Heidelburg University feels impelled, as a mathematician, physicist and Sanskrit scholar, to put on record his comment on the following sloka couched in alphabetical code language. He gives the value of π *(pye)*.

गोपीभाग्यमधुव्रात शृङ्गिशोदधि सन्धिग ।
खलजीवितखाताद गलहालारसंधर ।

On the face of it, it is a hymn to Lord Krishna. Actually this gives the value of π *(pye)* as 3.14159265358979323846264338822792. **It shows how deeply the ancient Indian mathematicians penetrated into the subtlety of their claculations even when the Greeks had no numerals above 1000 and their multiplications were so very complex which they performed with the help of their counting frames, by ad-**

ding so many times the multiplier. Prof. Sengupta, former Professor of Mathematics in Calcutta University, has clearly shown after comparing Greek and Hindu methods in spherical astronomy, of the independence of Hindu Astronomers and that Hindu method is not derived from any Greek source. "Hindu astronomy in its scientific form is original and not borrowed from a foreign source. There is evidence that some crude form of Greek astronomy was transmitted to India and went by the name of the Romaka or Poulasa Siddhanta but they were rejected by our Astronomers." For instance, conversion of a vulgar fraction say 1/19th of its equivalent recurring decimal fraction, involves 18 steps of cumbersome working according to the current system, but requires one single and simple step of mental working according to Vedic *sutras.* So if you go to the Vedic period, I think they had very good knowledge of Astronomy and during the period of Siddhantas, there may have been some sort of a stagnation.

Mr. Murthy : Not stagnation—May I conclude that at the time of the Vedas, the Siddhantas had correct knowledge of Mathematical Astronomy and all that and only after these people Aryabhata, Brahmagupta came, they spoiled the whole thing or they had forgotten the ancient. They did not know the Vedas and therefore they presented wrong values say value of π (pye) as 10 or 3 which Brahmagupta has said and Sulbhasutras of ancient time—8th century B.C.—also gave the wrong values, and this is the first time I am hearing that the value of *pye* is corrected to so many places.

Dr. Raman : Regarding the accuracy of planetary movements of course they based their calculations on mathematics as we do now. The Moon's synodical revolution according to *Surya Siddhanta* is 29.530587946 days. The period given by modern astronomy differs by 7/100ths of a second so that in 5000 years the difference is about 1 . With this accuracy they felt they could study positions of planets in the various Rasis, and the consequent effects they envisaged.

Mr. Murthy : The *Surya Siddhanta* has been corrected from time to time. I would just like to read this about Surya Siddhanta. "The latest *Surya Siddhanta* has been the Almagen of India for the last 15 centuries and has been acknowledged as an authority on all matters of phenomena. All the subsequent works on Astronomy—Indian Astronomy of course—have been more or less based on it and it is very much venerated in India as being a direct revelation from the Sun. But it would be unreasonable to adhere to it in future when the great discoveries, the accurate observations and the refined methods of calculations of modern European astronomers are available to us. **We must venerate and admire it as an ancient relic testifying to the high degree of excellence attained by ancients under very adverse circumstances.**" Already Panchangas based on the nautical almanac have gained considerable popularity among the educated men for their perfect agreement with easily observable phenomena, such as eclipses and conjugation of planets. I will just say this that I had an interview with one of the Panchanga makers, one or two of them, one admitted that he used French tables in preparing his Panchanga, the other said nautical almanac was used in giving data about the eclipses and even the latest Panchanga, you give 9.04 minutes as the starting of the eclipse and 9.04 minutes cannot be by any means got by means of your Ghatis and the ancient calculations.

Dr. Raman : Now, if accuracy is the only basis, then all sciences including Physics and Chemistry started with primitive instrumentation but does it then invalidate those sciences?

Mr. Murthy : I have said that Astronomy is continuously improving. Why Astrology is static—I have said that point.

Dr. Raman : Astrology cannot be static because we all are adopting only the modern calculations. What can be adapted to suit modern conditions have been adapted. What cannot be used have been rejected. But in acutal practice, some astrologers say that you have Vahana Yoga, that you have Gaja Yoga and so on, if the predictions are given, we cannot blame it on Astrology. It is as much a science as for instance medicine is.

Mr. Murthy : In the case of medicine, a certain research is made and a man thinks that you can try. He will first try it on a number of rats or a number of rabbits. When he is satisfied that it is alright he will give it out to the world, and the Government is very particular in seeing that proper tests are made and otherwise it will be considered as spurious drug and precautions will have to be taken because it is a matter of life and death. It is not merely a dictum of a certain person.

Dr. Raman : I find that penicillin in one case causes death and in another case, causes relief.

Mr. Murthy : Quite right.

Dr. Raman : Penicillin has been tried and teseted in a number of cases but why should one...

Mr. Murthy : It is the same in all the cases because, you are not interacting dead elements. There is a human cell which reacts ....

Dr. Raman : So you have an excuse....

Mr. Murthy : No excuse and every medicine...

Dr. Raman : Or explanation.

Mr. Murthy : A man dies after taking a cup of Panaka—can't say why—There is a reaction. It is not a bad thing.

Dr. Raman : I know. Similarly a certain combination, it may apply in one case and a certain combination, it may not apply in another case.

Mr. Murthy : Quite right Sir.

Dr. Raman : Just a minute. If you want statistics, and if you think statistics has not been done, I submit, that you collect 1000 horoscopes and then you yourself can make statistical studies to disprove Astrology, as one of the eminent scientists in Western country Michel Gaquelin tries to do. That can be done but I say....

Mr. Murthy : You say that statistics have been collected in Western countries.

Dr. Raman : And also in India.

Mr. Murthy : Large number of statistics have been collected and all that.

Dr. Raman : Yes.

Mr. Murthy : If that is done, it is alright. I say that statistics have not been collected.

Dr. Raman : To give one instance, as to the validity of these astrological principles, you know nowadays, by sending the space vehicles, scientists have been able to measure solar radiation, intensities and so on. Now the scientists have been able to find that the outburst of solar flares have a very significant effect on terrestrial phenomena. So when there is a solar flare, the effect of the solar flare is being transmitted to the earth through the solar wind and when the solar flare impinges on the earth's magnetic field, there is a disturbance of the ionic content. Now scientists have found that when the solar flare bursts, and it impinges on the earth's magnetic field, many people die from heart attacks and many people will have nervous breakdowns and Maxwell Johnson has been able to discover that a certain juxtaposition of Mars and Mercury coincide with solar flares. So we can mathematically calculate that Mars and Mercury will reach the juxtaposition on such and such a day, about that time and there are solar flares, and there are the heart attacks. Now, the astrological principle says

हृद्रोगं मम सूर्य

They associate the Sun with the heart trouble. Intuitionally what the ancients may have perceived is being experimentally proved by some of these Western thinkers.

Mr. Murthy : I lay stress on that some. I want many. I want many people to do it. As I told earlier, an experiment on a frog was conducted by some scientist in the 16th century. But it is done in our colleges even today. So experiments or statistics, statistical experiments on the solar flare affecting the human heart must be conducted daily and continuously.

Justice Tukol : I mean the reason why that is not done is all those who are astrologers are not of the same calibre, not are they mentally so equipped as to carry on the sort of experiments by collecting statistics. It is only given to a few people who have got expert knowledge of both the subjects, *viz.*, Astronomy and Astrology that can be expected to do justice by collecting statistics and giving us the verifications of the planetary positions as *vis-a-vis* the incidents that occur.

Dr. Raman : Now to give you some more statistical information conducted by Michel Gaquelin, who is the Professor of Statistics and

Psychology at Sorbonne University, what he has done is—he has collected hundred thousand horoscopes and he finds that high frequency of births of doctors coincide with the position of Mars in the meridian, and low frequency of births of actors; similarly high frequency of births with the position of Jupiter in the meridian and low frequency of births when Jupiter is in the meridian—for doctors and painters. Similarly, for scientists he finds high frequency of births when Saturn is in the meridian and for writers and actors, he finds a low frequency births. This way he has done quite a bit of statistical evidence to show that certain juxtapositions of planets at the time of birth predispose one towards an aptitude for certain types of professions and he says we could use this information to enable one to pursue his studies in the direction and derive the maximum of benefit. So even according to astrological considerations, planets in the tenth house are supposed to indicate profession. But in actual practice, many astrologers may be erring but that is no reason for a reflection on Astrology.

Justice Tukol: So from the discussion, it apears to me that everything need not be open to

What is Rationalism?

Rationalism does not, however, either begin or end with the mere adoption of a critical attitude to established beliefs in religion or philosophy. The Rationalist seeks to overthrow accepted beliefs only in so far as he concieves physical verification. There are many things in the world which could be understood; many phenomena, I should say, which could be understood more by intuition and so far as Astrology is concerned, though many statistics have been collected by way of horoscopes and the verification of the juxtaposition of the planets *vis-a-vis* the incidents in the individual lives and the lives of the country, have been made in the foreign countries, in India, I think we have yet to advance in the collection of statistics and verification of the consequences so as to establish that even those who are studying the field of Astrology or Astronomy and allied sciences should have oppourtunity of knowing the scientific connection between the two.

Dr. Raman : The cosmic-terrestrial relations which form the basis of Astrology may transcend recognised principles of Westren Science. But a scientific approach to the problem gives the proof of Astrology. What we want critics to do is to ap-

them to stand in the way of a true constructive explanation of man's relation to the Universe and to his kind. He believes, in short, that right thinking is the key to right conduct, and that, as Mr. J.M. Robertson puts it, you cannot "rationalize conduct without seeking to rationalize creed." Rationalism—the acceptance of the reason as the final arbiter in all matters relating to the formation of opinion—involves the adoption of an essentially positive and affirmative, though wisely discriminative, attitude towards the materials of experience. Of course, the mere intention to be reasonable does not always succeed in its object. Al-

proach the problem scientifically not irrationally, basing their conclusions on subjective factors.

Justice Tukol : Mr. Narasimha Murthy is also saying that there should be scientific approach.

Dr. Raman : Again experimental evidence has been collected by many scholars interested in the study of Astrology and it is astonishing how those, who looked down upon it, have ignored all such evidence and stuck to their orthodox view. We have been able to collect a number of horoscopes and study them statistically and reject what is not valid and retain what is valid. This work could profitably be done by the Universities with all the resources and funds they have.

> though we can all reason fairly well up to a certain point, most of us reach that point all too soon. Hence, increasing accuracy and adequacy in the use of our reasoning powers should be our constant aim. And if we are to achieve that aim in any marked degree we must voluntarily undergo certain disciplines in supplement of those afforded by our present defective system of education.
>
> **—Thomas Paine in**
> *"The Age of Reason"*

E. Piqued Rationalist Resorts to Lies

(Society**, a Bombay-based journal, in its October 1984 issue carried a write-up on Dr. Raman titled "B. V. Raman's Star- Spangled Life and Predictions" It was, on the whole, a true and fair assessment of Dr. Raman and his attainments. It also carried several correct predictions Dr.Raman has made in his life and appreciative references to his missionary crusade for Astrology. Mr. Narasimhiah, a Bangalore rationalist, was so upset by this that he post-haste scribbled an article in the* ***Society, *November 1988, making cheap gibes at Dr. Raman. He wrote "His International Conference of Astrology, utilised as a felicitation function to himself in December 1983 was a flop, thanks to the systematic campaign, by the right thinking people, in Bangalore, against the fraud of Astrology. The conference was considered to be international since his son Dr. B. Sureshwara attended it coming all the way from the United States of America...." and many more lies referring to Dr. Raman.*

I rang up the Editor Mr. Binoy Thomas from Bangalore and asked him if he would carry my rejoinder refuting Mr. Narasimhiah's blatant lies in his journal. He promised to do so and the February 1985 issue carried not only my rejoinder blasting the awful lies Mr. Narasimhiah had so shamelessly written about Dr. Raman but also the reproduction of a very aptly worded letter from Dr. Sureshwara of Illinois which showed to what contemptious levels this self-styled rationalist could stoop to vent his personal animosity against Dr. Raman. We reproduce relevant excerpts from the rejoinder below, courtesy, ***Society****. We place on record our thanks to Mr. Binoy Thomas for presenting both sides of the issue to his readers, thereby showing a high sense of fairness and impartiality.* ***Editor)***

THE NEW RAMAN EFFECT

Dr. Narasimhiah's rejoinder (***Society***, November 1984) made familiar but painful reading. That he is entitled to his opinions on Astrology or any other science under the sun none can dispute. But what is in extremely bad taste is his distortion of certain facts and the presentation of even blatant lies in relation to Dr. B.V. Raman.

Referring to the International Convention on Astrology, he describes it as a flop, because to use his own words "thanks to the systematic campaign by the right thinking people in Bangalore against the fraud of Astrology". I was present throughout the two-day delibe ations and I can give an eyewitness account of the nuisance these followers of Dr. Narasimhiah made of themselves at the portals of the Banquet Hall of the Vidhana Soudha where the Convention took place. Just before the deliberations began a noisy group of about 5 or 6 persons started shouting anti-Astrology slogans. One would have thought they were hooligans and rowdies (judging by their dress and demeanour) of the kind one usually encounters in theatres peddling tickets in black. The police however hounded out the group in a matter of minutes. So much for Dr.Narasimhiah's campaign and right thinking people at the Convention!

The second fact he deliberately misrepresents is, he says the Convention was considered international because Dr.Raman's son Dr.Sureshwara "attended it coming all the way from the United States of America". I wonder where he gets his ideas from. Dr.Sureshwara did not attend the conference. But there were as many as 100 overseas delegates from England, Sweden, Germany, Canada, the U.S.A., Malaysia, Sri Lanka, Singapore and Bangladesh who participated in the Convention to make it a grand international meet of astrological savants. Besides delegates from all over India also took part in it.

The people of Bangalore led by the Committee for the Felicitation of Dr.B.V. Raman headed by Justice A.R. Somnath Iyer (former Chief Justice of Karnataka) and comprising of such distinguished gentlemen as Justice Nittoor Srinivasa Rao, Govind Narain, Veerendra Patil, Ramnath Goenka, Dr.M. Chenna Reddy, Dr.V.K.R.V. Rao and other luminaries had decided to honour their distinguished fellow citizen Dr.B.V. Raman. The International Convention was held as an adjunct to the Felicitation function. To impute the motives of fraud to these intellectual and public personalities is an insult to the entire people of Karnataka.

A LETTER FROM RAMAN'S SON

This has reference to the article "Narasimhiah, Bangalore's Miracle-buster Challenges B.V.Raman" in November 1984 issue of SOCIETY.

Dr. Narasimhiah should verify facts before he writes or says anything. The International Conference on Astrology at Bangalore was attended by delegates from both within and outside India. I, son of Dr.B.V.Raman, did not attend the conference. Therefore, Dr.Narasimhaiah is wrong when he writes that I attended the Conference. I question his credibility and judgment on many of the things he has written, especially when he cannot verify a simple fact like my not attending the Conference. Those who stretch truth to discredit a branch of learning, an individual, or a group are just hypocrites and nothing else.

There is nothing new in what Dr.Narasimhiah has said in the article. Today it is fashionable for some to identify himself or herself as a 'rationalist'. Many of these 'rational' persons appear to have made their main goal in life to continually degrade anything pertaining to Indian Culture, Hinduism and Hindus. It is because the Hindus are tolerant, that many of the so-called 'rationalists' are able to make stupid and irresponsible statements.

Their 'rationalism' quickly evaporates when it comes to non-Hindu religions and cultures. It is simple because the other religious groups and cultures would not tolerate any direct or indirect insults or attacks on their group or beliefs. If these so-called 'rationalists' truly believe in universal applications of their beliefs, I would like to see them express their 'rationalist' views on the beliefs of not only Hindus, but also others. Otherwise, the conclusion is, they lack courage of conviction, and sincerity in whatever they say or write.

Dr.Narasimhaiah is a talented and educated individual. He should direct his talent and energy not at publicity generating efforts such as 'challenging' the faiths, and beliefs of millions of Hindus, but at action-oriented service in the suffering poorer and weaker sections of society. We have seen enough of lip service and words by politicians and others. Dr.Narasimhaiah with his educational background can effectively initiate educational and other programmes to assist the deserving poor. Of course, that needs a lot of effort, and it will not generate the same publicity as the gimmick of 'challenge'.

In any case, the public will understand sooner or later that the main objective of many of the 'rationalists' is simply to get free and cheap publicity. And by making every issue sensational, they double their 'popularity' and 'public appeal'.

It appears it does not matter to them whether they hurt the feelings and faith of a vast number of people, and all they care is generation of continuing publicity for themselves.

Yours sincerely,
(Sd.)
B. SURESHWARA

Reference to Mr. A.N. Banerjee's and Mr. S.R. Bommai's speeches have also undergone malicious twists. While Governor Banerjee described Astrology as a statistical science and not exact, Mr.S.R. Bommai called on the astrologers to word their predictions in cautious language. Statesman and politician respectively, they are not expected to be as thoroughly science- knowing as men from specific areas of science are. I think it would be appropriate at this stage to point out to Dr.Narasimhiah, that with the discovery of Heisenberg's Principle of Uncertainty and the surfacing of quantum physics, the very concept of the exact sciences has received a death blow. It is true Dr.Narasimhiah received a doctorate for his thesis some three decades ago, but it is unfortunate he has not kept pace with the latest developments of science. Several theories prevailing then have been set aside and clinging to these outdated theories can do more harm than good to the cultivation of his scientific temper.

A Convention attended by three to four hundred delegates and nearly 2000 citizens drawn from all walks of life cannot be called a flop.

One of the more serious charges Dr. Narasimhiah makes against Dr. Raman is that his challenge to the latter to predict events has not been accepted. Dr. Narasimhiah sounds like a garrishly painted matinee hero who throws out 'challenges' left and right from his pedestal on the silver screen. This would be the rating his challenges deserve. However, coming to the facts themselves, there has been no challenge to Dr. Raman from Dr. Narasimhiah. Even otherwise for the sake of argument, how can he arrogate to himself the task of a judge of an individual's competence or the validity of a science. Surely, it would be the height of absurdity to claim such omniscience. No one in his senses would care a hoot for challenges of this kind. On the contrary, a few years ago when Swami Krishnateertha, Secretary of the Karnataka Jyotisha Parishad invited Dr. Narasimhiah to a public debate on Astrology, the latter backed out at the last minute. Dare he 'challenge' a specialist in cancer to cure a particular case of cancer? Dare he challenge specialists in other fields of knowledge?

While claiming to not blowing his own trumpet, Dr.Narasimhiah unabashedly reels out distinctions that have supposedly descended on him of their own accord. Belonging to a minority group in a country of caste-politics has its own distinct advantages !

I shall give just two instances where I had an opportunity to watch his 'scientific temper' at work.

One was at the Seminar on 'Science and Superstition' organised by the Youth Writers and Artists Guild in mid 1977 at the Institution of Engineers at Bangalore, under the Chairmanship of Dr.V.K.R.V.Rao. Dr.Raman, Swami Adidevananda and Dr.Narasimhiah and a few others were the speakers. Angered by Dr.Narasimhiah's charge against Astrology that no one had forecast the Emergency, I walked up to him with a copy of the forecast of the event made 10 months in advance in THE ASTROLOGICAL MAGAZINE. This man claiming to be a rationalist just scampered away hastily refusing even to look at it, let alone peruse it.

His favourite quote from Swami Vivekananda (***Society***, November 1984, page 59) is pulled out of context. The Swami had the highest regard for the ancient science of Astrology. (*Complete Works of Swami Vivekananda*, Vol. IV, pages 372-373). "In America there is the best scope for caste (real *jaati*) to develop, and so the people are great. Every Hindu knows that astrologers try to fix the caste of every boy or girl as soon as he or she is born. That is the real caste — the individuality and Jyotisha (astrology) recognises that, and we can only rise by giving it full sway again", the Swami says. Men who quote Vivekananda to tarnish Astrology should remember this!...

"The history of science is fraught with cases of orthodox scientists rejecting the theories and findings of contemporary scientists which did not fit in with the theories prevailing then. Copernicus, Galileo, Michelson, Morley were all looked down upon because they took a stance that did not respect the reason of contemporary scientists. When will orthodox scientists learn they have never been and never will be champions of truth? As Whitehead in *Science and the Modern World* puts 'Science has never shaken off its origins in the historical revolt of the later renaissance. It has remained a predominantly antirationalistic movement based on a naive faith.....Of course, the historical revolt was justified... it was a sensible reaction, but it was not a protest on behalf of reason."

Dr. Narasimhaiah is no rationalist or scientist. A highly prejudiced don, he is making use of his official position to brainwash young minds with his personal biases and prejudices. Like all self proclaimed reformers in our country, he will question Hindu beliefs and Hindu saints and never non-Hindu beliefs and practices. What about the faith-healing at the Dargahs and the healing sessions of the Hendersons? He dare not. Their communities will not tolerate him like we do.

Lastly, a word on his attack of the predictions made by Dr. Raman. These predictions are based on planetary movements and their correlations to human activity. It is to the credit of Dr.

Raman that he does not make categorical forecasts. No man of intellectual stature will do it. A parallel will illustrate the point. A cancer specialist with all the equipment at his command and the patient, fully reposing his faith in him will still not promise categorically, a cure. All he will say is, "I shall do my best. The rest is in God's hands". That is the reason why Dr. Raman uses the words 'may and possibly' and not 'will' and 'shall'. Only politicians and dons backed by them spill promises with a liberal usage of these words. Not true scientists who know both the scope and limitations of human skills and knowledge.

(Courtesy: ***Society*** February 1985)

INDIA AND WESTERN SCIENCE

"From its modern awakening with Sri Ramakrishna and Swami Vivekananda, Eastern mysticism has begun to adapt its revelations to the entirely different cultural framework provided by science and technology, without in any way sacrificing what is valid in its traditional understanding of the phenomemon itself. " *(The Eye of Shiva: Eastern Mysticism and Science p.120)*

—Amaury De Reincourt

F. Some More Hypocrisy

i) The Space Tamashas

In 1979, India's first booster-rocket SLV-3, launched on 10-8-1979 with much fanfare came plummeting down into the Bay of Bengal within 5 minutes of take–off (10-8-1979 at 7.55 a.m. IST. at Sriharikota).

MR. CITIZEN
By RAMAMURTHY

The only thing that is soaring into space with a steady velocity is the Indian price-line!

Courtesy : Deccan Herald dated 15/7/1988

You Said It
by Laxman

Don't feel so bad, professor! There is a vast improvement over the last attempt. This one fell 30[illegible] metres farther.

Courtesy : TIMES OF INDIA dated 16/7/88

This scientific failure costing crores of hard-earned money only proved a simple astrological truth in electional Astrology.

Malefics Saturn and Rahu are in Lagna, a deadly thing to have.The Moon in the 8th is never advocated in Muhurta as leading to premature death or termination (For details, refer ***Planets and Our Space- Programme supra)***

On 24-3-1987, again from the same site, SROSS-I was launched to watch which the Prime Minister of the country and a whole lot of other big-wigs had gathered.

The weekday was Tuesday and for the time of launching (12-10-noon) Gemini rising had the Moon in the 8th. Tuesday is fateful astrologically for any new venture. The launch met with a premature and watery grave and at a whooping cost of 28 crore rupees when it came plunging into the sea within a bare 164 seconds of take-off. Any student of Astrology would have thrown up his arms in protest at the choice of the time and date of these launchings.

And for this the space-scientist concerned was given a special award. This simple demonstration of Astrology is proof against all criticism. It, even to the chagrin of the scientist, proves the truth of the Yogas in his own chart which fetched him laurels for a dismal performance.

LAB BLAB **Mohan Sivanand**

"Thanks to satellite technology, Dourdarshan now shows us a new picture every day – the Insat 1B picture".

Courtesy : Indian Express, Science Supplement dated 23-8-88

ii) Weathermen Caught Napping

The deluge of July 9, 1987 at Mancherial predictably caught our Meteorology Department unawares. Two bogies of the Hyderabad-Nizamuddin Delhi (Dakshin) Express were washed away in flash floods on this fateful night about 245 kilometres from Hyderabad when the train was just about to cross the rail bridge across the Gangaregedi rivulet. About 53 people were killed according to official sources.

It was a flash alright, for us laymen. But we are not most certainly going to accept this explanation from the Meteorology Department. **Pampered and fed at great expense to the exchequer what were these weather prophets doing?**

Courtesy : Indian Express Science Supplement dated 22.3.1988

With all the resources they have at their command, the highly expensive and sophisticated weather gadgets and the countless men working for them, what were these men upto? Aren't they paid to warn of weather vagaries of the magnitude and nature of the Mancherial deluge in which so many lives were lost?

Just look at the forecast appearing on page 15, *THE HINDU*, dated July 8, 1987. The forecast **is said to be "valid until the morning of July 9". That means it includes the pre-dawn 2 hour-period on July 9 when the flash-flood came like a bolt from the blue. The meteorological forecast said "Rain or thundershowers will be fairly widespread over coastal Karnataka, Telangana, scattered over interior Karnataka, Coastal Andhra Pradesh, Lakshadweep and isolated over Rayalaseema, Tamil Nadu and Pondicherry."**

The train having travelled 245 kms from Hyderabad towards Delhi was far from anywhere near the coast. That means the weather predicted for the region was" rain or thundershowers". Not even thunderstorms but look what happened! It certainly needed cheek to make this kind of prediction!

A sudden deluge which kills more than 50 people and which washes off the track itself from under the train is not even remotely anticipated. The Department owes an explanation on its fatally poor performance. This is just one amongst numerous instances when the weathermen fool the people with their totally unreliable forecasts leading to catastrophic and disastrous consequences. This, based on "scientific" knowledge and methods! Scientists who have such a high opinion of their scientific knowledge and methods and who do not accept the limitations of science should ponder over their failures and descend from their ivory towers and humbly approach Astrology.

Not a word of criticism from the "rationalists" who shout themselves hoarse over astrologers. Most rationalists are biased, rather ill-informed with inflated egos and a strong conditioned sense of righteous indignation which, when roused, fumes and frets and make them run amok.

What is important is what is going on in the Meteorology Department if it cannot play any effective role in deciphering weather changes. No answers will come because that is how it is today

Flunky Forecasts from the Weatherman.

IN ABSOLUTE defiance of INSAT pictures and charts at the Meteorological Department, the City's winter sky has held true. But take a look at the forecasts daily over the last three days. "Generally cloudy with spells of rain" on Thursday, "partly cloudy" on Friday and "mainly cloudy" for Saturday while the sky stayed gleefully blue. It seems we are in luck. Whoever said that weather was predictable anyway?

—Indian Express (20.12.1987)

in our country when uncomfortable questions are asked.

Science is meant not to glority personal egos; science is meant to unravel the secrets of Nature and to use this knowledge to help mankind. But what many of the scientists are doing now is the exact antithesis of the fundamental purpose of science.

(Reproduced from **The Astrological Magazine** January 1988)

iii) Another Instance of Hypocrisy

A lot of nonsense on Astrology has gone into a book *Science, Non-Science and Paranormal* produced by a local "rationalist" assisted by a mathematics teacher in a local college.

Parts of the book carry flashes of sense. For instance, the "rationalist" who has also edited the volume, quotes a scientist saying science is identified by its methods and not by its attainments. Immediately, he contradicts this statement by quoting out of context half-a-dozen predictions saying these went wrong and Astrology is therefore, not science. But unfortunately, scores of predictions which have proved correct have been just wished away perhaps to impress his personal prejudices on the readers. A genuine science-man, on the other hand, would have taken note of the overwhelming number of correct preditctions and gone on to study why these predictions came right and how. The "rationalist" only made a fool of himself by this gimmick *

NEWSLETTER JUNE 1988 11

COMPUTER HOROSCOPE

Computer Horoscope in the South Indian/North Indian style cast in 5-pages computer printout giving the following details :—

(i) Scientifically computed accurate positions of the Sun, the Moon, Lagna (Ascendant) and all the planets including Uranus, Neptune and Pluto
(ii) Nakshatra and Paada, Janma Tithi, Rashi, Yoga and Karana
(iii) Balance of Dasha at birth according to the Vimshottari sytem
(iv) Rashi kundali and Navamsha Kundali in South/North Indian style
(v) Arambha, Madhya and Antya of all the 12 Bhavas, and
(vi) Bhava Kundali.

Send details of date, time and place of birth. Fees Rs. 30/-

For trade enquiries for the Horoscope Software Package on SPECTRUN Home Computer or to act as collection centres contract :—

Dr. Shirali Balachandra Rao, M.Sc., Ph.D.
2388, Jnana Deep, Subramanyanagar Main Road
Rajajinagar, 2nd Stage, Bangalore-560 010.

Courtesy : Canara Union Newsletter dated June 1988

Now on to his man, Friday, Mr. Balachandra Rao. This man prepares horoscopes for a fee on the sly while decrying it before the rationalist for either fear or favour, we do not know. Given above is a copy of Mr. Rao's advertisement for his horoscopic-wares which expose to what levels one can descend in the name of 'scientific temper'. This advertisement appears periodically in **The Canara Union Newsletter,** Malleswaram, Bangalore.

For every single wrong prediction, dozens of space and science disasters can be shown. Astrologers are human and failures are there sometimes. But in fact the significant number of correct astrological predictions indicate probabilities far in excess of what can be achieved by random chance.

A fool who thinks that he is a fool is to that extent a wise man; but a fool who thinks of himself as wise is indeed a fool.

The fool desires undue reputation, precedence among monks, authority over dwellings and honour among the families.

"Let both laymen and monks think that this was done by me. In every work, great and small, let them follow me" - such is the aspiration of the fool; (thus) his desire and pride increase.

Through all his life, a fool associates with a wise man, he still remains ignorant of the truth as the spoon, the flavour of the soup.

—Dhammapada

CHAPTER SIX

THE KOVOOR STORY–THE DENOUEMENT

Y. Keshava Menon

Columnist Leon has been, from the time Kovoor started stalking this land from across the Strait throwing challenges right and left, pointing his index finger unerringly at the patently irrational terms with which he was hedging the contest. As far as we know only one person is so far reported to have fallen victim to his wile and lost a cash deposit of Rs.1000. No astrologer seems to have been involved.

Kovoor has now met a diamond of a man he could not cut. This is set out in some detail in a rare signed editorial in the prestigious Malayalam Weekly, **Malayala Nadu,** which had over a period of time, featured Kovoor and his work sympathetically. The rare editorial, in the issue of the journal of the 16th January 1977, was prompted by the Editor's total disillusionment with the Kovoor religion.

It so happened that a popular literateur based in Bombay, Sri M.P. Narayana Pillay was prepared to take up Kovoor on his challenge. Sri Pillay would demonstrate through an eminent Yogi at any appointed place of Kovoor's choice the miracle of man walking on water. Kovoor nominated Quilon (Kollam) for the demonstration and demanded the cash deposit. Sri Pillay sent in the cash to Sri S.R. Nair, the Editor of **Malayala Nadu**, a known admirer of Kovoor with a request that he act as the moderator for the contest after ensuring that Kovoor's lakh of rupees was readily available and nominate the time, date and venue for the performance of the miracle.

When told of Sri Pillay's final acceptance of the contest, Sri Nair was invited to meet Kovoor at the Government House, Quilon. Present at the meeting were, besides Kovoor and Sri Nair, Comrade M.N. Govindan Nair, the Communist leader who is also a Cabinet Minister in the Government of Kerala, political leaders Anandan, Mohan and K. Karunakaran (Editor of the **Daily Janayugam**), Thoppil Bhasi, the matinee idol, choreographer, dramatist, playwright, producer and director, Sri Panicker and a few of the followers of Kovoor's Rationalist Philosophy. Incidentally, Thoppil Bhasi is reputed to be the man behind the film **Punarjanmam** (Rebirth) which featured Kovoor live.

When Sri. S.K.Nair stated Sri.Pillay's case Kavoor reared up "On just one man's say-so, why should I sell off my valuable properties in Ceylon to stake the lakh of rupees in cash?" Kovoor said that his word that within 15 days of his losing the contest, should such a contingency arise, he would bring a lakh of rupees from Ceylon should be accepted. This statement, charged with unnecessary vehemence, stuck at the throat of those present.

Minister Govindan Nair intervened to say that bringing a lakh of rupees from Ceylon on an errand of this nature was an improbability. He cited the instance of a neighbour whose sole earning member in Ceylon was not permitted to remit paltry sums for the maintenance of his aged parents in India. On Kovoor contesting this statement, the Reserve Bank authorities at Ernakulam were promptly contacted on the telephone. It was then established that transfer of such a sum of money from Ceylon, for the avowed purpose was a total impossibility.

On Sri Pillay being told over the telephone that a stalemate had arisen on terms of the contest, Sri Pillay pointed out to those assembled that he had already put down Rs. 1000 in cash as demanded of him and he would be further incurring expenses of a few more thousands in

Are Astrologers Charlatans?

Sir,- Following Dr. Kovoor's line of reasoning (16th Oct) I think that cardiology too is humbug. Let Dr Kovoor produce a single cardiologist who on seeing an electro-cardiogram (ECG) can tell within 5 percent error the sex and age of the patient!

The fallacy in Dr. Kovoor's "test" lies in his absolute ignorance of science. Just as an ECG is an indicator of the patient's heart and circulatory system so the horoscope is the indicator of a person's destiny. Just as a cardiologist can make a wrong diagnosis, so too an Astrologer can make a wrong diagnosis (prediction). After all he is a human

bringing the yogi and his attendants over and escorting them back.

To this, Kovoor petulantly retorted, "If Sri Pillay's Yogi is a miracle performer why should he not produce the lakh of rupees for him from thin air rather than take all the pains to come over and take a risk?" With this he stalked out of the place followed by his adherents.

The editorial concludes "I am now in a quandary and led to believe that you do not have a lakh of rupees in the first place. Please do not churn our mind, thoughts and soul any more and create ulcers for which there might not be any remedy even in rationalism. I published your articles and statements hitherto accepting your genuineness *prima facie*. **Please do not put human faith on trial any more."**

Confirming the fact delineated in the editorial is an independent report by Thoppil Bhasi and a statement of Sri Narayana Pillay himself.

being and as prone to fallibility as any other engineer, physician, surgeon or Dr. Kovoor!

Coming specifically to Dr. Kovoor's charge against Dr B.V. Raman, **this is a clear example of hypocrisy. He has cleverly selected the one year in which Dr. Raman failed and ignored 37 years of accurate (published) record of predictions** (bold ours)

To quote just one astonishing prediction: In the period October 1972 to December 1972, Dr. Raman in his forecast 'IN THE USA' published in **The Astrological Magazine** of the same period said "as Saturn enters Aridra constellation, in May 1974, Nixon will be forced to resign". This predic-

In the meantime, came the blast from no less a person than Acharya Rajneesh. This was the real *coup d'etat* for the Doctor which only Acharyas may divine.

"Why does Kovoor," asks the Acharya in the course of an interview with the ***Current***, the popular Bombay Weekly, "spend his last days on negativism?"

To the saint, it is simple logic. "You say that there is no God. That can only be a matter of faith, for you cannot prove it. You accuse the other fellow of being irrational because he says that there is God. Your rationality is thus on a par with the other fellow's." (The words are mine to simplify the whole process of thought of the Acharya).

The Acharya deplores that an aged man of over 80 as Kovoor claims he is should engage

tion came just before and after Nixon had won the U.S. Presidential election with the largest majority in American history and a clear 20 months before he actually resigned as predicted. Name ONE newspaper or magazine Dr. Kovoor, which has politically or otherwise anywhere in the world made such a prediction! There are hundreds of other accurate predictions but for reasons of space I give only a few: the assassination of Shaikh Mujibur Rehman and King Faisal of Saudi Arabia as well as the attempts on the life of President Ford were accurately predicted.

Besides every issue of **The Astrological Magazine** carries the legend- "Those who know Astrology can only indicate in a way what will take place in future, who else except the Creator can say with certainty what will definitely hap-

himself in this negative process of denials in his last days.

Kovoors do more for Astrology than is commonly imagined. By his several challenges going totally unnoticed by astrologers led by Dr.B.V.Raman who sat back like a sage receiving the darts as flower offerings, Kovoor is today a sad man—a little wiser let us hope.

Reproduced from **THE ASTROLOGICAL MAGAZINE**, *April 1977.*

pen?" If a man is a charlatan and out to fool people why should such a legend be published in every issue at all? No, Dr.Kovoor you can only fool some of the people, sdme of the time, but you can't fool all people all the time!

Bombay.

— V.R. PRABHU

Courtesy: Free Press Journal, dated 22-10-1976

CHAPTER SEVEN

HOW I WAS GREETED BY 'SCIENCE' : STRICT SCEPTICISM

Michel Gauquelin

In science, the important thing is not only to discover phenomenon, but above all to repeat it a sufficient number of times for it to be properly established. When I published my first statistical results in 1955, revealing a new relationship between man and certain planets, I had of course already made sure of the phenomenon by various experiments in France. But all I had done was to discover them. This is why this work, which presents the extension of my research from France to four other countries of Europe, takes on the value of a confirmation.

A link between man and the planets...When we envisage such a relationship, we automatically

---

In his latest book *"Written in the Stars"* Michel Gauguelin's studies establish the link between man and planets. Thirty years have passed since he first began his experiments to disprove Astrology but now he has ended up accumulating invaluable data proving the correlation between astrological data and human life. This volume published in 1988 is an impartial but amazing record of the study conducted by Gauquelin which proves the validity of the basic tenet of Astrology— of the link between man and planets. These findings are based on a collection of more than 100,000 cases and 30 years painstaking, scientific endeavur.

think of Astrology. And such positive and negative passion is attached to that word in the eyes of those who are stirred up by the question, that they can no longer make any objective judgement of the scientific facts presented to them. This is why this work is also valuable as a response to all those who only wanted to see in my work a 'fortunate' stroke of luck, which was *a priori* unworthy of being examined.

Scepticism, which is the 'done thing' in adversaries of Astrology, is nine times out of ten based on an exaggeratedly scientistic concept of the relationships between man and nature. Indeed, Mr.Dauvillier, for example, a professor of

---

The complete data used by Gauquelin is said to be available on magnetic tape and can be checked by anyone against the source data in the public domain and on the original birth- certificates accessible at Gauquelin's laboratory in Paris according to the postscript to the book by Geoffrey Dean.

In fact, there is no doubt whatsoever about the validity of Gauquelin's methodology, as three members of the CSICOP (Committee for the Scientific Investigation of Claims of the Paranormal which publishes the*Skeptical Inquirer*) to which local rationalists make frequent references in their attacks on Astrology, Professors Abell, Paul Kurtz and Zelen have finally acknowledged in 1983, in an article that " Gauquelin adequately allowed for demographic and astronomical factors in predicting the expected distribution of Mars sectors for birth times in the general population ". (Ref.'The Abell-Kurtz- Zelen'Mars Effect' Experiments: A Reappraisal' *The Skeptical Enquirer*, 1983, pages 77-82.)

cosmic physics at the College de France, wrote to me, in a letter which in other respects was most polite*.'What immoderate human vanity it is to believe that the destiny of a mammal born on a little planet could be linked to the course of the celestial bodies! Just put the sun, the earth, and the human race and life into their places in the galaxy, and you will see how futile these beliefs are... '. Every word is saturated with a kind of primary materialism. Look again: 'the vanity of this mammal born on this little planet...' What has vanity got to do with anything here? There are facts and there are experiments. We have to examine them, that is all.

In any case, it does too much credit to the consequences of my results to think, with horror or delight, that there is any risk of them overturning everything that is currently known. It is too much to believe that they might, if recognized to be correct, modify the thought processes of a scientist worthy of the name. In the case of sceptics, this excessive credit (or indignity) which they heap on me comes from their habits of thought, which prevent them from reasoning about anything other than what they already know about the laws of the universe. They confuse an unresolved problem with a 'false problem and flee from it, giving their current knowledge as an excuse. Here is Mr. Dauvillier's testimony once again: 'If such influences existed, they would not

* All the quotations which follow are taken from letters I received and have preserved in my files.

act on the arrangement of chromosomes at the moment of birth, but at conception. Now, the laws of genetics show us that these associations are chance ones'. Nevertheless, this scientist is presented with numerous easily verifiable statistics showing the importance of the moment of birth... That they should appear to him to be incredible, or even absurd, I can easily accept. But one should at least assess the results before affirming the opposite!

There is more to come: Sylvain Arend,an astronomer at the Brussels observatory, asserts by way of sole scientific criticism: 'Professional astronomers have studied the problem *a priori[!]*.As far as they are concerned, the planets are celestial bodies which have cooled down and which in essense merely reflect the radiation which they receive'.He adds: 'Moreover, it can be seen [!] that human destiny depends on human and not astral factors'.

The thought process is always the same: peremptory apriority (which is admirable in a scientist), negative proof on the basis of known 'radiations'and complete refusal to study the question. The most astonishing thing is still to come. All these gentlemen, for whom there is nothing left to discover about 'radiation', have been working together for several years on a committee with the publicly recognized aim of examing evidence such as mine!

From the pen of Paul Couderc, an astronomer at the Paris Observatory, we read:

'For a long time, a permanent scientific commission, founded by the American Association of Scientific Societies, has undertaken to study the laws put before it: it is prepared to examine any propositions concerning the influence of planets on individuals'; and further on : 'A Belgian committee for investing phenomena held to be paranormal, made up of thirty scientists from all disciplines,* was formed in 1948 to study precise programmes of simple, controllable experiments.' And Courdec concludes : 'I am at the disposal of anyone to pass on to the Belgian committee any precise statement of laws, since these experiments deserve to be examined by scientists—they have been in the past and will continue to be.' †

I hastened, of course to forward my work to these two committees, and to Couderc himself. I expected that my results would surely be examined by these men of science. Did not my work contain first and foremost an experimental critique of Astrology which no one had ever before really undertaken? With these men of science, I hoped to set up a discussion not of the practical aspect of horoscopes, since I was backing up their argument on this point, but at the strictly

---

* Compromising, amongst others, S. Arend (see above), M. Boll (see below) and P. Couderc himself.

† Paul Courdec, *L'Astrologie*, P.U.F., 1951, pp.76 and 77

scientific, experimental and verifiable level of my experiments.

I am still waiting....

After some time, having received no reply, I ventured to enquire about the progress of the matter. I was berated with accusations of self-importance. 'What!' replied Marcel Boll, 'do you really think that the scientists would stop all work and amuse themselves for ten days going over your work with a fine tooth comb? ... this is self-justification mania!'

Are the scientists on these committees really so overburdened with work? Not according to Paul Courdec who—contradiction of contradictions!—made this disillusioned remark : 'Unfortunately these scientific commissions do not have enough work'. Yet he himself never even acknowledged my repeated requests for examination. I was told he had better things to do. Be that as it may, it is clear that this astronomer is perfectly willing to spend time writing a whole book on the blunders of astrologers, but not to look into 'a programme of simple, verifiable laws' that he himself called for.

It is very easy to draw a conclusion from all this: the adversaries of Astrology love to criticize it, but they have no intention whatsoever of broadening the debate in order to check the facts set before them. Their committees of 'scientific investigation' do not aim to serve science, but only to spread amongst public opinion the deceptive appearance of science.

But deploring the indifference and scepticism of certain scientists would be a sterile, and hence unscientific, attitude. In order to claim the right to be examined and read, you have to set everything in motion. To find the necessary credence, you have first and foremost to pursue research in order to obtain more and more convincing sets of proof.

This is why I had to increase the amount of birth data studied, and repeat the experiments over and over again, broadening the scope of my research to several countries. After all, perhaps the quantity of my data was not yet sufficient. And you could ask what would happen to all this fine reasoning if fresh observations destroyed the first ones.

My contradictors had not waited for the results of these experiments to come, but had replied in advance: 'If the statistics show a semblance of correlation.' Dauvillier wrote to me, 'this can only be a fluctuation showing that the data are not sufficiently numerous.' As for Marcel Boll, he prophesied: 'Your conclusions are nothing more than a serialized novel, the worst kind of justification, and this solution is hopeless, since if you repeated the same investigation in Great Britain, Germany, the U.S.A. or the USSR, you would wriggle out of it with ease (faced with different results), by citing national idiosyncrasies.'*

That was a challenge that I just had to take up. The results of fresh research that I am publishing now are a direct response to Messrs Dauvillier and Boll: they fully confirm, and extend to a European scale, the French results published in 1955.

Courtesy: "*Written in the Stars*" by
Michel Gauquelin

---

* Note of 1987 : Some 30 years ago, Marcel Boll was a well-known scientific writer in France, ranking with Martin Gardner in the USA, for example.

CHAPTER EIGHT

PLANETS AND PERSONALITY*

Michel Gauquelin

Planetary Heredity

I maintain that the child's temperament is related to the position of the planets at the time of his birth. But relationship does not necessarily mean direct and almost instantaneous influence. When he comes into the world, the child is fully formed, with all the potentialities inherited from his parents. It is difficult to accept the idea that the heavenly bodies could act on the chromosomal structure of the child's cells, could disrupt and redistribute them, to the point of

---

* Gauquelin began his studies with 576 cases of doctors who were members of the *Academic De Medecine*. He then took up 508 cases of notable doctors. He found Mars occupied a prominent position in their charts. He extended his investigations to 570 well-known sportsmen, then to 494 members of the Chamber of Deputies and stage by stage covered painters and and scientists in his study. He found Jupiter dominant in the charts of actors, lawyers, judges, Mars significantly placed in the charts of the sportsmen, military men and doctors. Saturn was strong in those of priests and scientists. However, at this stage Gauquelin's studies were confined only to France.

Well-known mathematicians and statisticians who examined the results of these studies were impressed but said if the findings could be replicated in data from other countries, Gauquelin's fingings would be really significant.

modifying his character. At the conception, perhaps, the heavenly bodies might (who knows) have affected the chromosomal lottery. But after the encounter between the ovum and the sperm, the whole game is played according to the genetic plan. In reality, if he were born two weeks earlier, the same child would just as well have become a doctor, sportsman or painter, according to his temperament.

This is why—looking at the question from a scientific point of view, I do not think that the planet adds anything to the child being born. At the very most, it is perhaps an 'indicator' of a temperamental tendency which will lead him later

---

So, Gauquelin geared up to the challenge and set about working on cases outside France. This covers about 15,000 cases—Italy 7,000 Germany 3000, Belgium 3000, and Netherlands2000 plus 2000 more French births. This was no easy task and at every stage Gauquelin had to face many problems. These plus the original group of 7000 births were divided into 40 specific groups. He found Mars, Saturn or Jupiter had just risen or reached their culmination at these births, the planet depending upon the group to which the births related, the division being on the basis of occupation. The results of these findings are given in detail in"Written in the Stars" and show an unfailing cosrrespondence between planets and personality. Some of these findings were independently tested and corroborated by researchers, some of whom include the 'Para Committee' in Brussels in 1967, 3 members of the CSICOP, American Sceptics Committee in 1977 and Prof.Dr. Arno Muller, Saarland University, in 1988.

Reproduced above are excerpts from "Written in the Stars".

to succeed in a career which suits his character. What leads to success in professional life is hereditary predispositions, allied to a combination of favourable circumstances. To integrate the planet into the system, we have to take account of heredity. Psychology—and particularly the work of Eysenck—teaches us that there is an hereditary basis for personality.[1] Since the position of the celestial body represents a factor in character, one explanation proves to be possible: that this factor is hereditary. Thus the position of the planet at birth would also have to be hereditary.

As early as 1955, I had intended to put this idea into concrete form. But, for practical reasons, it was only from 1959 that any truly empirical research could be undertaken, this research being announced in the last chapter of *Les Hommes et les Astres*. My first results appeared in 1961 in a German journal[2]. But the fundamental work on this subject remains my

Heredity Planetaire (Planetary Heredity), which was published in 1966 with a preface by Professor Giorgio Piccardi, the director of the laboratory of physico-chemistry at the University of Florence, in Italy.[3] I am pleased to announce that an updated version of this work has just been translated into English and published.[4] In that work I give a detailed report on the results of an investigation carried out on some 30,000 birth dates and times for parents and their children, collected from the birth registers for Paris and several places in the Paris area. I noted a predisposition in children to come into the world when a planet is rising or reaching its culmination, if the same planet was positioned in the same zones of the sky at their parents' births.

The tendency to have a planet in 'Gauquelin plus zones' in one's horoscope appears to be hereditary, hence the title of my book: planetary heredity. True, this tendency is not very pronounced. A very great quantity of data is required to bring it to light. Sometimes— and this was the case for an investigation I published recently— the effect is not observed, and this could lead us to doubt its very existence.[5] The future will doubtless show us how to explain this regrettable instance of non- replication. Most often, however, the effect can be observed in a manner which is statistically very significant.

What appears certain, in any case, is that planetary heredity can only be observed for Mars, Jupiter, Saturn, Venus and the Moon, precisely the five temperament -planets, and not with the others which are further away from us: Uranus, Neptune or Pluto, nor for Mercury either, a very small planet which is swamped by the Sun's fires. All this appears to confirm the hereditary nature of the five planetary types described above, to the exclusion of any other. Moreover, if both of the child's parents are born with the same planet in 'Gauquelin plus zones', then their child has twice as much chance of being born under the same planetary configuration. This last observation, if confirmed, is in accord with the classical laws for the transmission of hereditary factors. But it is not opportune to go to further lengths on planetary heredity in this work. The curious reader will, if he wishes, find further information on these investigations in the recent English translation of my book *Planetary Heredity*.[4]

Midwife Planets?

Little by little, my work encouraged me to propose a physical model for the planetary effects; a very fragile model, it is true and not without contradictions; nothing more, in fact, than a proto-theory[6].

The child seems to be endowed with a 'planetary sensitivity' which induces his coming into the world at a 'chosen' moment. How can this be explained? In medicine it is known that once the moment of birth has arrived, the slightest little thing—the introduction into the organism of a medicine in a homeopathic dose, for instance—can set off the start of labour. This 'slightest little thing' could be linked to planetary factors, so that the child could react to a cosmic 'call sign' to which his planetary type would make him more sensitive than to any other. Playing the role of a catalyst or filter, the midwife planet would partly determine the time of birth. This is the most likely mechanism: birth being imminent, the mother's uterine contractions are started up and guided by harmonal secretions from the foetus passing into the mother's blood; the foetal secretions themselves being partly stimulated by the 'midwife' planet passing through the Gauquelin plus zones.

Certainly, this is a very daring model, perhaps too much so, and one which makes astrophysicists shudder. It is certain that it raises a shower of difficulties which have not yet been overcome. In a recent book, I have indulged in self-criticism of my explanatory model; I refer the reader to this.[5] The most shocking thing from the astrophysical point of view is that I have not established any significant correlation for the Sun, whose influence on the earth and its inhabitants is by far the most important. So by what means could the planets, which are miniscule by comparison, act this role of catalyst or filter that I have described? There is however a promising sign: when the geomagnetic activity of the earth (which depends on sunspots and solar eruptions) increases, the planetary effects on heredity can, it seems, as much as double in frequency.

This explanatory model also makes biologists shudder. Here, however, the promising signs seem more numerous. The role I attribute to the foetus, for example, is based on the most recent medical observations. They are, for example, expressed in this succinct phrase of Professor Robert Debre, a renowned paediatrician and a member of the *Academie de Medicine*: 'It is the foetus that orders the mother to expel it!;[7] or rather, in the words of the chairman of an international congress of obstetrics, Dr. G.S. Dawes, of the University of Oxford: 'Finally, there is evidence that suggests that the foetus normally initiates the process of parturition, thus liberating itself from the intra-uterine environment which has protected it'. I can note in passing that these experts are merely reformulating in modern scientific terms the intuition of Hippocrates who asserted, five centuries before Christ: 'When the time comes, the child stirs, breaks the membranes holding it and comes forth from its mother's womb'.

. . . . .

Yes, any other theory: the search for a physical model for planetary effects is, I fear, an almost unsurmountable task in the state of current knowledge, because of the small material means I have at my disposal in order to achieve it. But, as William of Orange asserted in a famous maxim: 'It is not necessary to hope in order to undertake, nor to succeed in order to persevere'.

. . . .

It is worthwhile abandoning for once the 'scientification' of my results in order to examine the 'symbolic' hypothesis. At the beginning, I had little belief in it and wrote to this effect. But certain pieces of empirical evidence have shaken my antipathy for this way of seeing things. Alongside the theory of the celestial bodies as physical causes, we shall discover that the doctrine of heavenly bodies as signs or symbols is full of enigmatic indications which cannot be blindly ignored simply because we wish to remain

reject my discoveries in the name of logic. The reality of facts alone should be our Ariadne's thread in this obscure labyrinth of astral influences where so many great minds have wandered hopelessly but with the deep conviction that there was a way out of the labyrinth, perhaps even many ways out.

. . . .

A planet in the 'Gauquelin plus zones' is certainly linked to the child's predispositions. There is simply no need to search for a physical relationship between planet and child. As a consequence of universal sympathy, the child is born in his own time. If human beings come into the world under the same astral configurations as their parents, it is because they are obeying the same signs. The influence of the celestial bodies, in the astrological sense, is not really an influence; it is simply a *significant coincidence* between the planet and the child. That is the true meaning of planetary effects, the only possible astrological doctrine. In other words, the planet 'signs' the child; it does not influence him.

. . . .

As early as 1955, when I observed my first results, it was already pretty obvious to me that there was something astonishingly true about this planetary symbolism. But the time had not then arrived to speak of it, because it was simply an impression that I was not able to prove scientifically. In my research, I had observed Mars dominating the births of men of war and sports champions, Jupiter being dominant with actors, Saturn with scientists and the Moon with poets. And, it is true, many military men and champions turn out to be 'martial', many actors 'jovial', many scientists 'saturnine' and many poets 'lunar'. Can we really speak of coincidences? It seems difficult.

. . . .

How could I demonstrate to others what appeared to me to be terribly evident? My impression would have to be confirmed by objective research. Fortunately, the character traits method made it possible to identify the psychological patterns which correspond to the positions of the planets in 'Gauquelin plus zones'. The Mars, Jupiter, Saturn, Venus and Moon types have been defined and published. Thanks to this method, it had become possible to compare astrological tradition with the thousands of traits in our catalogue; in particular, to test the validity of the keywords that astrologers attribute to planets which are *strong* in the birth horoscope. It was going to be possible to judge my hypothesis, or rather, my initial impression. Already, in 1974, in my work *La Cosmopsychologie*, with regard to our description of the planetary types, I had published the astrological significance of the heavenly bodies according to the *Tetrabiblos* of Ptolemy, the great astrologer of antiquity.[12]

This was just a first step. In 1977, I suggested to my then-wife Francoise, now Schneider-

Gauquelin, that she undertake a more systematic investigation. Using the data provided by our catalogue of traits, she tested the validity of the keywords attributed by ten astrologers to the bodies of the solar system. She demonstrated in accordance with my hypothesis, that a significant proportion of planetary symbolism had an objective reality, at any rate for the five celestial bodies for which psychological types had previously been demonstrated. This work gave rise to the publication of a monograph by my laboratory[13]. This monograph has since been reproduced in the form of a book for which I wrote the preface [14]

The results of my investigation were very positive for Mars, Jupiter, Saturn, Venus and the Moon. When they bear the 'ancient' astrologers' keywords, the celebrities in my groups were born much more frequently 'with the right planet in the right place', that is, in the Gauquelin plus zones, than would be allowed by chance.

REFERENCES

1 Eysenck H., *The Structure of Human Personality*, Methuen London, 1970.

2 Gauquelin M., 'Die Planetare Hereditat',*Zeitschrift fur Para psychologie und Grenzgebiete der Psychologie*, 5, 2/3,1961, 168-193.

3 Gauquelin M., *L'Heredite Planetaire*, foreword by Prof. G.Piccardi, Florence University, Planete, Paris,1966.

4 Gauquelin M., *Planetary Heredity, ACS Publications, P.O.Box 16430, San Diego, CA 92116, USA, 1988.*

5 Gauquelin M.,*Planetary Heredity, A Reappraisal* on 50,000 subjects, New Birthdata Series, Volume 2,LERRCP, Paris, 1984.

6 Seymour P.A. H., *A Causal Mechanism for Gauquelin's Planetary Effect, Plymouth, 1986, (another very recent mathematical model for a theory by an astronomer).*

7 Debre, Prof. R., in *France-Soir*, 12 April 1975.

8 Dawes G.S., Chairman's opening remarks, *Foetal Autonomy*, CIBA Foundation, 1969.

9 Andre J., Rendez-vous planetaries, *La Science et ses doubles*, Autrement, Paris, 1986,pp 46-53.

10 Gauquelin M., *Cosmic Influences on Human Behavior* Stein & Day, New York, 1973, (*Updated edition, Aurora Press, New York, 1985)*

11 Seznec J., *The Survival of the Pagan Gods*, Princeton University Press, 1972.

12 Gauquelin M., *La Cosmopsychologie*, Paris,Retz.1974.

13 Gauquelin F., *Traditional Symbolism in Astrology and the character-Trait Method*, Series D, Vol. 7, LERRCP, Paris 1980

14 Gauquelin F., *The Psychology of the Planets* foreword by M. Gauquelin, Astro Computing Publications, San Diego, 1982.

15 Startup M., The Accuracy of Astrologer's Keywords- Part1 & Part 2, *Correlation*, 1981, 1,1, 36-43 & 1,2, 24-36.

One is born into a herd of buffaloes and must be glad if one is not trampled underfoot before one's time.

* * * * *

Great spirits have always encountered violent oppoition from mediocre minds.

* * * * *

16 Gauquelin M., Planetary Influences: An Empirical Study of the Acuracy of 'Ancient' Astrologers' Keywords, Correlation, 1982, 2,2,4-11.

17 Parr J., *Tambulane's Malady and other Essays on Astrology in Elizabethan Drama* University of Alabama Press, 1953.

18 Couderc P., *L' Astrologie, P.U.F., Paris, 1951.*

19 Sachs A., Babylonian Horoscopes, *Journal of Cuneiform Studies, 1952, 6, 2, 49.*

20 Curry, P., Astrology and Philosophy of Sccience, *Correlation*, 1981, 1,1,4-10 (and *Astrology as a Scientific Research Programme* unpublished M.Sc. thesis, London School of Economics, 1980).

21 Lakatos I., *The Methodology of Scientific Research Programmes*, Cambridge University Press; ed. J. Worral & G. Currrie, 1978, (quote in Curry, 1981).

The struggle against the persistent and overwhelming majority of fools and of those who exploit them as tools is indeed a tough one and with little prospects. But the fight is necessary for without it mankind will be in worse plight.

— *ALBERT EINSTEIN*

CHAPTER NINE

ASTROLOGY, SCIENCE AND SCIENTISTS

Kumar Babu B.E.,M.S.

The alignment of planets on the same side of the Sun a few years ago gave the media an opportunity to take some cheap potshots at Astrology. Though it had been astronomers who had been making a big deal of this so called alignment, imaginary predictions were attributed to astrologers. For example the *New York Daily* News said that *"Indian Astrologer B.V.Raman predicted that Los Angeles would be destroyed by an earthquake."* This was nothing more than a fabrication because we have repeatedly been advising our readers to disregard the big fuss that astronomers have been making regarding this alignment. In our editorial in the January 1982 issue of THE ASTROLOGICAL MAGAZINE we stated "It is our opinion that no special significance be attached to this so-called line-up. And we would like to make it clear that we do not endorse the opinions of either Western astronomers or astrologers anticipating such catastrophes as a nuclear war, extinction of life and destruction of cities by earthquakes, etc. One need not get scared at such sensation-mongering predictions made in this regard".

There is no doubt that this was primarily done for its headline value but it is symptomatic of a deeper psychological disease that is afflicting not only the media but the public in general. The psychological basis for the media making unfair and underserved comments on Astrology probably resides in the newsman's (and the general public's) awe of scientists. This awe is so obsessive that newsman who are supposed to verify the truth of a report before publishing it become totally tongue-tied when they are in the presence of scientists and take anything a scientist says as Gospel truth. And unfortunately since the scientific community, with a few honorable exceptions, has been less objective when it comes to Astrology we can't really expect anything better from the media either. Is Astrology a science ? Are scientists justified in trying to bar the entry of Astrology into the comity of sciences? We will attempt to answer briefly these and other questions.

Critics of Astrology have always had "valid arguments" to prove Astrology is not a science. It is important here to realize that a subtle distinction exists between what is valid and what is true. The connection between truth and validity is this. If all the premises of a valid argument are true then the conclusion is true. The thing to note is that the "premises" must be true. If a review of criticisms of Astrology is made one will invariably find that the arguments flow from faulty initial premises. A case in point is critics finding fault with Astrology on the basis of the newspaper report above— when the report itself was totally wrong.

Quantification is the introduction of numbers into the definition of concepts and the formulation of laws. There is no doubt that physics is the most thoroughly quantified of all sciences and there is a proclivity in some scientists to take for granted that in all areas quantification alone is a necessary and sufficient condition for a subject to be classified as a science. In Astrology, psychology and in biological science quantification is not very prevalent.

In itself quantification is no magic key. If the material warrants it, then its advantages are obvious. Advocates of quantification get annoyed when other sciences do not make an effort to quantify. Understandable as it is, the annoyance does not always make their arguments more judicious or temperate. Deduction from quantified laws is easier; this is one reason why quantification is desirable. But to say that a subject can't be classified as a science unless it can quantify is totally illogical.

There are those who think that scientists are always objective and fair and would have accepted Astrology if it merited being called a science. This is far from the truth and is very clearly brought out by Theodore Gordon in his book *'Ideas in Conflict'* where he says "some of the ideas which are now the very jewels of our existence were absolutely rejected by prominent spokemen of their age. For all our vaunted scientific achievements and publicized open-mindedness, radically new ideas have few supporters. Ideas which did not coincide with the preconceived mainstream of scientific, political or religious thought were fought with militant and abusive dedication. Socrates, Galileo, Maxwell, Planck, Lister and Roentgen, all of these and others faced the establishment. They proposed the unusual, the mutant idea and they were rejected first,

"......The scientists have attempted to introduce a logical and codified reception system by which newly proposed data can be rationally examined before being accepted as truth. This is the scientific method which purports to open its arms to all new ideas to give them a fair test. This method implies that there are no cliques in science, that an idea will stand on its own worth, not on the opinion of pre-eminent scientists. Yet this approach has failed repeatedly because scientifists are people who, even as you or I, are impressed by titles, rank, glory, and can suffer the ego-starvings jealousies....".

The whole edifice of science is built on the ability to prophesy. Natural laws are, after all, formulas for predicting. Some scientific disciplines permit relatively exact predictions; others predict with less precision. These latter disciplines, including Astrology, are those in which causality is not properly understood. However over the course of time considerable evidence has accumulated linking terrestrial phenomena with planetary motion and in time causality may be understood better. It is impoosible to list in an article of this nature all the accumulated evidence but we will sample some of the latest findings.

Ralph Morris, a professor of pharmacology at the University of Illinois Medical Center, studied more than 100 patients over 5 years and found that bleeding ulcers and chest pains became more frequent in two thirds of the patients at times of the Full Moon. His findings were published in the January 8,82 issue of *the Journal of the American Medical Association* where he says "People who have problems, such as ulcers, should be more careful and take their medicine during full-moon periods". Prof Morris thinks that incidences of health problems may be linked to changes in gravitational and electromagnetic fields. He says that while no one has pinpointed a cause and effect relationship there is considerable support for a theory that speculates that magnetic interaction between the earth and the Moon may affect physical and emotional processes. He further thinks that this interaction could affect humans because of electrical charges and metals such as iron in the body. Support to the theory that the Moon could influence humans comes from J.Allen Hynek, Professor Emeritus of Physics and Astronomy at Northwestern University. His studies show that increases in arson, violent crimes and strange behaviour in mental hospitals occur when the Moon is full.

Professor Frank Brown, Dept. of Biological Science at Northwestern University says that"all life is sensitive to the electromagnetism of the atmosphere. Humans, he says, are" just a plethora of magnetic fields ....", and studies have shown that changes in the magnetic field can, for instance, affect metabolism. Other researchers like A.P. Krueger of the University of California, Berkeley point out that ion levels are known to change 100 fold during electrical storms and that positive ions in the air can drastically increase the levels of serotonin, a biochemical associate with a widerange of stress and anxiety reactions in animals.

Jupiter has always been considered by astrologers to be a very special planet in a horoscope. Modern science reiterates this in the February 82 issue of *the Science Digest* which says"Jupiter is probably the only planet that is slowly contracting and thus generating thermal energy which radiates into space at twice the rate it receives energy from the Sun. Because its very strong rapidly rotating magnetic field interacts with the solar wind, Jupiter emits intense radio waves. This in conjunction with the fact that human beings are influenced by eletromagnetic fields should be sufficient to cause even the most hard-nosed skeptic to investigate whether planets may, after all, have some influence on the destiny of man. This may he disturbing to some who believe that man is master of his own destiny. Even here modern science seems to indicate that we are not really totally in control of our destiny.

For instance Sarnoff Mednick, Professor of Psychology at the University of Southern California, says that his research (including measurement of brain waves etc.,) has shown that some people have a genetic predisposition to commit crimes. In a study involving 9000 children he said one could predict the onset of criminal behaviour as much as 10 years in advance.

These and other scientific findings have shown and continue to show that the microcosm and the macrocosm are not after all that far apart. Dr.Fritjof Capra, a distinguished physicist at the University of California says, "Any living system, from a bacterium to a brain, from a beehive to the biosphere, is complete in itself and is also a component of the Cosmos. Two basic themes emerge again and again from the study of living and nonliving matter and are also repeadly emphasized in the teaching of the mystics—the Universal interconnectedness of and interdependence of all phenomena."

Some researchers speculate that planetary influences may be due to energy beyond the presently known limits of the electromagnetic spectrum, perhaps even on another still undiscovered spectrum. But others are uncomfortable with the idea of a force apparently not governed by the known laws of physics. These others have an established view of the world and how nātural laws work and they are afraid of any new view point that in any way threatens their comfortable and settled perceptions of the world. As Beverly

Rubik, a San Francisco State University biophysicist says, **"Everyone thinks the scientific community is cool, calm and collected but there are people who would rather crucify you than see their world view destroyed."** It is possible that using our subconscious minds may be the only way of obtaining a complete understanding of the effect of planetary motion on human affairs. Our ancient sages must have realized the limitations of the conscious mind when they gave more importance to "Jnana" (transcendental experience)than to "Vidya" (or knowledge). Princeton Psychologist Julian Jaynes likens the conscious mind to a flash light searching around a dark room. The flash light (if it could think) since there is light in whatever direction it turns, would have to conclude that there is light everywhere while the truth was that the room was dark!

The bitter denunciation of Astrology by some scientists reminds us of what philosopher William James said many years ago about his scientist colleagues at Harvard. We quote, "There is included in human nature an ingrained naturalism

The Scientist's Dilemma

We are living in a period of such great external and internal insecurity and with such a lack of firm objectives that the mere confession of our convictions may be of significance, even if these convictions, as all value judgements, cannot be proven through logical deductions.

and materialism of mind which can only admit facts that are actually tangible, of this sort of mind the entity called 'science' is the idol. Fondness for the word 'scientist' is one of the notes by which you may know its votaries; and its short way of killing any opinion that it disbelieves in is to call it 'unscientific'."

There have been a number of 'Investigating Committees' which have been formed — all with the express intent of debunking Astrology and other paranormal phenomena. Dr.Hynek ridicules these committees with this observation, **"What sort of a scientific investigation is it that assumes the answer before starting ?". The answer to a research problem should never be anticipated to such a degree that it strongly influences the approach to the problem. Ridicule can not and should not be an accepted part of the scientific method.**

In each epoch of man's history there has been a smugness of knowledge that is not apparent to most participants of that age. It is an

> There arises at once the question: should we consider the search for truth or more modestly expressed, our efforts to understand the universe through constructive logical truth—as an autonomous objective of our work?.....
>
> This, in a sense, religious attitude of a man engaged in scientific work has some influence on his whole personality. For apart from the knowledge which is offered by accumulated experience and from the rules of logical thinking, there exists in principle for the man of science no authority whose decisions and statements could have

unawareness of things not properly understood. Things that are bewildering and unthinkable at that point in time but holding answers for the future. That is why it is essential that scientists study the puzzling phenomena of today, not dismiss with ridicule, with humility and dignity.

themselves a claim to "truth". This leads to a paradoxical situation that a person who devotes all his strength to objective matters will develop from a social point of view, into an extreme individualist who at least in principle has faith in nothing but his own judgement. It is quite possible to assert that intellectual individualism and the thirst for scientific knowledge emerged simultaneously in history and remained inseparable eversince.

— Albert Einstein

CHAPTER TEN

ASTROLOGY AND OUR SPACE PROGRAMME*

Gayatri Devi Vasudev

July 13, 1988 was indeed one of the darkest days, in the life of our space programme. Even as the 150 Kg ASLV-D2 satellite shot into the sky and the scientific community gathered at Sriharikota cheered shouting 'success, success', a pall of gloom descended over it within a mere 150 seconds, when the Augmented Satellite Launch Vehicle (ASLV-D2), carrying a stretched Rohini series Satellite plunged into the Bay of Bengal, hissing fumes!

Except for isolated instances of bold write ups on the failure, the media, by and large, preferred not to criticize the dismal performance of our science-men. On the contrary many consoled the scientists that programmes everywhere had had to face failure and one even went so far as to pat the space scientist on his back and prod him **to redouble his efforts**. As in the past the Failure Analysis Committee was entrusted with the task of finding out what went wrong, where and why.

The ISRO Chairman drew consolation from the fact that failures have also occurred in U.S. and European space programs but conveniently

---

* Reproduced from THE ASTROLOGICAL MAGAZINE, October 1988

avoided comparing the success-failure ratio of our programs to that of other countries! **ISRO's shocking 66 per cent launch failure is the highest**. Against this background, it was ridiculous for the ISRO chief to say that the Polar Launch Vehicle Program will remain unaffected.

The Government (presumably on the advice of our space scientists) uses 'technology spin off' as a justification for the colossal amounts of money being spent on the space program. This technology spin-off includes nationwide television, better telephone systems and sophisticated cyclone warning systems. Apart from the fact that *none of these things have materialized*, all the spin-off items can be purchased from the U.S., Russia and Western Europe at a fraction of the cost. As an example, Singapore has no space program but its telephone systems far outclass those of every city in India. It is apparent to us that the government is afraid of displeasing the powerful 'space/science lobby' that seems to be omnipresent. **The 7th plan assigns 700 crore rupees to space when basics like drinking water, sanitation etc., are in short supply in every city of India. Imagine the benefits if that money was invested in improving our country's water supplies.**

The 'space lobby' is a creation of ego bound Indian scientists who start 'prestigious' projects (that have very little relevance to the country's real needs) in order to advance their careers. Career advancement is easy in India if you start expensive projects even if you do not complete them. Large segments of the Indian press appear to understand little about the state of technology development outside the country. So much so that any press release from a National Laboratory or an Indian University is immediately accorded headline status!

Our Rishis who gave us such sciences as *Vaimanika Sastra* (crudely translated as aeronautics) also gave us *Jyotisha* a beacon of knowledge to show light where conventional methods of 'information gathering' must stop due to various limitations. There is general scientific agreement that at any given point in time science has a degree of incompleteness resulting in some inconsistencies and *Jyotisha* is no exception. Hence it is surprising that some 'scientists' display such ignorance when dealing with Astrology.

The ASLV-D2 was launched on an Amavasya (new Moon)— a most unsuitable time astrologically. Though the launch probably had severe technical problems—not surprising because of the low calibre of some of our scientists— the inauspicious launch time itself magnified the technical problems. Dr. Ram Shrivastava, Professor of Physics at the Holkar Science College,Indore and Founder Member of ICEPS (International Centre for Educational Physics Experiments in Space) echoed a fundamental dictum of Muhurta or electional Astrology when he said "No space scientist would dare to launch a satellite on a new Moon night when the earth tilts in the direction of the Sun and the Moon resulting in severe tides."

In fact, Dr.Shrivastava's warning to the Minister of State for Science and Technology had been arrogantly dismissed by the concerned Minister with the words he (the Minister) did not know if "the scientist was well-known or reputed". Had Astrology been applied, "the hard-earned money of the nation would not have been thrown into the Bay of Bengal". It is all the more appropriate now for thoughtful decision makers to seriously consider Astrology as a planning tool in projects of national interest.

The failure of the ASLV-D2 brings four points into sharp focus: (1) a new vindication of astrological principles, (2) a lack of understanding of the term 'science' of some newsmen, (3) failure of the news media to critically review our scientists' performance and (4) the guilty silence of men in responsible positions on the tremendous wastage of public money.

A few days before the launch, many a newspaper carried columns on how foolproof this venture was: and one went on to say "This second ASLV being in effect the first operational one, no chances are being taken" and further wrote, naively, of the Failure Analysis Committee constituted by the ISRO Chairman to find out what went wrong with SROSS-I and that it would do everything to ensure the success of SROSS-II

The truth of our observations made in the June 1975 issue of THE ASTROLOGICAL MAGAZINE when India's first space-craft was launched from a Soviet cosmodrome has now been borne out. We had observed: ".....This has occurred just on the eve of the country coming under the second and more significant phase of *sade-sathi* influence of Saturn. Obviously this is a period of great saturnine strain on Indian affairs and **we are hesitant to join the chorus of sooth-sayers amongst our politicians and scientists that "Aryabhata" now in orbit, and "Rohini" the second Satellite to be put into orbit would serve the nation in its development efforts.** This inference becomes fortified if the chart cast for the time of launching Aryabhata is carefully assessed. Lord of the Ascendant Moon ruling Aryabhata is in the Ascendant in the constellation of Saturn who in turn occupies the 12th without any benefic aspects. But Jupiter, lord of the 9th, aspects the Ascendant. Obviously this disposition indicates that the launching could act as a shot in the arm to our country now under the grip of moral degeneracy and economic chaos.

"Mercury, the planet of science ruling the 3rd and 12th houses, is in the 10th in exact conjunction with the Sun, lord of the 2nd, the constellation of Ketu being involved. The exaltation of the political planet in the 10th is significant in as much as the experiment in space while strengthening the image of the rulers and diverting public attention, will not have much relevance to the current problems of India's economic and social development....

JUPIT.	SUN MERC.	KETU VENUS	SAT.
MARS	Chart 1 RASI		ASCDT. MOON
	RAHU		

	SAT. KETU	VENUS	SUN MERC.
MARS	NAVAMSA		
			MOON ASCDT.
	JUPIT.	RAHU	

"What are the uses of 'Aryabhata' and how do they benefit the country?" are questions that naturally arise in our minds. Lord of the 4th (agriculture) and 11th (benefits) is no doubt placed in the 11th but he is in conjunction with Ketu aspected by Mars and subject to Papakartari Yoga being hemmed in between the Sun and Mercury on one side and Saturn on the other. Because Mars is a yogakaraka its prestige as a member of the Space Club will be enhanced but it will not find a practical application in the course and content of economic development as a whole...

"Aryabhata" was put into orbit under the directional influence of Saturn which will last for nearly 14 years. Saturn as lord of the 7th is in the 12th while in the Navamsa his affliction is not less pronounced. Therefore, it occurs to us that we should not expect much useful result from this experiment.

Every single word said above has come out true. The relevance of this project to our economic and social life is dubious. Its role in improving agriculture has been zero. What initially started at 4 crores of rupees is now mounting with each venture, the present costing 23 crores of rupees and taking into account the 15 months of work by space-science men it would probably run into several more crores.

In a country where millions die for lack of food and countless children are ravaged by disease and malnutrition, putting public funds to such prestige-boosting exercises and expensive luxuries is an appalling and disgraceful commentary on the Government's priorities.

Reproduced below is a table from a national daily which is to say the least amusing. Incidentally, the June 1981 launch is described as a success although the mission ended in less than 10 days against a life expectancy of 90 days!

LANDMARKS IN SPACE PROGRAMME

DATE	SATELLITE	FUNCTION	LAUNCHER RESULT
MAR.19,1975	Aryabhata	Scientific	U.S.S.R.Success
June 7,1979	Bhaskara-1	Earth observation	U.S.S.R.Success
Aug.10,1979	Rohini	Earth observation	SLV-3 Failure
July 18,1980	Rohini	Earth observation	SLV-3 Success
June19,1981	Apple	Communi - cation	Ariane Euro-pean Success Space Agency
Nov.20,1981	Bhaskara II	Earth observation	U.S.S.R.Success
May 31,1981	Rohini	Scientific	SLV 3 Failure
Apr.17,1983	Rohini	Scientific	SLV-3 Success
Mar.24,1987	SROSS-I	Technology and Appli - cation	ASLV Failure
Mar.19,1988	IRS-IA	Remote sensing	U.S.S.R.Succes

Courtesy : THE HINDU (14-7-1988)

Seven of these launches are described as successful and no one still knows, the spacemen included, what that means. If putting a satellite at colossal cost to the exchequer in the sky is decribed as a success, well... And the term failure in all the 3 cases is a disastrous plunge down into the sea within minutes of take off. Perhaps, the launches did not come down immediately is what success means according to this table. Incidentaly, the Table is indulgent to ISRO in enumerating its success and needs correction.

Earlier on 10-8-1979 'Rohini' SLV-3 also came plummeting into the Bay of Bengal within 5 minutes of take-off. A horoscope (Chart 2) cast for this launch has serious afflictions.

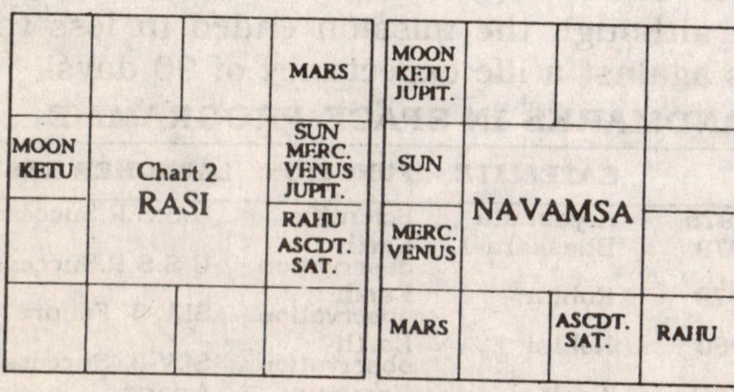

The Lagna is Leo, occupied by powerful Saturn and Rahu while the Moon is in the 7th. All the benefics are relegated to the 12th house.

In the parent launch (Chart 1), the Dasa lord Saturn is in the 12th house in Aridra and its ruler Rahu is debilitated in the 5th house. Rahu in the 5th is a severe affliction that can give problematic offspring (in this context the series may have a chequered career) some times, at other times, a mental euphoria of success where it is not,phantasical plans, wild imagination and hypochrondria also. Saturn as Dasa lord made the successful projects practically useless and the failures, abysmally dismal. Saturn Dasa ends in August 1989. The present Bhukti is that of Jupiter and is the last one in Saturn Dasa going by the name of *dasa-chidra*. Saturn, the 7th and 8th lord and a first rate malefic, is placed in the 12th house. His blemish is slightly redeemed by being in Jupiter's constellation, although Jupiter is himself caught between malefics. Jupiter and Saturn are in Nakshatra*parivartana* which is not too bad but the chart suffers from severe strokes of *balarishta* and the Dasa of a *maraka* planet running can hardly support the grandiose objectives envisaged in our space programmes.

'Bhaskara I', which marked Experiment two of the space scientists, was launched on 7th June, 1979 at 16 hours (IST), again from a Soviet cosmodrome. Its function was described as earth observation and that included "studies in hydrology, metelorology, forestry and other related areas of economic developments". 'Bhaskara' was an improvement on 'Aryabhata' in that it cost Rs. 6.5 crores (the launcher being a gift from USSR), took 4 years to build and involved 600 men who worked on it in different space centres in the country. This was in Venus Bhukti of Saturn Dasa in Chart I. Venus as 11th lord is afflicted by Ketu. The Dasa lord Saturn is in the 12th in the house of expenditure and as a malefic allows for unwarranted spending or to put it more plainly, creates losses.

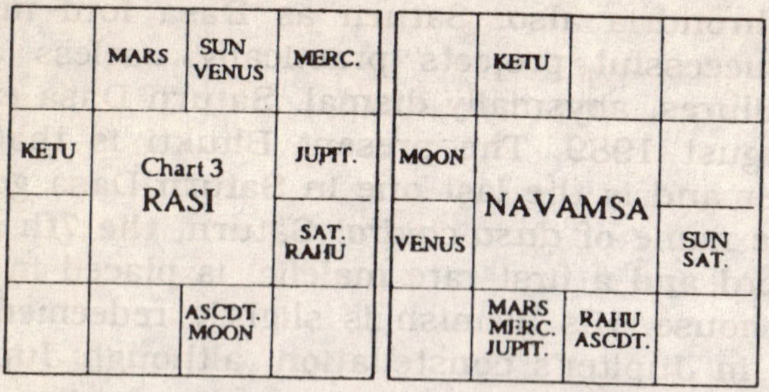

In 'Bhaskara's chart (Chart 3)' discussed in the August 1979 issue of THE ASTROLOGICAL MAGAZINE,we wrote, "Lord of the Ascendant Venus is in the 8th in his own sign in association with the Sun, lord of the 11th and the constellations involved being Krittika and Mrigasira respectively. This disposition suggests that the launching of 'Bhaskara' can at best act as not only a shot in one arm to the sagging spirit of our scientist as the pace of our progress in space science is far from spectacular, but also strengthen the image of our rulers whose amateurish methods of governing have placed India under the grip of moral degeneracy not to speak of economic chaos and political confusion. Mercury, the planet of intelligence, thinking, communications, weather and intellectual acumen, is ideally placed in the 9th as lord of the 2nd and the 7th. This is a silver lining as Mercury's position denotes that

'Bhaskara' will contribute to some extent to the advancement of knowledge pertaining to weather....

"What is the main mission of 'Bhaskara' and how does it benefit the 'common man' and the weaker sections about whom our politicians shed crocodile tears day in and day out? The satellite is said to identify mineral occurrence areas. The fourth rules minerals, agriculture, etc. It is aspected by exalted Jupiter, lord of the 3rd and 6th. But lord of the 4th Saturn is with Rahu in the 8th from the 4th. This is not an encouraging disposition though Saturn and Rahu are posited in the 11th.

"... In fact, Ketu in the 5th can only mean imaginary uses and nothing more..."

Saturn, the 5th lord, ruling intelligence is eclipsed by Rahu. It is also the house of investment and Saturn's affliction by the nodes confirms the unwise investment of both grey-matter and resources which finally showed up as a big failure.

'Rohini' D2 launched in April 1983 is said to have been an unqualified success for ISRO. One just cannot be satisfied by such statements. One is also curious to know why it was called successful. Simply because 'The Rohini D2 took more than 2500 imageries which were used for identification of features of Bhadravati forests in Karnataka, snow cover in Sutlej and vegetation in northern Andhra Pradesh" although this data was of practically no utility compared to the cost of acquiring it. The same data could have been provided by U.S. satellites currently orbiting the earth for a nominal cost. The same crores if employed to improve agriculture would have paid spectacular dividends both in terms of produce and in terms of improving the life of the poor farmer. But none of it. These space programmes provide information using which a paper is written, read at an international conference, and the reader given a citation amidst the clicking of cameras and the clapping of hands. A single ego is bloated out of all proportion and that at what cost to the exchequer? Some space project this!

'Rohini' D2's predecessor's performance is also described as a success thereby making a mockery of this term if we look into the facts of the Rohini Satellite which went up on July 19, 1981. Its" mission ended in just 9 days as against the envisaged 90 days due to low attitude problems".

Now when the media heralded the second ASLV Launch on July 13, it was received with crossed fingers by the astrological community. More so because of the sad choice of the lunar day being Amavasya, in the context of the first developmental flight of the ASLV also going up in smoke. This was barely a year ago when according to the spacemen, the operational launch vehicle had failed to "achieve its mission's objectives". In spite of that, said the press, which seemed to have clearly succumbed to the story doled out to it by the 'scientists', that "much of the technology developed for the ASLV could be tested during its 3 minute flight and the performance was found to be satisfactory" even if in common parlance it had failed even before the end of this 3 minutes of providing profound enlightenment!

According to the FAC the failure of the mission was due to an occurrence which had only an exceedingly low probability. **Chances or no chances and in spite of all the detailed research and investigation by the FAC, SROSS-II went the same way as its predecessor, because the orthodox scientific community of our country did not have an open enough mind to consider the use of Astrology. There has been, never before, such rigidly of outlook as we now have in our officially designated scientists.**

SROSS-I was launched on March 29, 1987 in Jupiter Bhukti of Saturn Dasa of the parent chart. The chart (Chart 4) for the time of blast-off has some interesting features.

The weekday was Tuesday. The Moon is in the 8th, a powerful combination for *balarishta*. Apparently *abhijit*, the Sun in the 10th is himself afflicted by Rahu. The Moon in the 8th is one of the *doshas* frowned upon in electional Astrology. In fact, the principle is *Sarveshukaryeshusasi balatayah* that no matter what the venture, the Moon must be rendered strong.

The same mistake was repeated at the launching of ASLV_D2 (Chart 5) rendered worse by the lunar day being *Amavasya*, *Amavaasyaa*

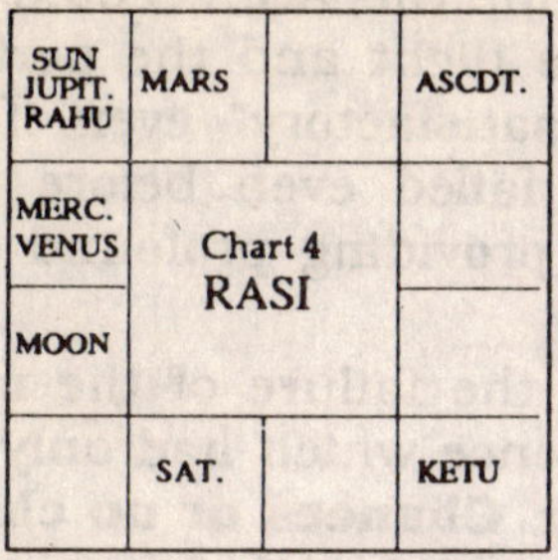

niraarambha sarvaarambhesh varjitam—meaning the new Moon day should be rejected for any enterprise. We may also note the concentration of the malefic influences of the Sun, the Moon, Mars and Saturn on the 8th or house of destruction. The 8th lord Mercury is in Aridra ruled by Rahu. Any tyro in Astrology could predict that ASLV- D2 would meet with instantaneous death.

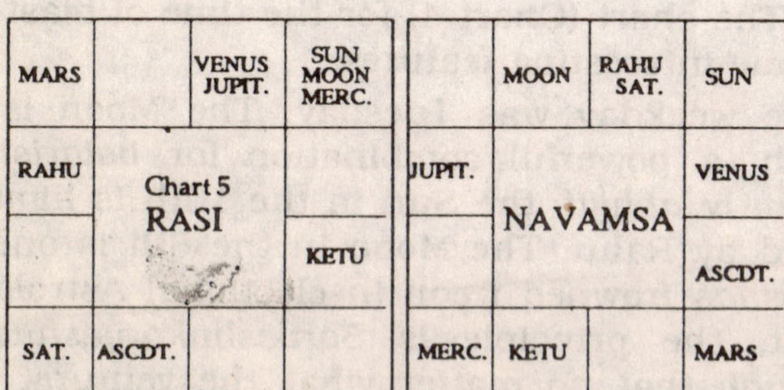

The Ascendant is in a martian sign Scorpio. Both Aries and Scorpio ruled by Mars are taboo for any undertaking. *Panchaka* works out to 4 which is unsafe. Now let us take a look at its previous project shown by the 11th house Virgo (ruling elder siblings). Virgo is afflicted by the combined aspects of Mars and Saturn. The 11th lord Mercury is also aspected by both malefics showing the fate of its predecessor.

Apart from the fact that the launch-off times were astrologically unsound the last Bhukti of Saturn Dasa (Chart 1) now running does not seem to indicate smooth sailing for the space projects of our country.

Chart 1 has an interesting melee of planetary dispositions. The Lagna and Lagna lord are both in Cancer, the constellation occupied by both being Pushya ruled by Saturn. Saturn as a functional malefic and placed in a *dusthana* transfers his inhibiting qualities to the Lagna. Therefore results of the space project will be nebulous, non-profitable, entail heavy losses and be marked by a string of failures. Yogakaraka Mars who is also the 10th lord (ruling achievements) is in the 8th house and this does not speak much of future performances either. Results include "many breaks in career, If the 10th lord is fortified, he will occupy a high office in his field but only for a short time. If a malefic planet afflicts the 10th lord, the person has criminal propensities and commits offences. Saturn here makes the person an undertaker or otherwise employed in burning ghats, grave yards etc". These are for individual charts but can be suitably adapted to the project although they cannot be read too literally. The 10th lord Mars is afflicted by being in Rahu's constellation and Rahu is afflicting the house of intelligence from his sign of debility. This suggests impaired thinking and inability to comprehend realities. The 10th lord in the 8th, house of death, is hardly indicative of laudable achievements. On the contrary it points to more dismal performances.

In Chart 1 Jupiter in the 9th is the only saving grace of a jinxed space program. It may give an occasional sample of a semi- successful launch and nothing more. But Jupiter Dasa is practically ruled out this century and this disposition of Jupiter ceases to be relevant.

Mercury Dasa can be interesting for Mercury, though 12th lord, is in the 10th with exalted Sun (2nd lord) and can normally give rather gratifying results in terms of achievement. But within a year of the advent of Mercury Dasa, transit Saturn will have moved to Capricorn bringing the chart under affliction again. This could therefore give another spell of frustration and gloom for our space 'scientists'. The Sun, 2nd lord joining 12th lord Mercury in a constellation of Ketu will fire the ambitions of the spacemen so much as to expend astronomical amounts to put their plans into action but most of it ultimately going up in smoke, LITTERALLY!

> Phenomena come to us disguised in their frameworks of time and space; they are messages in cipher of which we shall not understand the ultimate significance until we have discovered how to decode them out of their space-time wrappings.
>
> **Sir James Jeans (The Universe Around Us).**

CHAPTER ELEVEN

HOW I WAS CONVINCED ABOUT ASTROLOGY

Late Dr. S.A. Bhise, D.Sc.,Ph.D.

(Dr. S.A. Bhise was an eminent scientist and a great inventor. His inventions in the realm of mechanics were largely to do with the casting and composing of type. American and European scientific journals conceded that he had satisfactorily solved the intricate problem of multiple type-casting and he was dubbed "the Edison of India". In the chemical line he developed processes for reducing iodine to its atomic non-poisonous and water-soluble form. According to *Scientific American*, "the work of Dr. Bhise should dispel the illusion, that the Indian brain sadly lacked inventive faculty". Such an eminent scientist's personal experiences with astrologers, must be of great value to the advocates of Astrology for Dr. Bhise's opinions are not coloured by misconceptions and prepossessions which characterise the utterences of modern scientists on Astrology.)

As a youth I had not the slightest faith in Astrology. This despite the fact that my parents firmly believed that the stars exert an influence on human affairs. They used to consult astrologers frequently.

However, I kept an open mind on the subject. In the event of coming across evidence which proved conclusively the soundness of astrological principles, I would gladly recognize the science as valid, I told my friends. I meant every word of it.

Thus, when, in 1895, in the twenty-seventh year of my life, I was afforded an opportunity to observe astrological evidence at first hand, I proceeded to investigate the matter with all scientific impartiality at my command.

In the course of my sojourn at Lucknow, whither I had gone as a piligrim, I heard that a famous astrologer and palmist had taken up residence in the city. In order to "kill time", I went to him one day. I told him quite frankly of my scepticism. But I assured him that in the event of his furnishing conclusive evidence of his claims, I would cheerfully confess my conversion.

The man was a venerable Brahmin pandit and since I was from distant Bombay, he was a total stranger to me. It was scarcely conceivable, therefore, that anything he said was based on previous information.

He regarded me solemnly for several seconds, carefully examined my palms, and asked whether I had two hours or more to spare. "Here is one thing at any rate that I can safely predict. If you can spare the time, you will leave here fully convinced".

"I called his bluff" and he set to work. The first thing he did was to take impressions of my palms on a sheet of paper. Then he studied the lines on the soles of my feet. Finally, he completed an involved series of mathematical calculations and said:

"I am now going to ask you several questions, please answer nothing but 'yes' or 'no'.

"Did you lose your father when you were twenty-six years of age?" (I answered in the affirmative, attributing the guess to the fact that he knew me to be on a holy pilgrimage and such journeys are usually undertaken on behalf of the disembodied soul of one's late parent and occur after the first anniversary of the death).

"Did you complete your formal education at the age of twenty-one and enter the civil, military or private service soon afterwards?" (This too, I attributed to mere guess work. Such a program is quite the usual thing for the educated Hindu).

"Did your first wife pass away several months before your father?" (This was more than mere guess work. I was now intensely interested).

Tell me, " I asked him, "would you care to cast my horoscope? Could you undertake to tell me the approximate date of my birth and, at the same time, tell me something of what the future has in store for me? I have all the time in the world at my disposal at the present moment, and I shall be glad to pay you well for your services."

"Frankly", - the pandit smiled benevolently as he said this "I am very much interested in your case. I would regard it as a privilege to cast your horoscope. But I warn you I shall have to spend considerable time making the necessary calculations."

Two hours later, the good Brahmin was ready with his report.

"At the time of your birth, Pisces was in the Ascendant".-

I was mildly surprised. - "You were born in April 1867." - The adjective mildly no longer applied - "You came into this world on the 29th day of the month, shortly before sunrise." At that my amazement knew no bounds. - "As nearly as I can calculate it", he ruthlessly continued, "You were born at 4-30 in the morning."

My scepticism was at an end. I frankly and enthusiastically admitted this to the astrologer. I entreated him to enlighten me with regard to the future.

The sage was silent for several minutes. Then he said: "Within less than a year, you will be given an unexpected opportunity to travel to a far distant land, north-west of India. This will mark the beginning of a new career. It will be entirely at variance with that of your father." Within six months I left for England. - "You will reside in foreign lands for many years. And you will become celebraated for your work. You will derive a comfortable living from your labours. never, however, be truly a man of wealth. You will achieve considerable success in some kind of humanitarian work, in work of a medical nature among other things. You will incline increasingly toward an interest of philosophy and matters occult. You will ever be striving anxiously and earnestly—independently to boot—to achieve something worthwhile. Assistance will be offered you more largely by foreigners—than your own people. You will have plenty of secret enemies. No one, though, will be able to do you any harm. You will devote the best part of your life to the fulfilment of some important task or mission. After a hard struggle you will succeed. You will owe your success to financial and moral support rendered you by foreigners unexpectedly. You will neither gamble nor speculate nor become addicted to any vice. You will live an exemplary life. After reaching a ripe age you will be survived by grown-up sons and daughters and grandsons and grand-daughters.

"Scorpio in relation to Saturn occupies a peculiar position in your horoscope. On this account, you will never sanction religious orthodoxy, so called. Rather, you will become a religious and social reformer of note. When you will have passed your sixty-fifth birthday, you will devote the great part of your time to the study of philosophy and the occult sciences. To facilitate your studies you will retire from all commercial activity. In fact, you will virtually renounce all worldly interest. According to the planetary aspects of your horoscope and lines of your palms, you are destined at this time to illuminate the weary ways of the world with a new, important concept, a concept which will either take the form of a philosophical or spiritual truth or be translated into a measure of reform. Your accomplisment will be accorded wide renown.

Your memory will persist in the minds of the world at large for many years after your death".

A large part of the foregoing has already been substantiated, especially the last. Within the past few years, I have not only proposed a concrete "measure of reform " (viz., the World Globe Temple) but I have also devoted considerable time to the study of philosophy and religion with a view to write a "Philosophy of Reason". I intend to retire from all temporal affairs within two or three years.

My enlightment encompassed a period of more than three hours.

My mother verified the hour of my birth for me on return to the hotel, in as much as I was not myself fully aware of it and I found my Lucknow friend's rough horoscope, when I was once more back in Bombay, totally almost line for line with that cast at the time of my birth. The only exception I could note was that of the position assigned to the Moon; the Lucknow astrologer identified a particular phase as existing with Aquarius in the ascendancy whereas the man my father had engaged showed it in relation to Pisces. Then, of course, there was six minutes difference in the time of birth.

From that time to this very day I have been a staunch believer in Astrology and Palmistry. I have constantly in the interest of science, attempted to sift the truth from the falsities.

My horoscope..... with the first announcements in the Indian press of the Chicago world fair of 1893, I became conscious of a burning desire to make a trip to the United States. Since I had no way of knowing whether or not I would be afforded the opportunity for such a journey - as a matter of fact, my circumstances at the time seemed to indicate anything but the likelihood of my leaving India in the near future - I consulted a prominent Bombay astrologer. As I have already pointed out, I had not the slightest faith in Astrology at the time; it was only out of curiosity. The good man at once pronounced the the Aries Ascendant horoscope the more reliable. He proceeded to predict, on the strength, of it, that I would never leave India.

On the other hand, the Lucknow sage, as I have already indicated, cast my horoscope with Pisces in the Ascendant and, on the strength of Saturn's position during Scorpio's ascendancy, he prophesied my spending the greater part of my life achieving success abroad.

Needless to say, the fulfilment of the Lucknow prognostication has resulted in Hindu astrologers with one accord discarding the horoscope with Aries in the Ascendant and accepting that dominated by Pisces.

The following are positions of the planets as determined by Hindu astrologers:

There is the conjunction of Venus and Mercury, during the ascendancy of Pisces, which is considered highly beneficial. As a result of it, I have acquired international repute as India's pioneer and inventor. In addition, I have secured myself a significant position in social and scientific circles generally. The publicity accorded me by the press, I might state, has at no time in recent years been inconsiderable.

Pisces appears in my horoscope incidentally, in the first house.

The Sun's position in the second house, with Aries in the ascendent, is indeed an exalted one. In accordance with it I have at all times beer able to earn a comfortable living. I have had lit tle trouble securing adequate financial backin for my inventions. Unlike so many accidental in ventors, I have never had the experience of bein given anything other than an executive post or the board of directors of the company organised for my contrivance's exploitation. I have been either president, vice-president, or some other officer, with a proportionate share in the company's earnings. However, it has not been destined that I mass wealth or make any appreciable savings. The Sun's position is scarcely favorable as can readily been; the Sun in the house of wealth is considered favourable to spiritual rather than temporal well-being.

Mars appears in the fifth house with Cancer in the ascendancy, which is by no means too favourable. On account of it, I was forced to end my formal education with graduation from high school. Owing, however, to the opportunities for observation and enlightening contact afforded in the occident, I have been able, I believe, considerably to increase my store of knowledge. I have been granted honorary academic degrees and membership in sundry engineering and learned societies.

Rahu, the earth's node, apears in the sixth house, with Leo in the ascendancy. This is a decidedly good omen. According to Hindu Astrology, Rahu in the 6th house raises a man of the most humble origin to the position of a powerful potentate and enables him to crush his enemies with ease.

I, for one, did not reach such an exalted position as that of king or dictator. However, it is true that I was born in India, a land scientifically centuries behind the times, and that despite the almost insurmountable obstacles arising out of this contingency I have "beat" a number of European scientists and inventors "at their own game". It is also a fact that I have had any number of enemies, the greater portion of whom have been characterised by duplicity. Yet, with the help of the Almighty, I have consistently prevailed against them.

I am told by Hindu astrologers that H.H. Sayaji Rao, Gaekwar of Baroda has a horoscope which, too, shows Rahu in the sixth house. On this account it is believed he ascended to the throne. Needless to say, he was aided by other powerful planetary aspects as well.

Saturn is shown in the ninth house with Scorpio in the ascendancy. Saturn is a slow-moving planet. Its chief function is to increase the beneficence of the influences peculiar to the house in which it finds itself and in my case these influences pertain to travel and to religion.

As regards travel, I have made several long voyages from India to England and return, and from England to the United States. All in all, I have spent more than thirty three years of my life, the greater part by far, in travel and residence abroad. In the house directly opposite, the third, Saturn is in exceedingly bad aspect, to which fact I have absolutely no assistance from brothers, sisters or relatives.

With regard to religion, I have throughout waged relentless war against orthodoxy, so-called and deceitful dogma. I have devoted not a little time to matters philosophical and had endeavoured with more or less zeal to effect social and religious reforms. It is interesting to note in this connection that the *sadesati* of Saturn in my case begins somewhere in 1933, the year in which I am contemplating the inception of a drastic change in my way of life.

When I was about five years of age, we removed to Bombay, to a house which my father had had built next door to a family of Christian persuasion. A very real friendship sprung up between our neighbours and ourselves and I used very often to have tea with them, often afternoon. My further contact with a faith other than Hindu was obtained at Christian Missionary School at which my education commenced.

In the course of my residence abroad, my contacts have been almost exclusively with Christians and Jews and it is by them that I have been helped most considerably in my work.

The conjunction of Jupiter and the Moon and Ketu (the Moon's node in relation to the earth) with Aquarius in the ascendancy, in the twelfth house of my horoscope represent the expenditure of money. Due to Jupiter's favourable aspect in this case, my money was rarely spent for any reason other than one of necessity, that is; for up-keep of the home, for worth-while causes, etc.

Since the Moon is the ruler of the mind, and, in this case is found in, Aquarius, I have constantly been engaged in intellectual pursuits, in the solving of scientific problems and the study of philosophical and occult subjects. Astrologers term me an "Aquarian" as a matter of fact.

The effect of the Moon, however, is complicated by the phenomenon of Ketu, the eclipse aspect as I have already stated. By virtue of this land, I have often been in "hot water" (the occidental astrologer does not take such concurrences into account and cannot, therefore, help but be in error).

In 1896 I first acquired a full knowledge of Ketu's significance in my horoscope. It was from the lips of no less renowned a Hindu Gujarathi (astrologer) than the aged Nursi Joshi, of Bombay. He warned me that my inventions and ideals were bound at all times not only to meet with misunderstanding and distrust but with jealousy and envy - to breed for me enemies of a cowardly nature who, not having the courage confront me with their indictments in public, would resort to a whispering campaign against me. He assured me at the same time that I was certain to emerge from all this triumphant. He even went so far as to say that every obstacle in my path would serve only to assist me on my way.

Since the Moon's eclipse is caused by the shadow of the earth itself, enemies would be found among my fellow countrymen. It would be only on exceedingly rare occasions that help would be forthcoming from India.

Nursi Joshi concluded by telling me that the instance of Ketu in the twelfth division is exceedingly rare, and that the only other such case of which he was aware was that of H.H. the Gaekwad of Baroda.

Thus it came about that I have on numerous occasions suffered set-backs through misunderstanding only to secure an even more advantageous position within a short while. My ideals, motives, and activities have not only been misjudged by outsiders but also by my family circle, who certainly should have known better. I have been blamed with distressing frequency for fancied wrongs which time invariably proved the result of none of my doings.

Due to its somewhat unusual aspects, my horoscope has been carefully studied by astrologers on three continents. Several years ago, it was published in a number of astrological journals.

Among those to whom I am especially indebted for convincing proof of Astrology's validity are:

The Sage of Lucknow; Narsi Joshi, Hareshwar Mahadev Joshi Jivanram Chithnavis (all three of Bombay), Alan Leo and Robert King of London; Swami Rajah of Atlantic City; Belle Bart and Theodore Nyland of New York.

— *Reproduced from* THE ASTROLOGICAL MAGAZINE *(October 1948 and November 1948.)*

In America there is the best scope for the caste (real *jaati*) to develop, and so the people are great. Every Hindu knows tht astrologers try to fix the caste of every boy or girl as soon as she is born. That is the real caste—the individuality, and Jyotisha (Astrology) recognises that, and we can only rise by giving it full sway again.

— *Swami Vivekananda (Complete Works Vol. IV page 372-373)*

CHAPTER TWELVE

SRI AUROBINDO ON ASTROLOGY

edited by K. Channabasappa

ASTROLOGY is in the general mind associated with that class of subjects which goes under the name of the occult,and along with others of its class it has long been discredited by modern "enlightenment", one does not quite know on what gtounds or with what rational justification. It has its psychic and mystical side, but that is not its ordinary presentation; there it claims to be a science like any other with fixed processes and an exact and definite system of rules which ought to be perfectly capable of verification or of disproof by experiment and induction like any othere science. Its basis is astronomical and mathematical, its data perfectly open and positive and in no way hidden or occult,nor does it at all shrink back from the test or hide itself in secrecy and mystery. It does not indeed give ordinarily the why, but only the how of the causes and effects it professes to establish, but so it is with all other sciences; they do not give the reason for things, but only their processes.

Yet Astrology is supposed at some indefinite time in the march of human mind to have been exploded along with such things as witchcraft and demonology, not to speak of the existence of spirits and the immorality of the soul — and there is a sort of idea that it has been disproved and therefore put aside as a superstition which no reasonable man can even look at except with a lofty disdain, much less stoop to investigate with an open mind its truth or falsity.

Still the anathema of science has not been able to destroy it. In Europe it has revived, and in India it has always survived. It is not indeed the habit of educated Indians to profess explicitly their belief in it; they fight shy of that as a rule, but it is largely consulted by numbers of them, as also by many Europeans. This is an anomalous position which ought to be corrected. Either Astrology is a true science and should be investigated, proved, improved where defective and generally rehabilitated in opinion, or else it is a pseudo-sience and should be investigated and disproved so as to cut the ground away finally from all secret belief or open credulity.

As a matter of fact Astrology has never been scientifically disproved, nor has any rational ground ever been advanced for treating it as a pseudo-science. It simply came to be assumed at a certain period and under certain intellectual influences that it was a childish superstition. Or if there were any grounds,then it was left aside because astrologers were charlatans, because many, perhaps most predictions went wrong, but most of all because it was thought that in the nature of things, in any rational theory of the universe the planets simply could not have any influence on our characters, lives and actions. None of those grounds are sufficient. If many astrologers are charlatans, so also have there been many quacks in the field of medicine; at one time indeed not only did they pullulate; but the system of medicine itself seemed so defective that there were plenty of clear and enlightened minds who were inclined with Moliere to denounce the whole thing as a gross pseudo-science, an elaborate and solemn system of ignorance, humbug and quackery. Supposing that view had prevailed it could not, merely because men are too vitally interested in healing their ailments and preserving their bodies and know no other way of doing it, that would not have done away with the truth underlying the science.

That many predictions go wrong, proves nothing essentially, against Astrology any more than the constant failure of doctors to heal diseases proves anything essential against their science. The first reason of this failure may be that a number of practising astrologers are either charlatans who speak to please their clients rather than predict by scientific rule—of that kind there are perhaps many—or else ineffieient and ignorant men who practise only by rule of thumb, perfunctorily and with a main eye upon their fees. But if even capable astrologers fail often, that also only proves that either the science or their way or treating it is largely empirical or that some of its rules and theories may be errors. But every science has to pass through its empirical stage and some—as again, the science of medicine have hardly emerged from it, and every science too burdens itself in its progress with false generalisations, incorrect theories and imperfect rules which have afterwards to be discarded or amended. As the main point in medicine is whether herbs and metals and other remedies have or have not certain effects on the body and whether their working can be substantiated by experience in a suffieient number of cases to establish a regular relation of cause and effect so it is in Astrology with the fundamental question of planetary influences upon earth and its creatures.

The *apriori* argument from the rational theory of the universe cannot stand. There is nothing essentially irrational in the idea that in this solar system, so closely linked together, there may be mutual influences of all the planets upon each other or that the beings of a particular planet are powerfully influenced or even dominated by influences from the others. The question remains, the *apriori* rationality being admitted or at least not summarily dismissed, first, whether it is so in fact and secondly, how far those influences go and of what nature they are. Astrology affirms that they not only effect our bodies, but also our psychical being. If matter and mind were entirely independent entities having no influence or determining effect upon each other, then such a result could not be: but that is not the case. According to the materialistic view of the universe which claims to be the sole rationalistic view, mind is itself an effect of matter and all its states and movements are determind by matter. There is nothing then impossible, planetary influence being once admitted, in the action of material bodies producing psychical conditions on the earth and thereby determining our psychical states and movements. In a more truly rationalistic view mind and matter are always influencing and determining each other; here too, given a universal mind and matter so acting upon individual matter and mind, the movements of the planetary system may be one or even the first nodus of their activities, and the assertions of Astrology become at least primarily credible.

Further, Astrology affirms that these influences determine the whole course of our lives and that the all-important element is time. That raises the major question of the influence of Time upon human beings and events; does Time determine the course of our lives and the states of our being and if so, how far and in what way? Or to put the question more precisely, as it is raised by Astrology, do or can the conditions reigning at given critical time, in this case the moment of birth, determine our physical and psychological conditions and the whole course of our future lives, or determine them to any considerable extent? And are the relative movements and therefore the mutual positions of the Sun and planets with regard to the earth and each other either the nodus or in some way the effective signs of these determinations? And, secondly, do the developing time conditions which come afterwards, by themselves or viewed in reference to the original conditions determine from moment to moment, from time to time the subsequent evolution of our primary physical and psychological conditions and the course of linked and successive circumstances which make up the history of our lives, and if so, again, are the relative movements and mutual positions of the Sun and planets at any given time the nodus or the effective signs of this late determination also? Can they therefore be taken for all practical purposes as determinants, or at any rate as sure signs by which the determinations of our life and being can be discovered? That is the question which Astrology raises, and it is evidently a perfectly legitimate and rational question: nor can we on *a priori* grounds condemn and put away an affirmative answer, which is based upon past expirence systematised into rules and theories, as a superstition or a childish folly. Granted that in things here there is a chain of cause and effect or at least, if causality is disputed, of antecedent condition leading upto subsequent condition— and that if and so far as we know that chain, scientific prediction becomes in that proportion pos-

Ancient Prophecies

There have been many occasions in the past 2,000 years when astrological predictions have come true. Hippocrates predicted a plague at Athens, and a plague swept the city. Alexander the Great was warned by astrologers to flee from the walls of Babylon where his evil star prevailed, but like Hitler he took their advice only when it suited him, entered the city, and met his end.

Courtesy: *Seeing into the Future* by Harvey Day

sible— two propositions which, unless we deny determination altogether, it would be difficult to dispute— there is no inherent improbability in the clue to happenings, human and other, on the planets being found in the motions of those planets. Astronomy is in a sense the primary physical science, for the first facts which give all the others their field are astronomical facts; it may well be that in the psycho- physical field the same rule holds and that there the first facts may be astrological.

The *a priori* objections disappearing, the next step is to ask ourselves whether there is a sufficient *prima facie* empricical case for inquiring into the actual truth of Astrology. This at present depends upon the experience of isolated individuals, a very unsatisfactory basis. But if this experience could be collected, sifted and published, I believe it would he found that a formidable prima facie case exists in favour of Astrology, much stronger than that which encouraged the Society for Psychical Reasearch to carry on its work in another psycho- physcial field to such important conclusions. I may state

Astrology Is Science

Mr. Morarji Desai observes thus about Astrology:

I firmly believe that the law of Karma governs the universe and therefore I believe in Astrology as a science. But I would not go so far as to claim that there are many practising astrologers who can make absolutely correct forecasts. Accurate predictions are indeed possible....

my own experience in the matter in the belief, justified by many instances, that it is only typical of the experience of hundreds of others. My first accidental contact with an Indian astrologer was not encouraging. This gentlemen was the most accomplished thought-reader I have ever seen: for he asked me to think my question without speaking it and not only successfully named the unspoken question I had fixed on, but three others which had crossed my mind, one of them only in the merest flash and without leaving any impression behind; this he pretended to do by mathematical calculation, an operation which I took leave to regard as humbug or professional parade. For when it came to his answers, I found that he was still doing thought-reading and not Astrology: he simply echoed the hopes or thougts in my mind and his predictions did not come within one hundred miles of the truth. Other practioners I have found to belong, a few plainly to the class of merely flattering charlatans but most to the ineffieient who read by rule of thumb and have made no profund study of their

> One's destiny is the sum total of the consequences of one's past actions or karmas. If we believe in the dynamic law of karma, we must admit that one's destiny is unalterable, unavoidable. Modern physical science, too, tells us that action and reaction are equal and opposite, that nothing in this world is lost, but only undergoes a change of form or value. It stands to reason thus that one's destiny is capable of being charted in advance by a good astrologer.
>
> *Coutesy: Times of India (11-4-65)*

science. **On the othere hand, with capable astrologers the results have been often of such a remarkable accuracy as to put quite aside any possibility of chance hit, mere coincidence, intelligent prevision or any of the current explanations**. I may instance the father of a friend of mine, a deep student of the science but not a professional, who predicted accurately the exact year, month, hour and even minute of his own death. In my own case accuracy was hampered by the inability to fix the precise moment of my birth; still some of the results were extraordinary. Two may be mentioned, from one and the same astrologer, which related to my public career. One, given when I had not yet plunged into the political vortex and my then obscure personality was quite unknown to the astrologer, predicted as an inevitable certitude of the future a political struggle with powerful non-Indian adversaries during which for a time even my life would fall under the shadow of danger. The other, given at the time of my first prosecution in the Bande Mataram case, predicted three

India And Western Science

"If we are to live at all, we must resume India's great, interrupted endeavour. We must take up boldly and execute thoroughly, in the individual and in the society, in the spiritual and in the mundane life, in philosophy and religion, in art and literature, in thought, in political and economic and social formulation, the full and unlimited sense of her highest spirit and knowledge. And if we do that, we shall find that the best of what comes to usdraped

successive criminal trials in each of which the prosecution would fail. I may instance also two predictions by the book in which *slokas* from Sanskrit astrological writings indicating the results of certain conjunctions or planetary positions were shown to be aplicable to my horoscope. One foretold specific chronic illnesses for the body of which there was no sign at the time, but long afterwards they put in their unexpected appearance and persisted. Another indicated very very precisely that one of my future activities would be to found a new spiritual philosophy and its discipline; at that time I had no knowledge of philosophy or Yoga and no turn or inclination in my mind which could make the realisation of this prediction at all probable. These are only the most precise examples out of a number. Supposing all well-authenticated evidence of the kind were to be collected, I am convinced there would be an overwhelmingly strong *prima facie* case and even a body of sufficently strong empirical proof to establish at least a nucleus of truth in Astrology.

in Occidental forms, is already implied in our own ancient wisdom and has there a greater spirit behind it, a profounder truth and self-knowledge and the capacity of a will to nobler and more ideal formations. Only we need to work out thoroughly in life what we have always known in spirit. There andnowhere else lies the secret of the needed harmony between the essential meaning of our past culture and the environmental of our future." (Yuva Bharati, Madras, Dec 1979.p33).

— *SRI AUROBINDO*

That would be the first step. For if Astrology is a science and is to take its proper place, the first necessity is to dissipate by an appeal to the empirical mind of the general public as well as of the sceptical thinker the great mass of unenquiring prejudice which now exists against it.

— *Reproduced from* **THE ASTROLOGICA MAGAZINE**
February 1975.

CHAPTER THIRTEEN

OUTWITTING THE STARS

"Mukunda, why don't you get an astrological armlet?" "Should I, Master? I don't believe in Astrology." "It is not a question of belief; the scientific attitude one should take on any subject is whether it is true. The law of gravitation worked as efficiently before Newton as after him. The cosmos would be fairly chaotic if its laws could not operate without the sanction of human belief.

"Charlatans have brought the ancient steller science to its present disrepute. Astrology is too vast, both mathematically[1] and philosophically, to

1 From astronomical references in ancient Hindu literature, scholars have been able to ascertain the dates of the authors. The scientific knowledge of the rishis was very great; in the *Kaushitaki Brahmana* we find precise astronomical passages indicating that in 3100 B.C. the Hindus were far advanced in astronomy, which had a practical value to determining the auspicious times for astrological ceremonies. An article in *East-West*, February, 1934, says the *Jyotish* or body of Vedic astronomical treatises: "It contains the scientific lore that kept India at the forefront of all ancient nations and made her the Mecca of seekers after knowledge. *Brahmagupta*, one of the *Jyotish* works, is an astronomical treatise dealing with such matters as the heliocentric motion of the planetary bodies in our solar system, the obliquity of the ecliptic, the earth's spherical form, the reflected light of the Moon, the earth's daily axial revolution, the presence of fixed stars in the Milky Way, the law of gravitation, and other scientific facts that did not dawn in the Western world until the time of Copernicus and Newton".

be rightly grasped except by men of profound understanding. If ignoramuses misread the heavens, and see there a scrawl instead of a script, that is to be expected in this imperfect world. One should not dismiss the wisdom with the 'wise'.

"All parts of creation are linked together and interchange their influences. The balanced rhythm of the universe is rooted in reciprocity," my guru continued. "Man, in his human aspect, has to combat two sets of forces - first, the tumults within his being, caused by the admixture of earth, water, fire, air, and ethereal elements; Second, the outer disintegrating powers of nature. So long as man struggles with his mortality, he is affected by the myriad mutations of heaven and earth.

"Astrology is the study of man's response to planetary stimuli. The stars have no conscious benevolence or animosity; they merely send forth positive and negative radiations. Of themselves, these do not help or harm humanity, but offer a lawful channel for the outward operation of cause-effect equilibrium that each man has set into motion in the past.

The so-called "Arabic numerals," invaluable in the development of Western mathematics, came to Europe in the ninth century, via the Arabs, from India, where that system of notation had been anciently formulated. Further light on India's vast scientific heritage will be found in Sir P.C. Roy's *History of Hindu Chemistry*,in B.N. Seal's *Positive Sciences of the Ancient Hindus*, in B.K. Sarkar's *Hindu Achievements in Exact Sciences* and his *The Positive Background of Hindu Sociology*, and U.G. Dutt's *Materia Medica of the Hindus*.

"A child is born on that day and at that hour when the celestial rays are in mathematical harmony with his individual karma. His horoscope is a challenging portrait, revealing his unalterable past and its probable future results. But the natal chart can be righly interpreted only by men of intuitive wisdom; these are few.

"The message boldly blazoned across the heavens at the moment of birth is not meant to emphasize fate - the result of past good and evil but to arouse man's will to escape for his universal thraldom. What he has done, he can undo. None other than himself was the instigator of the causes of whatever effects are now prevalent in his life. He can overcome any limitation, because he created it by his own actions in the first place, and because he possesses spiritual resources that are not subject to planetary pressure.

"Superstitious awe of Astrology makes one an automaton, slavishly dependent on mechanical guidance. The wise man defeats his planets which is to say, his past - by transferring his allegiance from the creation to the Creator. The more he realizes his unity with Spirit, the less he can be dominated by matter. The soul is ever free; it is deathless because birthless. It cannot be regimented by stars.

"Man is a soul, and has a body. When he properly places his sense of identity, he leaves behind all compulsive patterns. So long as he remains confused in his ordinary state of spiritual amnesia, he will know the subtle fetters of environmental law.

"God is Harmony; the devotee who attunes himself will never perform any action amiss. His activities will be correctly and naturally timed to accord with astrological law. After deep prayer and meditation he is in touch with his divine conscousness; there is no greater power than that inward protection."

"Then, dear Master, why do you want me to wear an astrological bangle? I ventured this question after a long silence; I had tried to assimilate Sri Yukteswar's noble exposition, which contained thoughts very new to me.

"It is only when a traveller has reached his goal that he is justified in discarding his maps. During the journey, he takes advantage of any convenient short cut. The ancient rishis discovered many ways to curtail the period of man's exile in delusion. There are certain mechanical features in the law of karma that can be skilfully adjusted by the fingerts of wisdom.

"All human ills arise from some transgression of universal law. The scriptures point out that man must satisfy the laws of nature, while not discrediting the divine omnipotency. He should say: "Lord, I trust in Thee, and know Thou canst help me, but I too will do my best to undo any wrong I have done'. By a number of means — by prayer, by will power, by yoga meditation, by consultation with saints, by use of astrological bangles — the adverse effects of past wrongs can be minimized or nullified.

"Just as a house may be fitted with a coper rod to absord the shock of lightning, so the bodily temple can be protected in certain ways.

"Electrical and magnetic radiations are ceaselessly circulating in the universe; they affect man's body for good and ill. Ages ago our rishis pondered the problem of combating the adverse effects of subtle cosmic influences. The sages discovered that pure metals emit an astral light which is powerfully counteractive to negative pulls of the planets. Certain plant combinations were also found to be helpful. Most effective of all are faultless jewels of not less than two carats.

"The practical preventive uses of Astrology have seldom been seriously studied outside of India. One little-known fact is that the proper jewels, metals and plant preparations are valueless unless the required weight is secured and unless the remedial agent is worn next to the skin."

"Sir, of course I shall take your advice and get a bangle. I am intrigued at the thought of outwitting a planet!"

"For general purposes I counsel the use of an armlet made of gold, silver, and copper. But for a specific purpose I want you to get one of silver and lead." Sri Yukteswar added careful directions.

"Guruji, what 'specifc purpose' do you mean?"

"The stars are about to take an 'unfriendly' interest in you, Mukunda. Fear not; you shall be protected. In about a month your liver will cause you much trouble. The illness is scheduled to last for six months, but your use of an astrological armlet will shorten the period to twenty-four days".

I sought out a jeweller the next day, and was soon wearing the bangle. My health was excellent; Master's prediction slipped from my mind. He left Serampore to visit Benares. Thirty days after our conversation, I felt a sudden pain in the region of my liver. The following weeks were a nightmare of excruciating pain. Reluctant to disturb my guru, I thought I would bravely endure my trial alone.

But twenty-three days of tortue weakened my resolution; I entrained for Benares. There Sri Yukteswar greeted me with unusual warmth, but gave me no opportunity to tell him my woes in private. Many devotees visited Master that day, just for a a darshan[2]. Ill and neglected, I sat in a corner. It was not until after the evening meal that all guests had departed. My guru summoned me to the octagonal balcony of the house.

"You must have come about your liver disorder." Sri Yukteswar's gaze was averted; he walked to and fro, occasionally intercepting the moonlight. "Let me see, you have been ailing for twentfour days, haven't you?"

"Yes, sir."

---

[2] The blessing that flows from the mere sight of a saint.

"Please do the stomach exercise I taught you."

"If you knew the extent of my suffering, Master, you would not ask me to exercise." Nevertheless I made a feeble attempt to obey him.

"You say you have pain; I say you have none. How can such contradictions exist?" My guru looked at me inquiringly.

I was dazed and then overcome with joyful relief. No longer could I feel the continuous torment that had kept me nearly sleepless for weeks; at Sri Yukteswar's words the agony vanished as though it had never been.

I started to kneel at his feet in gratitude, but he quickly prevented me.

"Don't be childish. Get up and enjoy the beauty of the moon over the Ganges." But Master's eyes were twinkling happily as I stood in silence beside him. I understood by his attitude that he wanted me to feel that not he, but God, had been the Healer.

I wear even now the heavy silver and lead bangle, a memento of that day — long-past, ever-cherished — when I found anew that I was living with a personage indeed superhuman. On later occasions, when I brought my friends to Sri Yukteswar for healing, he invariably recommended jewels or the bangle, extolling their use as an act of astrological wisdom.

I had been prejudiced against Astrology from my childhood, partly because I observed that many people are sequaciously attached to it, and partly because of a prediction made by our family astrologer: "You will marry three time, being twice a widower." I brooded over the matter, feeling like a goat awaiting sacrifice before the temple of matrimony.

"You may as well be resigned to your fate", my brother Ananta had remarked. "Your written horoscope had correctly stated that you would fly from home toward the Himalayas during your early years, but woud be forcibly returned. The forecast of your marriage is also bound to be true."

A clear intuition came to me one night that the prophecy was wholly false. I set fire to the horoscope scroll placing the ashes in a paper bag on which I wrote: "Seeds of past karma cannot germinate if they are roasted in the fire of divine wisdom." I put the bag in a conspicuous spot; Ananta immediately read my defiant comment.

"You cannot destroy truth as easily as you have burnt this paper scroll." My brother laughed scornfully.

It is a fact that on three occasions before I reached manhood, my family tried to arrange my betrothal. Each time I refused to fall in with the plans,[3] knowing that my love for God was more overwhelming than any astrological persuasion from the past.

---

3 One of the girls whom my family selected as a possible bride for me afterward married my cousin, Prabhas Chandra Ghosh. He is an officer of the Yogoda Satsanga Society (affiliated with SRF) in India.

"The deeper the Self-realization of a man, the more he influences the whole universe by his subtle spiritual vibration, and the less he himself is affected by the phenomenal flux." These words of Master's often returned inspiringly to my mind.

Occasionally I told astrologers to select my worst periods, according to planetary indications, and I would still accomplish whatever task I set myself. It is true that my success at such times has been preceeded by extraordinary difficulties. But my conviction has always been justified; faith in divine protection, and right use of man's God-given will, are forces more formidable than are influences flowing from the heavens.

The starry inscription at one's birth, I came to understand, is not that man is a puppet of his past. Its message is rather a prod to pride; the very heavens seek to arouse man's determination to be free from every limitation. God created each man as a soul, powered with individuality, hence essential to the universal structure, whether in the temporary role of pillar or parasite. His freedom is final and immediate, if he so wills; it depends not on outer but inner victories.

Sri Yukteswar discovered the mathermatical application of a 24,000-year equinoctial cycle to our present age[4]. The cycle is divided into an Ascending Arc and a Descending Arc, each of

---

4 Tese equinoctial cycles are expounded in Swami Yukteswar's book, *The Holy Science* (Yogoda Satsanga Society, O. Ariadah, Dakshineswar, West Bengal, India).

12,000 years. Within each Arc fall four Yugas or Ages, called Kali, Dwapara, Treta, and Satya, corresponding to the Greek ideas of Iron, Bronze, Silver, and Golden Ages.

My guru determined by various calculations that the last Kali Yuga or Iron Age, of the Ascending Arc, started about A.D. 500. The Iron age, 1200 years in duration, is a span of materialism; it ended about A.D. 1700. That year ushered in Dwapara Yuga, a 2,400-year period of electrical and atomic-energy development, the age of telegraph, radio, airplanes, and other space-annihilators.

The 3,600-year period of Treta Yuga will start in A.D. 4,100; its age will be marked by common knowledge of telepathic communications and other time-annihilators. During the 4,800 years of Satya Yuga, final age in an Ascending Arc, the intelligence of man will be highly developed; he will work in hormony with the divince plan.

A Descending Arc of 12,000 year, starting with a Descending Golden Age of 4,800 years, then begins for the world (in A.D. 12,000); man gradually sinks into ignorance. These cycles are the eternal rounds of maya, the contrasts and relativities of the phenomenal Universe[5]. Men, one by one, escape from creation's prison of

5 The Hindu scriptures place the present world-age as occuring within the Kali Yuga of a much longer universal cycle than the simple 24,00 year equinoctal cycle with which Sri Yukteswar was concerned. The Universal cycle of the scriptures is 4,300,560,000 years in extent, and measures out a

duality as they awaken to consciousness of their inseverable divine unity with the Creator.

Master enlarged my understanding not only of Astrology but of the world's scriptures. Placing the holy texts on the spotless table of his mind, he was able to disect them with the scalpel of intuitive reasoning, and to separate errors and interpretations of the scholars from the truths as originally expressed by the prophets.

(Reproduced from *Autobiography of a Yogi* Paramahama Yogananda.)

Day of Creation or the length of life assigned to our planetary system in its present form. This vast figure given by the rishis is based on a relationship between the length of the solar year and a multiple of Pi (3.1416, the ratio of the circumference to the diameter of a circle).

The life span for a whole universe, according to the ancient sears, is 314,159,000,000,000 solar year, or " One Age of Brahma".

The Hindu scriputes declare that an earth such as ours is dissolved for one of two reasons; the inhabitants as a whole become either completely good or completely evil. The world mind thus generates a power that releases the captive atoms held together as an earth.

Dire pronouncements are occasionally published regarding an imminent "end of the world". Planetary cycles, however, proceed according to an orderly divine plan. No earthly dissolution is in sight; many ascending not descending equinoctial cycles are yet in store for our planet in its present form..

CHAPTER FOURTEEN

WRITTEN IN THE STARS

The cupolas quiver with light in the dazzling sunshine, the bathers fill the air with the sounds of their matutinal ablution, and the jumbled, Oriental pageant of the water-front and Benares shows itself anew to my alien gaze. I idle down the Ganges in a heavy junk, whose prow is carved like a cobra's head. I am on the roof of a cabin, while the three rowers who are below pull their quaint oars.

A merchant from Bombay is my companion and, as he sits next to me, he tells me that he intends to retire from trade when he returns to that city. He is an extremely pious but equally practical man. While laying up treasure in heaven, he has not omitted to lay up treasure in the bank. I have known him for about a week and find him an amiable, genial and friendly person.

"I am retiring at the very age which Sudhei Babu predicted it would happen" he says, eager to explain.

This odd remark causes me, metaphorically, to prick up my ears.

"Sudhei Babu - who is he?"

"Do you not know? He is the cleverest astrologer in Benares."

"Oh, just an astrologer!" I grunt back a little scornfully.

For I have seen the breed squatting in the dust of Bombay's great open space, the Maidan; sitting in sultry booths at Calcutta; and foregathering wherever travellers pass through every little town I have visited. Most of them are dirty-looking creatures, with wild locks of unkempt hair. The recognizable print of supersitition and ignorance rests upon their faces. Their stock-in-trade usually consists of two or three greasy, well-fingered books and some vernacular almanac filled with incomprehensible signs. I have often cynically thought of their eagerness to direct the fortunes of other persons, when they themselves seemed outside the pale of good fortune.

"I am somewhat surprised at you. Is it safe for a business man to trust himself to the twinkling of the stars. Don't you think common sense is a better guide?" I add, in the tone of one giving good advice.

The other man half-shakes his head and smiles tolerantly at me.

"How, then, do you explain the prediction of my retirement? Who could have guessed that I would give up trade at such an exceptionally early age, for as you know I am only a year past forty?"

"Coincidence, perhaps."

"Very well; let me tell you a little story. Some years ago I met a great astrologer in Lahore and started a large business negotiation on his advice. At that time I was in partnership with an older man. My partner asserted that the affair was far too risky and he refused to agree with me. Because he would not enter into the transaction we dissolved partnership. I carried the business through alone. It was a startling success and brought me a small fortune. Yet unless the Lahore astrologer had strongly supported me, I, too, would have feared to enter the affair."

"Then you hold the opionion that......"

"Our lives are ruled by destiny and that destiny is shown by the positions of the stars!"

I slip my objections to his statement upon the thread of an impatient gesture.

"The astrologers I have seen in India are such an illiterate, stupid-looking lot, that I cannot imagine what beneficial advice they can give anyone."

"Ah, you must not confuse a learned scholar like Sudhei Babu with those ignorant men you have encountered. Truly, those men are charlatans but he is a highly intelligent Brahmin who lives in a large house of his own. He has made a deep study of the subject for many years and possesses many volumes of great rarity."

It suddenly occurs to me that my companion is no fool. He belongs to that type of modern Hindu who is enthusiastically practical and who does not hesitate to avail himself of the latest resources of Western invention. He is even ahead of me in some ways. He carries a magnificent moving-picture camera on the boat, whereas I can boast of nothing better than a humble pocket kodak; his servant produces a thermos flask and pours out a cooling drink, thus rebuking my lamentable forgetfulness of an excellent travelling requisite; and I know from his talk that he makes more use of the telephone when in Bombay than I have ever cared to do when in Europe. And yet he believes in astrology! I puzzle over the incongruous elements which compose his character.

"Let us understand each other. You fully accept the theory that every man's career and every worldly event is controlled by stars whose distance from our planet is so great that it beggars imagination?"

"Yes, I do," he answers quietly.

I shrug my shoulders, not knowing what to say.

He assumes an apologetic air.

"My dear sir, why not go and try him for yourself? You say in your country, 'The proof of the pudding is in the eating'. Find out what Sudhei Babu can discover about you. I have no use for the cheap charlatans myself, but I believe in that man's genuineness."

"H'm. I am sceptical about those who make a business of foretelleing. Still, I shall take you at your word. Will you take me to this astrologer?"

"Certainly, Come and have tiffin with me tomorrow and then we shall visit him."

We continue to float by broad palaces and old temples and little shrines bespattered with yellow flowers. I look indifferently at the broad stone steps crowded with bathing pilgrims and reflect that, though science rightly flatters itself with having put a check to superstition, I have yet to learn that a scientific attitude should put a check to investigation. If my companion can produce some evidential facts for the marked feeling of fatalism which he shares in common with most of his countrymen, I shall study them with an open mind.

The next day my amiable acquaintance brings me to a narrow, archaic street which runs through a heap of flat-topped houses. We stop before a rambling, old, stone-built stucture. He leads the way through a dark, low-roofed passage and then we climb several stone steps, which are no wider than a man's body. We pass through a narrow room and find ourselves on the veranda of a spacious inner courtyard, around which the house has been built.

A chained dog sights us and furiously barks a challenge.

An array of large pots, each holding some tropical flowerless plant, spreads along the veranda. I follow my companion into a dark, frowning room and nearly fall over some broken flag-stones at the threshold. As I stoop, I notice that loose earth lies sprinkled in the room as freely as it is sprinkled on the veranda floor. Does the astrologer find relief from his starry studies in plant-growing, I wonder.

The other man shouts for the astrologer, whose name is echoed back to us by the ancient walls. We wait for two or three minutes and assist the dog, by further calls for the astrologer, to punctuate the silence of this seemingly deserted building. I begin to think that we have come on a fruitless errand, when the sound of someone stirring descends from an upper floor. Soon after I hear shuffling steps approach our room.

The figure of a slight man, carrying a candle in one hand and jangling a bunch of keys in the other, appears on the threshold. There follows a brief conversation in the semi-gloom and the astrologer unlocks another door, through which we all pass. He draws aside two heavy curtains and opens the shutters which cover tall balcony windows.

The astrologer's face is suddenly illuminated by the light which falls through the opened windows. I see a man who seems more like a figure from the ghost world than one of flesh and blood. Never before have I seen anyone so" sicklied o'er with the pale cast of thought". His death-like coutenance, incredibly lean body and unearthly slow movments combine to produce a weird effect. The whites of his eyes are so pronounced as to heighten this impression, their whiteness offering a strong contrast to the jet-black pupils.

He takes his seat at a large table, whose surface is littered with papers. I discover that he speaks tolerably good English, yet it is only after some persuasion that I can induce him to carry on a direct conversation without the aid of a third party as interpreter.

"Please understand that I come as an enquirer, not as a believer," I begin.

He nods his thin head.

"Yes, I shall cast your horoscope and then you must tell me if you are satisfied."

"What is your fee?"

"I have no fixed charge. Some people of position pay me sixty rupees; others pay me twenty rupes. I leave the amount to you".

I proceed to make it clear to him that, before we bother about the future, I want to test his knowledge of the past. He agrees.

"For a while he busies himself with calculations over my birth date. After ten minutes he stoops to the floor behind his chair and searches among a disorderly pile of yellowed papers and palm-leaf manuscripts. Finally he draws out a little bundle of oblong, time-stained slips. He sketches a queer diagram on a sheet of paper and says:

"This is a chart of the heavens at the time you were born. And these Sanskrit texts explain the meaning of every part of the chart. Now, I shall tell you what the stars declare."

He scrutinizes the diagram with minute care, referes to one of the slips, and speaks again, in that low, emotionless voice which befits his personality so well.

"Your are a writer from the West? Am I correct?"

I nod in agreement.

He tells me thereafter about my youth and describes in quick succession a few happeings of the earlier years of my life. In all, he gives me seven important points about my past. Five of them are broadly correct, but the other two are utterly wrong. Thus I am able to check up on the value or worthlessness of his powers. The honesty of the man is transparent. I am already convinced that he is incapable of deliberate deception. A 75% success in an initial test in startling enough to show that Hindu Astrology calls for investigation, but it also indicates that the latter is no precise, infallible science.

Once again Sudhei Babu burrows among his scattered papers and then describes my character with a fair degree of accuracy. After that he pictures the mental capacities which have brought me to follow a profession congenial to them. Here again, when he lifts his intellectual head and asks, "Have I read correctly?" I cannot dispute his words.

He shuffles his papers, silently studies the diagram, and begins to speak of the future.

"The world will become your home. You shall travel far and wide, yet always you will carry a pen and do your writing work." And in this strain he discourses of what is yet to be. But I can run no investigating rule over his prophecies, so I am content to leave them where I find them - written in the stars![1]

1 One of his predictions, which I had instantaneously and sceptically dismissed as a ridiculous impossibility, has now received ample confirmation. But a second event has failed to mature at the date he gave for it. The others still wait for time's comment.

With his last words he again asks if I am satisfied. His fairly correct description of my past forty years on this amazing planet; his almost completely successful effort to show me my mental self these things silence the criticisms which I have come prepared to utter."

I want to ask myself, "Is this man merely drawing a bow at a venture? Is he doing nothing more than a bit of smart guess work?" But I must candidly confess that his prognostictions impress me. Yet time alone can tell whether there is any worth in them or not.

Is my western attitude toward the dark question of fate to tumble about me like a house of thin cards? What can I say about lthe matter? I move over to the window and stand there, staring out at the opposite house and jingling the silver rupees in my pocket. Finally I return to my seat and question the Astrologer.

"Why should it seem impossible to you that such distant stars can influence the lives of men?" he rejoins softly. Do not the tides respond to the distant moon in their ebb and flow? Does not the body of woman undergo a change every lunar month? Does not the absence of the Sun make men more liable to depressed moods?"

"Quite so. But that is a far cry from asserting the claims of astrology. Why should Jupiter or Mars care two annas whether I meet with shipwreck or not?"

He looks at me with an unruffled face.

"It is better that you regard the planet as being only symbols which stand in the sky; it is not they which really influence us, but our own past." He replies. "You will never understand the reasonable nature of astrology unless you accept the doctrine that man is born again and again , and that his fate follows him with every birth. If he escapes the results of his evil actions in one birth, they will punish him in his next; and if he does not retrieve a due reward for his good actions in one lifetime, he will surely retrieve it in the next. Without this doctrine of the continued return of man's soul to this earth until such time as it becomes perfect, the changing fortunes of different persons would seem the result of mere chance or blind luck. How can that be allowed by a just Deity? No — it is our belief that when a man dies, his character, desires, thoughts and will continue to exist until they enter a body of flesh once more and come among us in the form of a new-born baby. The good or evil actions committed in the former birth will be suitably rewarded or punished in the present or even future births. This is how we explain fate. When I said that you would be shipwrecked one day and in grave danger of drowning, that is the fit destiny which God, in His hidden justice, has portioned out to you because of something wrong which you did in a former birth. It is not the planets which force you into shipwreck, but the inescapable results of your former actions. The planets and their positions only act as a record of this destiny; why they should do so I cannot say. No man's brain could ever have invented astrology; it came to us from long ago, when it was revealed for man's benefit by the great seers and sages of ancients times."

As I listen to this plausible pronouncement, I hardly know what comment to make. He would bind one's soul and fortune to the stake of fate, but no healthy westerner will let himself be despoiled of the prized possession of free will. What inhabitant of the energetic Occident can wax enthusiastic over this belief that it is destiny, and not choice, which directs him to take his steps? I gaze in bewilderment at this lean dreamer, this sallow wanderer through remote signs of the zodiac. "Do you know", I tell him, "that in some parts of the South astrologers rank next to the priests, and that nothing of any magnitude can be done without previously consulting them? We Europeans would laugh at such a position, for we do not look kindly upon predictive methods. We like to think that we are free individuals and not the hapless victims of an inexorable destiny."

The astrologer shrugs his shoulders.

"In one of our old books, the *Hitopadesa*, it is declared: 'No one is capable of opposing the predestination of fate, which are written in the foreheads of men." He lets his words sink in. Then he continues:

"What can you do? We must bear with the the fruit of our actions." But I am dubious about this statement and express my feeling. The prophet of personal fortunes rises from his chair. I take the hint and prepare to leave him. He murmurs musingly:

"All is in the power of God. Nothing can escape Him- Who of us is really free? Whither can we go where God is not?"

At the door he adds hesitatingly:

"If you wish to come again we may talk further on these matters."

I thank him and accept the invitation.

"Verly well. I shall expect you tomorrow, after the Sun has gone down, about the hour of six."

Next day I return with the dusk to the astrologer's house. I have no intention of accepting all that he tells me, but neither have I formed any plans for rejection. I come to listen, possibly to learn, though the latter rests on how far his statements can be verified by experiment. And at this time I am ready enough to make experiments, but only if sufficiently strong reasons can be given for them. Yet Sudhei Babu's reading of my horoscope has stirred me to the perception that Hindu astrology is not superstitious nonsense, and that it may well warrant a deeper investigation. That thought represents the limit of my present attitude.

We sit facing each other at his large writing-table. A paraffin lamp throws a dim light upon the scene. Millions of other Indian homes are being lit to-night in the same way.

"I have fourteen rooms in this house," the astrologer tells me. "They are filled with ancient manuscripts, which are mostly written in Sanskrit. That explains why I need such a large house, although I live alone. Come and see my collection."

He removes the hanging lamp and leads the way into another room. Open boxes are ranged around the walls. I peer inside one of them and find it full of books and papers. Even the floor of the room is hidden under a multitude of paper, bundles of palm-leaf manuscripts and books whose covers are discoloured with age. I take a small bundle in my hand; each leaf is covered with incomprehensible, faded characters. We go from room to room and find the same scene everywhere. The astrologer's library appears to be in a state of hopeless disorder, but he assures me that he is familiar with the whereabouts of every book and paper. It seems to me that his house has gathered the wisdom of Hindustan. Surely much of the strange lores of India is contained in the almost undeciperable pages of these ancient rolls of manuscript and in these Sanskrit books! We return to our chairs and the other man informs me:

"Nearly all my money has been spent in buying those manuscripts and books. Many of them are very rare and cost me large sums. So it is that I am very poor to-day."

"What subjects do they deal with?"

"They deal with human life and divine mysteries, while many are concerned with astrology."

"Then you are also a philosopher!"

His thin mouth relaxes into a half-smile.

"A man who is not a good philosopher will make a poor astrologer."

" If you will pardon me for saying so, I hope you do not overstudy all these books. I was shocked at your pallor when I first met you."

"That is not surprising." he replies calmly. "I have not eaten for six days."

I express my conceren.

"It is not a question of money. The woman who comes every day to cook for me is away ill. She has been away for six days."

"Then why not call in another woman?"

He shakes his head firmly.

" No my food must not be cooked by a lower caste woman. I would rather not eat for a month than permit that to happen. I must wait till my servant's health is restored. But I expect her to return in a day or two."

I peer at him intently and notice that he wears the sacred thread of "The Sons of Brahma." The triple cord of woven linen which nestles under his chin is placed around the neck of every Brahmin baby and is never to be removed till death. So he is a Brahmin.

"Why trouble yourself with a superstitious caste restriction" I urge. "Surely your health is more important than that!"

"It is not superstition. Everyone gives out a magnetic influence which is quite real, even though the instruments of your Western science have not yet discovered it. The cook who prepares food throws her influence into it, unconsciously of course. A cook of low character will thus taint the food with bad magnetism, which passes into the person who eats the food."

"What a strange theory!"

"But it is true."

I change the subject.

"How long have you been an astrologer?"

"For nineteen years. I took up the profession after my marriage."

"Ah, I understand."

"No, I am not a widower. Shall I explain? When I was a youth of thirteen I prayed often to God for knowledge, and so was led to various people who taught me and to different books. I became so fascinated by study that I would sit up reading all day and far into the night. My parents arranged a marriage for me A few days after we were married, my wife got angry with me and said: I have married a human book!' On the eighth day she ran away with the man who used to drive our carriage."

Sudhei Babu pauses. I cannot help smiling at his wife's caustic comment, though her speedy elopement must have created a sensation in conservative India. But the ways of women are tortuous and beyond the compass of a man's mind.

"After a while I recovered from the shock," he continues, "and forgot her. All my emotions were blotted out. I went deeper than ever into the study of astrology and the divine mysteries. It is then that I took up my greatest study, the book of Brahma Chinta."

"Perhaps you will tell me what that book is concerned with?"

"The title can be translated as *Divine Meditation*, or as *The Quest of Brahma*, or even as *God-knowledge*. The entire work contains several thousand pages, but the part I study is only a section. It took me nearly twenty years to collect even that, because it exists only in scattered parts here and there. I have slowly obtained these different parts through agents in the various provinces of India. There are twelve chief divisions among its subjects, and many subdivisions. The chief topics are philosophy, astrology, Yoga, life after death, and other deep matters."

"Do you know if there is any English translation of book?"

He shakes his head.

"I have never heard of one. Few, even, are the Hindus who know of the existence of the book. Hitherto, it has been jealously guarded and kept secret. It came originally from Tibet, where it is looked upon as very sacred and only chosen students are allowed to study it."

"When was it written?"

"It was composed thousands of years ago by the sage Bhrigu, who lived so long ago that I cannot give you the date. It teaches a method of yoga which is quite different from all others which exist in India. You are interested in Yoga are you not?"

"How do you know that?"

For answer, Sudhei Babu quietly produces the chart which he constructed around my birthdate, and moves his pencil among the strange glyphs which represent planetary configurations and zodical signs.

"Your horoscope surprises me. It is out of the ordinary for a European, and not even a common one for an Indian. It snows that you will have a great tendency to study Yoga and that you will enjoy the favour of sages who will help you to delve deeply into the subject. Yet you will not limit yourself to Yoga alone, but become versed in other mystic philosophies."

He pauses and looks at me straight in the eyes. I recieve the subtle impression that he is about to make a statement which will be tantamount to a revelation of his inner life.

I am taken a back at this strange turn of affairs. I first come to Sudhei Babu to check up on the claims of Indian astrology; I come again to listen to his further defence of its basic postulate.

And now he unexpectedly offers to become my teacher in Yoga!

"If you will practise the methods of *Brahma Chinta* you will need no teacher,"he continues. "Your own soul will become your teacher."

I suddenly realize my mistake and wonder whether he has read my thoughts.

"You take me by surprise?" is all I can say.

" I have already instructed a few persons in this knowledge but I never regard myself as their master—only as their brother or friend. So I do not undertake to become your teacher in the ordinary sense. The spirit of the sage Bhrigu will simply use this body and mind of mine to communicate his teachings to you."

"I do not understand how you can combine the profession of astrology with the teaching of a Yoga system?"

His thin hands spread themselves upon the table.

" The explanation is this. I live in the world and serve it through my work, which happens to be astrology. Secondly, I refuse to be looked upon as a teacher of Yoga, because in our *Brahma Chinta* the only teacher acknowledge is God. He is the only preceptor we acknowledge. He, as the universal soul, is in us, and will teach us. Look on me as a brother, if you wish, but do not look on me as a spiritual preceptor. Those who have a teacher are too apt to lean on him and to depend on him instead of their own soul."

"And yet you depend on astrology for guidance, " I retort quickly, "instead of your own soul."

"You are not right. I never look at my horoscope now—in fact, I tore it up many years ago."

I express astonishment at this statement. He replies:

"I have found the light and do not need astrology to guide me, but those who still walk in darkness find it helpful. I have placed my life entirely in the Lord's hands. I carry that act to its proper conclusion by giving up all care about future or past. Whatever the Lord sends, that I accept as His will. I have given my whole self - body, mind, actions and feelings - to the will of the Almighty."

Suppose you are threatened with death by a murderous ruffian, would you do nothing and accept that as God's will?"

"When any danger arises I know that I have only to pray and instantly to receive His protection. Prayer is necessary but fear is not. I pray frequently and the Lord has marvellously protected me. Yet I have been through great troubles. Through all of them I was conscious of His help and I trust Him fully under every event. One day you, too, will disregard the future and become indifferent to it."

"There will have to be a remarkable change in me before that happens." I observe drily.

"That change will surely come"

"Are you certain?"

"Yes, you cannot escape your destiny. This spiritul rebirth is an event which comes from God, whether one looks for it or not."

"You say strange things, Sudhei Babu."

The idea of Deity is the unknown factor which enters into so many of my conversations in this land. The Hindus are essentially religious and I am often tantalized by the familiar way in which they introduce mention of God. It is possible for them to appreciate the view- point of a doubting Westerner, who has surrendered simple faith for complex reason? I realize that it will be unavailing and suit no practical purpose to throw up this question of Deity into agreement with the astrologer. I have no taste for partaking of any theological diet which he will probably place before me, so I turn the subject back to less controversial ground.

"Let us talk of other matters, for God and I have never met."

He looks at me fixedly, his peculiar black and white eyes searching my soul.

"The chart of your horoscope cannot be wrongly drawn or I might keep back my knowledge from an unready mind. But the stars move without fault; what you are unable to grasp today will linger in your thoughts for a time and then return with double force. I tell you again that I am ready to impart the way of *Brahma Chinta* to you."

"And I am ready to learn it."

What is the meaning of this mystery of chance, which, by the mere fortune of birth, puts one man in dirt-stained rags upon this road and another in silken robes in yonder river-side palace? Life is truly a dark enigma; I cannot comprehend it.

"Let us sit down here! " says the astrologer, when we reach the Ganges. We sit in the shade and look down the river upon the stretch of broad stone steps, rambling terraces and jutting platforms. Little groups of pilgrims are constantly coming and going.

The shapely forms of two slender minarets soar gracefully into the pearly sky to height of nearly three hundered feet. They mark the charming Mosque of Aurungazeb, that Muhammedan anachronism in this most Hindu of Hindu cities.

But the astrologer has noted my sad preoccupation with beggars, for he turns his sallow face towards me and says:

"India is a poor country." His voice is somewhat apologetic. "Its people have been sunk in inertia. The English race possesses some fine points and I believe that God brought them to our country for its benefit. Before they came life was unsafe; law and justice were often set aside. It is my hope that the English will not leave India; we need their help, but it should be given in friendship now, and not by force. However, the destiny of both nations must fulfil itself."

"Ah, your fatalism returns again!"

He ignores my comment and falls into silence. At length he asks:

"How can the two peoples avoid God's will? Day is ever followed by night, and night is ever followed by day. So is it with the history of nations. Great changes brood over the world. India has been sunk in sloth and intertia, but she will change until she bcomes filled with desires and ambitions, which ever precede activity. Europe burns with practical activities, but the strength of its materialism will pass away and it will turn its face towards higher ideals. It will happen to America.

I listen in silence.

"For this reason the philosophic and spiritual teachings of our land will travel towards the West like a wave of the ocean." he continues gravely. "Scholars have already translated some of our Sanskrit manuscripts and sacred books into Western languages, but many texts are hidden away in cave libraries in out of the way parts of India, Nepal and Tibet. Those, too, must eventually be made known to the world. The time will come before long when the ancient philosophies and inner knowledge of India shall unite with the practical sciences of the West. The secrecy of past times must give way to the needs of this century. I am glad that all this will happen."

I stare into the greenish water of the Ganges. The river is so strangely tranquil that it hardly seems to flow. Its surface shimmers in the sunlight.

He addresses me yet again:

"The destiny of each race of people must be realized, just as the destiny of every person must fulfilled. The Lord is omnipotent. Men and nations cannot escape from their self-earned fate, but they may be protected throught their troubles and even saved from great dangers."

And how does one obtain such protection?"

"By prayer, by keeping a child-like nature when one turns towards the Almighty, and by remembering Him not on one's lips, but in one's heart, especially before one begins any action. In happy days try to enjoy them as a blessing of God, and in troubles try to think that it is very much like a medicine to heal your inner disease. Fear Him not, as He is all merciful."

"You do not believe that God is remote from this world, then?"

"No. God is a spirit which is hidden in people and throughout this universe. If you see

RAMANA MAHARSHI AND ASTROLOGY

But Ramana could never let down the devotees who had cast their burden on him. The cases of Jagadisa Sastri and Rangayyar are worth recalling on this point. From his death bed Jagadisa Sastri, "the Sanskrit Pandit of Bhagavan's Court" wrote a final appeal in poem that "he would not accept any plea that *prarabdha* must follow its course and if only Bhagavan willed it His grace could cancel *prarabdha* and save him." Certain death was warded off. Rangayyar, a playmate of Ramana at Tiruchupuzi and later a staunch devotee, was stricken in a certain period

any beauty in Nature, a beautiful landscaspe, for instance, do not worship it for its own sake, but remember that it is beautiful because of the Deity present in it. See the Divinity in objects and people, and do not be so captivated by the outer forms that you forget the inner Spirit which gives them life."

"You mingle your doctrines of fate, religion and astrology in a peculiar manner, Sudhei Babu."

He gazes solemnly at me.

"Why so? These doctrines are not of my creation. They have descended to us from the most distant ages of the past. The tremendous power of destiny, the worship of our Creator and the lore of planetary influences were known to the earliest peoples. They were not such savages as you Westerners imagine. But have I not prophesied? The west will rediscover before this centruy closes how real are these invisible forces which enter into the lives of all men."

by a series of calamities. Astrologers saw no hope for him. Ramana not only made him stay with him but also insisted on his not leaving his presence for a long time. Once, when Rangayyar sought permission to go to the railway station and see off his relative, Ramana warned him to came there straight "without loitering anywhere or spending the night in town."He was thus saved from evil which there would have been no escape otherwise.

It is not that a specific prayer should always be addressed to Ramana. For, fate's blows are quick, sudden and totally upredictable. Then unasked Ramana would be

"It will be extremely hard for the west to give up its inborn notion that a man's will is free to make or mar his own life."

"Whatever happens is by His will and what seems like free will really works by His power. The Almighty returns to men the good or evil fruits of their thoughts and deeds in earlier bodies. It is best to accept His will, but one will not tremble under sorrows if one looks to him for the strength to endure them....."

(Reproduced from *Search in Secret India* by Paul Brunton)

there with his helping hand.... While seeing the palm of another devotee an eminent palmist wondered how this devotee was still alive. 'Could all my vast knowledge he wrong?', wondered the palmist. Then it dawned on him that Ramana had saved the life of his devotee even without the devotee's knowledge. Whether one prays or not Ramana knows what to do when and does it, but would never accept credit for it.

- Courtesy: *Divinity Here and Now*

A.R.Natarajan

CHAPTER FIFTEEN

ASTROLOGY VERIFIED

(The following is a reproduction from *Encyclopaedia of Tales* of the chapter on the experiences of the famous historian Meadows Taylor in Astrology).

In this chapter we shall strive for nothing less than to show that a great deal of what is boasted as "modern progress" is,in fact retrogression. Astrology may have fallen into contempt under the influence of improved modern science,but undoubtedly the time is coming when it will again have the attention it deserves and recover its ancient dignity as a sublime science. There is supposed by modern astronomers, to be some connection, not unlike that attributed by the old astrologers, between the position of the planets and the fortunes of our earth. Not of course, as used to be supposed in Christendom, and is still believed in this and other Eastern countries, that the lives of individual men are influenced, but that the period of perihelion, when the superior planets approach the Sun, is one of misfortune arising from natural causes. It is alleged that the history of great epidemics, for example, confirms this theory. The view is that at such time, the temperature and other conditions of our atmosphere are so seriously disturbed as naturally to engender irregularities. The next step will be for the modern astronomers to discover that no mere change in atmosphere temperature accompanying the conjunction of planets affects human destinies, but a far more important and occult power, the magnetic sympathy between the various planetary orbs.

Colonel Meadows Taylor, the well known author of "Confessions of a Thug, Tara" who had during his long career in India acquired an intimate knowledge of the natives of this country and gained their warm affection and respect as few Englishmen ever do, thus speaks of his experience of Astrology in three instances:-

"I hear you speak Mahratta, is it so ?"

"I am only a beginner" I replied; "but I dare say I can follow you"

"I am struck with with your face, " he continued, "and I should like to see your hand and cast your horoscope. Do you know when you were born?"

"I gave him the date, and he proceeded to examine first my forehead and then my left hand. 'It is a long and happy life on the whole ' he said; 'but there are some crosses and some deep sorrows; you are not yet married, but you soon will be, and you will have children - not many - some of whom you will lose. You will never be rich, nor ever poor; and yet much, very much money will pass through your hands. You will not now stay long here;but after many years you will return and rule over us. Fear nothing, your destiny is under the planet Jupiter, and you will surely prosper.'

"He added further details when he brought my horoscope some hours later, one which especially struck me being that I should become a Rajah, and rule over a large tract of country to the south."

This happened in 1828, and shortly afterwards Taylor's employment over the province of Nuldersy in which Tuljapoor is situate abruptly came to an end. He was some time afterwards appointed sole Administrator of the Shorapoor state during the minority of the king and subsequently when the Berars were ceded along with Nuldroog to the English he was appointed Deputy Commissioner of Berar and made his arrangements accordingly,but an express arriving from the Bombay Government a sudden change was made, and he was ordered to take charge of Nuldroog. This happened in 1853, and shortly afterwards when he visited Tuljapoor he met the old astrologer again. He thus writes:-

"On the day of my arrival, I had just breakfasted,and sat down to begin work in my cucherry, or office tent, when an old Brahmin came in, and for a time sat down quietly in a corner without speaking. Seeing that I was alone, he came up to my table, and peering closely into my face as he leant upon his staff, he said, 'Are you the Taylor Sahib who came here many years ago?'

"When I answered that I was the same, he produced a bundle of old papers, and asked me whether I recollected them. As I looked over them, I saw that I had put my initial to each of them, but forgot at the moment why I had done so; for in any case of inquiry or settlement it was my habbit to initial all the papers, and I thought these documents must relate to some old claim or suit to be revised, I was soon undeceived.

'Have you forgotten sahib', said the old man,'that I once cast your horoscope, and told you that you would return here to govern us after many years? And see! it was true! you have come; indeed, there is little difference in the time I recorded twenty- five years. I had not the exact data, if you remember, that I wanted, you could not give it to me.'

It was all true enough then I was the 'ruler' over them, and I then recollected how strange it had appeared to me at the residency when my destination was so suddenly altered from Berar to these western districts, on the requisition of Government of Bombay. The prediction had certainly been a strange one, and was as strangely fulfilled, even to the very letter of time.

"And you have been a 'rajah too', continued my old friend, "and have governed a country to the south for ten years; that I recored — see Sahib, and he pointed excitedly to the document. 'See there is no mistake there either!' "

"Not quite a 'Rajah' " I said laughing, "only manager of the country while the Rajah was a child".

'It was all the same, "returned the old Brahmin;" you were all powerful, and just like a

Rajah, and you governed the people. And you have seen sorrow too, Sahib; you were not married when you were here, and now you have lost wife and dear children, I hear? I wrote that. I saw it all plainly - it is here. And you are not rich they tell me? Yet lakhs of rupees have passed through your hands. Did I not tell you that too?'

"No, indeed," I replied, "I am not rich; indeed much the reverse,and I have had heavy sorrows."

'It could not be avoided' he said: 'no one could have mistaken what I discovered just 25 years ago. You were born for work not for the indulgence of wealthy idleness, and so you will continue. If you want these papers I will give them to you; if not, let them remain with me,' and so saying he took his leave. He soon afterwards went on a pilgrimage to Nasik and there died.

"I did not want the papers, and he kept them. I cannot account for his prediction. I only relate what happened. I told my old Serishtadar, Baba Sahib, about my horoscope and its results; but he was not in the least surprised.

'We Brahmins', he said 'believe in astrology, and you English laugh at it, but when one who understands the art casts a horoscope and calculates it scientifically, the result is seldom wrong. You were to have gone to Berar, and yet your fate has brought you here to Tooljapur again, at the very time appointed, twenty five years after, in spite of yourself and also of the Resident. Can you doubt, after this? Is there not more in astrology than you believe?'

I made no comment. How could I in the face of the simple facts that had occured?

The second instance is much more remarkable. Rather a curious incident occurred during this year (1846). A Brahmin who had been absent from Shorapoor for two years, came to me and said that he had cast up the table of my nativity, and had brought me the result. As I had never seen or heard of him before, and as he himself wished to know whether it tallied with my own experience hitherto, I was anxious to see the paper, which ran after this manner. I had not, nor could I have given him any sort of information as to the date of my birth or other particulars, as I did not know of his existence.

From birth under the Sun's influence. Neither favourable or unfavourable. I was weak and delicate, some times ill. Six years

Next under the Moon influence. Generally good; few crosses and those which occurred resulting in good. Ten years.

Next under Venus. Neither favourable nor unfavourable. The ordinary run of life. Seven years.

Next under Saturn. Bad, losses. Grief. No worldly advancement. No wealth. Never long in the same place; unsettled, frequent disappointments. Eighteen years.

Deduct on account of astrological months five years, two months. End of troubled period, thirty five years, two months.

Since when I have been under the influence of "Brihasput" or Jupiter, of whose sway one year is already past, and it will continue from its commencemnt, sixteen years.

Add to the previous calculation the one year of Jupiter, and the result is - thirty six years; which was my exact age.

The Brahmin enquired whether that was about right, as he had been rather bothered in the calculations regarding the Moon's influence which could not be rendered with as great certainty as the others. No one here knew my age, that I was aware of; but the result seemed to me very curious. I wished to know how the calculations had been made; but my friend could only explain them in Sanskrit, and this I did not understand. I sent the paper home to my father, and it afforded a good deal of interest and amusement to friends at home."

The third instance is the most remarkable.

CHAPTER SIXTEEN

ASTROLOGY: ITS ORIGIN

Vedanga Jyotisha : Oldest Tract

Vedanga Jyotisha is the oldest tract on Astrology and found in the *Rig* and *Yajur Vedas.*

The position of the equinoxes given in it enables one to fix the date of this treatise of the Hindus. This same information also helps us to fix the date of the beginnings of the accurate visual observations of the sky by the Hindus. According to *Vedanga Jyothisha*, Mrigasira, a star in the Orion group of stars, was the position of the equinox marking the beginning of the spring season at about this time. By noting the present position of the equinoxes (the spring equinox is now in Pisces) and from the rate of their retrograde motion of 50 1/4 seconds of angle per year, the difference between the present position of the equinox and that of the equinoxes as given in *Vedanga Jyotisha* can be worked out and this places it at about 4000 years before Christ. In other words, Hindu Astrology can be traced to this period in India.

Nakshatras

Very early in the history of mankind, the Vedic Hindus in Bharatavarsha were the first to study systematically the movements of the Sun, the Moon and other *grahas* in the sky. These movements were studied against the background of the stars. The ancient Hindus saw that, night after night, the Moon or Chandra, shifted its position among the stars. Watching its movements closely, they saw it came back to its original position every 193rd days. So, they divided the path of the Moon in the sky into 27⅓ equal parts. Constellations on or about the path of the Moon were related to the Moon's daily motion. Thus the lunar zodiac of the Hindus came into being. It was made up of 27 constellations corresponding to the star or groups of stars by which the Moon was seen on each successive night. These stars (may be one or more) were called Nakshatras.

The brightest star of each Nakshatra was called Yogatara.

The Yogatara (or asterism chosen to mark out each Nakshatra) was chosen either because it was most clearly visible to the naked eye or because it had some other feature that attracted the eye such as, for example, peculiarity of configuration.

These 27 Nakshatras chosen lay approximately on the ecliptic, never too faraway from it.

These 27 Nakshatras are: Aswini, Bharani, Krittika, Rohini, Mrigasira, Aridra, Punarvasu, Pushyami, Aslesha, Makha, Pubba, Uttara, Hasta, Chitta, Swati, Visakha, Anuradha, Jyeshta, Moola, Poorvashadha, Uttarashadha, Sravana, Dhanishta, Satabhisha, Poorvabhadra, Uttarabhadra and Revati.

Movement of the Sun

The ancient Rishis also saw that the Sun and the other *grahas* never moved very far from the course of the Moon. They used this fact to regard the 27 divisions in the sky as many milestones to chart the course of the other *grahas*.

They saw that the Sun too apparently moved amongst the stars. They noticed that a particular star which rose or set with the Sun did not do so after a certain number of days. So, they chalked out the Sun's course and found it also had a periodic movement like the Moon's. Only the time it took was 12 times that of the Moon's cycle. Therefore 27 lunar constellations were divided into 12 Rasis. The Sun took one month to cross each Rasi or 2 1/4 Nakshatras.

Solar Month

The period taken by the Sun to cross each Rasi was called a solar month.

The solar month was named after the asterism in which the Full Moon took place that month. The solar month in Mesha when the Full Moon occurred in Chitta Nakshatra was called Chaitra and so on.

Lunar Zodiac: Hindu in Origin

The phenomenon of precession, known in the *Vedas*, was known to the Hindus several centuries before the Christian era. The Hindus invented *sunya* or zero and this was a sensational attainment for it "liberated the human intellect from the bars of the counting frame". This symbol *sunya*, the sciences of *geometi*, *trikonameti* and *bijaganita* were carried over by early Arab travellers to India to the West. The same Arabs also carried the Nakshatra system and the lunar zodiac to the West.

These sciences in the course of their transit from India to the West via Arabia acquired new names. *Geometi* became geometry, *trikonameti* became *trignometry* and *bijaganita* became *algebra.* The Nakshatra system was christened *Menazil* system. They borrowed the system from the Hindus and improved upon it calling each Nakshatra or lunar mansion *Menazil al yamr.*

The Chinese also, one of the oldest civilizations, borrowed the lunar zodiac from India calling it *Sieu.* According to Prof. Weber, there is no evidence whatsoever of the lunar zodiac in China earlier than 250 B.C. This period in the history of Hindu astronomy is a very late period indeed. That clearly proves that the lunar zodiac was purely the discovery of the Hindu astronomers.

Many western historians and their slavish Indian counterparts make the sad mistake of attributing all knowledge of Astrology and astronomy to the Greeks. But the Hindus knew and practised Astrology much, much earlier and there is evidence of this in Vedic literature. The same historians who think Greece and Chaldea discovered Astrology unfortunately and conveniently overlook the fact that history does not admit of intellectual trade or even political intercourse betwen India and Greece till after the date of Alexander's entry into India which is about 300 B.C. **That means, their theory that India learnt her Astrology from Greece becomes baseless and concocted as we have already seen that *Vedanga Jyotisha* is at least about six thousand years old.**

The Solar Zodiac: Greek Origin Theory Mischievous:

In one of the hymns in the *Rig Veda*, the Sun is described as the 12 spoked wheel. The 360 days as well as the same number of nights are called his 720 children. The very fact that the Hindus could, so early in the history of the world, visualise the number of days to a year speaks of their astronomical attainments.

The commentator Sayana explains the 12 spokes referred to in the sloka as the 12 signs of the zodiac. There are the *12 Adityas* or solar entities of the Veda. They are said to be the offspring of *Aditi* meaning endless which means an enclosure like the ecliptic. The reference to the *Adityas* is to the manifestations of the same Sun in the 12 stages of his journey or simply the 12 divisions into which the ecliptic is divided.

The equinoctial and solistical points are important points on the ecliptic. In the *Vedas* these points are called as the 4 *Adityas* — Agni, Indra, Mitra and Varuna. In different hymns of the *Rig*

Veda, Indra is always associated with Agni. Agni is the point of intersection of the celestial equator and the ecliptic. The Vedic Hindu had a very good concept of the equinox, not merely as the time when day and night are equal but also as the junction of the ecliptic and equator.

In the *Rig Veda*, Agni is described as the leader of the hosts of gods, implying that the year begins when the Sun is at the vernal equinox or Agni. The 4 *Adityas*, Agni, Indra, Varuna and Mitra, though lords of different signs, are described as one in the sense that each can occupy the position of the other on account of precession. *Rik*(I 164-66)

Nakshatras:Arcs, not Stars

In the very early Vedic times, the Nakshatras were essentially longitudinal segments of the ecliptic. The constellations were a relatively later discovery chosen to symbolize and identify the divisions.

Weekdays First Conceived by Hindus:

The *Rig Samhita* is believed to be the world's oldest extant record. The date ascribed to it is 14th century B.C. by Colebrooke. But Indian scholars call it *apourusheya* or not composed by any human. Modern scholars, on the basis of astronomical data found in it, are now veering to this conclusion.

The *Rig Veda* (47-18) gives the period of precession as 28,800 years. The *Puranas* declare several Indras (equinoxes) have ruled over the world implying that the equinox has made several complete revolutions round about the ecliptic with respect to Aswini. The statements show in no unmistakable terms, the Hindus grasp of astronomical phenomena.

The Rig Veda consists of 3parts: The *Samhita, Brahmanas and Upanishads.*

The *Samhita* is divided into 10 *mandalas*. Each *mandala* consists of a number of *suktas*. Each *sukta* consists of *mantras* of different metres varying in number. Of these *suktas*, the *Purusha Sukta* is a very popular one and recited daily by almost every devout Hindu in his morning prayers.

This *sukta* is a description of Purusha, Kala Purusha or Time Personified. It contains many facts about time and divisions of time.

In the 15th mantra of the *Rig Veda* but apearing as the 7th in *Taittiriya Aranyaka* we find the week defined and related to the month. It says:

Saptaasyaasan paridyah, meaning the 'month is made up of 7 weekdays', and *Trisapata samidhah kritaah* which means 'and three more seven days' these with the Full and New Moon days constitute the month.

This is the oldest reference to the weekdays which are 7 in number. The *sloka* describes the month as constitued by 7 days plus three more (units) of 7 days plus the Full and New Moon days to make 30 days in all.

Many historians obsessed with the Greek origin will find these facts hard to digest. They have usually gone by western theories which are many times fanciful, not corroborated by facts and absolutely unconnected with original works.

Such historians and their slavish votaries mistakenly believe that the zodiac was formulated first by the Babylonians in 700 B.C. and the word horoscope is from the Greek word *horoskopos*. What they fail to comprehend is the issue is not the ethymology of the word horoscope but the origin of *Jyotisha Sastra*.Manilius' *Astronomicon* and Plotemy's *Tetrabiblios* (140 A.D.) are the earliest Greek works on Astrology or *Jyotisha*.

Further, the theories of Astronomy that Ptolemy puts forth in his *Almagest* are simply childish compared to ancient Indian attainments in Astronomy. For instance Prolemy begins with the theory the earth is fixed and the planets revolving around it. When he finds he cannot explain the appearance of Venus in the sky before sunrise and sometimes after sunset he changes the theory to one where he conceives of a long bar connecting the earth and the Sun and the planets hanging in between. This system of Ptolemy laid the foundations for European Astronomy. By this time in India, the theory of the earth spinning on its axis, the ecliptic....etc., were all familiar to even students of elementary

Astronomy. How can one be so naive and so biased as to attribute all knowledge of Astroloy in India to Ptolemy with his silly theories of the earth.

With their advanced theoris of the Universe (which are today accepted as correct) the Hindus were the founding fathers of Astrology when the Greeks were still stumbling in the dark with their knowledge of the skies misconceived and wrong. Vedic Astrology had gained such strong roots in India and its reputation had spread so far and wide that even Hippocratus who lived in about 400 B.C. borrowed not only his *materia medica* from us but also learnt Astrology here*. In India, a horoscope was an absolutely necessary diagnostic tool and helped decide the line of treatment as well. It was the Arabs and Moorish astrologers who took Astrology from India to Europe during the middle ages.

According to Balagangadhar Lokamanya Tilak, the Indians, the Iranians and Greeks originally were all Vedic Aryans. Later the Iranians and Greeks migrated westwards, the scholars among them taking with them Hindus Astrology amongst other subjects. Many Greek words are derived from Sanskrit. From *shukra* in Sanskrit is derived *kupris* in Greek. *Chakra* in Sanskrit is *kuklos* in Greek. The Sanskrit *tatra*

---

* *A Study of the Heliocentrie Science* by Swami Abhedananda

becomes *turas* in Greek**. Many historians, with an in-built inferiority complex, have knowingly or unknowingly worked to distort fact by attributing many Sanskrit astronomical terms to Greek. Such scholars unfortunately, are ignorant of both Sanskrit and Astronomy and are incompetent to comment on either subject. Perhaps these 'scholars'could study the available original works and scholarly studies of those proficient in both Astronomy and Sanskrit which could help them shed their highly prejudiced views of the date and origin of Astrology.

Prof. Weber, in fact, traces Indian literature to the period when the Indians and the Iranians lived together. According to Tilak *(ibid)* the Parsis separated from the Indian Aryan (from the geographical region known as Akhanda Vishala Bharata) in the Orion period, that is, between 3000 to 2800 B.C.

Says Tilak (pp. 206 *The Orion*) "The Greeks and the Parsis have retained no traditions of this period, for the simple reason that they carried with them only the calendar which was in force when they left the common home, while the Indian Aryans have preserved all the traditions with a super-religious fidelity and scruplousness......" Further on (p. 307) he says talking of the Orion period (4000 B.C. to 2500 B.C.) "The Greeks and the Parsis appear to have left the common home

** *The Orion* by B.L.Tilak

during the latter part of this period as they have retained most of these legends and even the attributes of the constellation of Mrigashiras otherwise called Agrayana, Orion or the Pauryeni...."

Prof. Max Mueller in his *Biographies of Words* (pages 288- 289) gives a list of about 60 mythological names common to Greek and Sanskrit. Many historians tend to represent this list as implying the Sanskrit words are derived from Greek. Actually, it is just the other way round as Tilak points out in his book *The Orion*.

Vedanga Jyotisha, some historians wrongly believe, is only about Astronomy. It gives details of when sacrifices must be performed and tells us about auspicious and inauspicious periods. These periods are determined on the basis of the solar and lunar movements and come, as such, within Astrology. It is not known exactly when but *jataka* or horoscopy also evolved with *muhurta*. The latest, no matter how unwilling one is to accept the antiquity of Astrology, can be 1400

GEOLOGIST USING MANUSCRIPT FINDS WATER

Armed only with a 6th century manuscript, an Indian geologist is discovering groundwater reservoirs with amazing success, using trees and termite hills as clues.

"My technique may be unorthodox", says E.A.V. Prasad, a professor at Sri Venkateswara University in Tirupathi in South India, "but it works."

The challenge came four months ago when the Gujarat state's water supply and sewerage board (GWSSB) asked

B.C. to 500 B.C. *Jataka* is a term that frequently appears in Buddhistic literature. Buddha's own birth was interpreted horoscopically by the scholars in king Suddhodana's court and that is far, far anterior to the Greek Astrology of Manilius. For one who is open-minded, the references to the horoscope of Sri Rama in *Srimad Ramayana* will place Astrology even earlier. By then Astrology was a well developed science, so its origins must date back very very early in the history of Aryavarta.

Even the most reluctant critic will have to concede that horoscopy in India is indigenous and the latest period that can be given is 600 B.C., the Buddha having been born in 623 B.C The great poet Aswaghosha who belongs to the 1st century B.C has written 2 books in Sanskrit, *Buddha Charita* and *Soundarananda*, both of which are admitted authentic by historians (I 31-32).

In the first chapter of *Buddha Charita* (I 31-32), it says that "renowned pious scholars as-

him to locate water in Jamnagar, a chronically drought-stricken district, in the western Indian state.

Surveying the surface vegetation in village Kamballia, Prasad spotted a date palm enwinted with a banyan tree. He asked the GWSSB to drill a borehole 15 feet north of the tree.

Water gushed out of the well at the rate of 2000 gallons per hour (GPH).

sembled at the king's palace and told king Suddhodana that his son would be a great man and save the world from sorrows".

There can be no doubt as to the origin as well as antiquity of *Jyotisha.* It was born and developed in India. According to scholars, well-versed in Sanskrit as well as Astrology, *Jyotisha* is at least 6000 years old.

In village Haripar, Prasad identified a termite mound colonized with vegetation and had a hole drilled 10 feet north of it. Its yield was even higher: 3000 GPH.

Within 10 days, Prasad located 51 well sites in 30 villages that had been classified as "no source" villages. Drilling has been completed in 15 sites.

While modern scientists depend on costly equipment and satellite pictures to detect groundwater, Prasad says he depends on "bio- indications" listed in "Brihat Samhita" written by Varahamihira, a philosopher and sage who lived about 1500 years ago.

According to Varahamihira, the presence of termite mounds indicates water below. His clues also include half a dozen animals and some 30 different trees, important among them being a species called "phreatotypes", whose roots penetrate to reach water, no matter how deep.

- Courtesy: SPOTLIGHT (30-4-1988)

CHAPTER SEVENTEEN

INDIAN ASTROLOGY*

Sepharial

(Sepharial was a noted writer on Astrology and a contemporary of late Prof. B. Suryanarain Rao. Sepharial had always kept an open mind on Hindu Astrology. The following is reproduced from his book *The Science of Foreknowledge* to bring home to the handful of Indian astrologers who have no correct conception of their own great heritage, the antiquity, importance and indigenous character of Indian Astrology and how, in the interests of astrological science, a hotchpotch mixing-up of the Indian and the European systems has withstood the test of time and experience and has certain features which can usefully be incorporated into the western system. - Ed. *A.M.*)

It has been asserted that " we can find a dozen writers who allege that the Hindus got their Astrology from Chaldea and Egypt, but not one authority can we find who controverts this". Frankly, I should like to examine the credentials of these twelve "authorities". I am prepared to find that not one of them has familiarity with the subject of Astrology, either European or

* Reproduced from the THE ASTROLOGICAL MAGAZINE, December 1961.

Hindu. My personal intercourse with Jyotish Sastris (astrological experts) and pandits of India confirmed me in this belief, and what I have seen of the work of Orientalists does not impress me to the contrary.

When the *Suryasiddhanta* has been closely studied from first to last, the Orientalist is as far from any conçeption of the basic principles of *Jyotish Vedanga* (Astrology) as a new-born babe. Bailly has given us a very good rendering of the astronomy of the Hindus in his *Astronomie Indienne*, but he and all other Orientalists are silent about the subject of Hindu Astrology. The fact is that, never having touched the subject in their own language, they wisely refrain from involving themselves in the more intricate system of the East as expounded in the Sanskrit Sastras.

Though no "authority" from a mere linguistic point of view, I venture to contradict the dictum of those twelve writers who allege (but do not prove) that the Hindus got their Astrology from either Chaldea or Egypt. I will advance my arguments against this allegation.

1. No Orientalist has yet disposed of the fact that Sanskrit is the oldest Indo-European language, the parent language of the Aryan race. None has shown, nor can show, that Accadian the principle languages of the ancient Babylonians is of greater antiquity than Sanskrit, or the Babylonians more ancient than the Aryans. The language of any people is the direct outcome of its thought, for it is embodied

thought, and hence expresses all those particulars and peculiarities of environment which induced the thought of the people, their religious beliefs, their social polity, and all that goes to make up the round of their lives. Such is the Sanskrit in which the *Vedas* are written. And of Sanskrit it may be said without fear of contradiction that it is at once the most complex, complete, and highly inflected language within our knowledge. The Chaldean and Hebrew tongues are in comparison with it as the lisping prattle of a child is to the mature diction of a philosopher. The Astrology of the Hindus is all written in Sanskrit, Translations have been made into the vernaculars, into Hindi, Telugu, Tamil, Marathi, Canarese, but all primarily are traceable to the teachings of the Hindu sages, Narada, Garga, Parasara, Varahamihira, and others.

2.1 It is true that India, under the princes, enjoyed a free commerce with the surrounding nations, and that certain traditions may have passed current among them. But we have to remember that this commerce was restricted to one caste of Hindus - viz., the *Vaisya*, or merchantmen. The landlord was never allowed to travel out of his country. Yet it is these Brahmins who, as hereditary Sastris, are responsible for the entire *Jyotisha Sastra*. Even at this day it is only the Brahmin who is permitted to expound the *Vedas*, and previous to the invasion of India by foreign nations the literature of the country was exclusively in the hands of the Brahmins.

3. If Claudius Ptolemy derived his Astrology from the Chaldeans, or if the methods advocated as original with the Chaldeans had any tradition in Egypt, certain it is that neither Chaldean nor Egyptian Astrology had tradition in India, **for the sole and sufficient reason that the astrological methods of the Hindus are essentally and fundamentally different to all that is reputed Chaldean and Egyptian.**

In the first place their zodiac is not related to the equinox, but counts from the fixed star Revati, which is now about 19° 35'17" east of the vernal equinox. (Mr. B. Suryanarain Rao makes Ayanamsa 21° 44'47". I have used the epoch K.Y. 3600 as given in the *"Kalasankalita"* tables. Precession 50 1/2 " per annum - Sepharial). The calculation of periods is based on the 27 Nakshatras, or asterisms, and are reckoned from the place of the Moon at birth. What are called "Chaldean Directions", based on the diurnal aspects of the planets after birth form no part of Hindu Astrology. How, then, can it be said that the father has been taught by his children?

It must not be thought that because the Hindus do not relate their zodiac to the equinox they were ignorant of those considerations which determine our Western methods. They were, apparently, well informed concerning the precession of the equinoxes and solstices, and the proper motion of the stars. They knew to make fairly accurate observations and did not neglect the study of astronomy. The *"Kalasankalita"* tables show this to be the case.

In Varahamihira's work, entitled *Brihatsamhita*, there is a passage which not only determines the date of that writer, but of that Parasara whom he quotes. Mihira says: "The summer solstice is now in the first point of Kataka and winter solstice in Makara but the summer solstice was at one time in the midddle of Aslesha according to former writers." Kataka is the constellation of Cancer; Makara is Capricornus; Aslesha is Leo. From this we learn that the constellation of Aries corresponded with the sign Aries when Mihira wrote his treatise on Astrology - *viz.*, in the year A.D. 498 - and also that observation had been made over 2,000 years before that date, when Taurus was an equinoctial and Leo a solstitial constellation. The two zodiacs are distinguished by the Hindus by the name of *Sayana* and *Nirayana*, that which has motion and that which has none. It is well known that at the beginning of the year the worship of Maya under the figure of the Bull (Apis) was performed by the Egyptians in the month of May in honour of the Sun's entry into the constellation Taurus, the solar disc between the Bull's horns being emblematic of the astronomical fact.

The Hebrews must have witnessed this ceremony during their captivity in Egypt, since they sought to perpetuate this custom in the worship of the golden Calf after their exodus. The incident is in accord with the astronomical fact, for the Sun came to the equinoctial point in the constellation Taurus during the period of their captivity. It is evident however that the celebration continued with the Egyptians after the equinoctial point had left Taurus and had passed into Aries, for Moses, who was "learned in all the lore and language of the Egyptians", put the Hebrews straight in this matter by instituting the Pasach (Transit), or passover to coincide with the true equinox. He prohibited the Worship of the Bull and instituted the symbolism of the Ram. The equinox had precessed from Taurus into Aries 170 years before the Exodus. Before the Pharaohs there were the Hysksoi or Shepherd kings, and before the Hyksoi in Egypt there were the "Former writers" on Astrology in India, referred to by *Mihira*. This carries us back to close upon 2700, B.C. at which time we find the Hindus already in possession of an astronomy and Astrology to writings upon which Mihira constantly refers.

The Sanskrit kadjan, or palmyra book, is more ancient than the hieratic papyrus of Egypt. So far as the records of Assyria go they do not approach the antiquity of the Hindu Sastras. Mr. Wilde has laboured to show that the "day for a year" method of directing was in vogue among the Chaldeans and hence with the Babylonians. This may well be, seeing that Daniel, the chief astrologer at the court of Nabakollassar (Nebuchadnezzar) declared that, in the first year of the reign of Darius, King over Chaldea, he "understood by books the number of the years" of desolation propheised by Jermiah and we find him making use of a period of "70 weeks" to indicate a period of 490 years, *i.e.*, 70x7=490 days. But if this were the method in vogue among the Chaldeans, it is certain that they were not the preceptors of the Hindus, for, as I have said, the latter have no such time-measure in their astrological books.

4. The insular character of the Hindus, and the exclusive nature of the Brahmin caste, is opposed to the idea of the Chaldean tradition which could only have been effected by commerce or by means of Mogbeds sojourning in India. In such cases the tradition would have left philological landmarks easy of recognition.

That our Astrology came to us, from whatever source, by Latin tradition is evident from the names of the signs and planets in use by us. In the same manner, had the Babylonians communicated Astrology to the Hindus, the names would have been received by the latter along with the tradition. Where are the landmarks? Prof. Max Muller takes the contrary view in his famous derivations:

Deva-Pitar Deo-pitar (Sanskrit), Zeus-patar (Greek), Deus- pater(Latin,) Jupiter(English).

There are two names for Jupiter in common use among the Hindus, one *(Brihaspati)* being the designation of the celestial Father, the other *(Guru)* being the appellative of the earthly preceptor or "God-Father",*i.e.*, Deo-pitar. *Brihaspati* means "Lord of Increase" from *brih* (to expand) and *Pati* (Lord). It is identified with the Lord of Creation, Brahma, the latter name having the same root, the Hindu Trimurti or Trinity being Brahma (Jupiter), Vishnu (Mars), and Siva (Saturn); literally the Expander, the Pervader, and the Resolver. They have for consorts Sarswati, Lakshmi and Parvati respectively. Hence the unique symbol of Biune Trinity is associated with the seven celestial bodies.

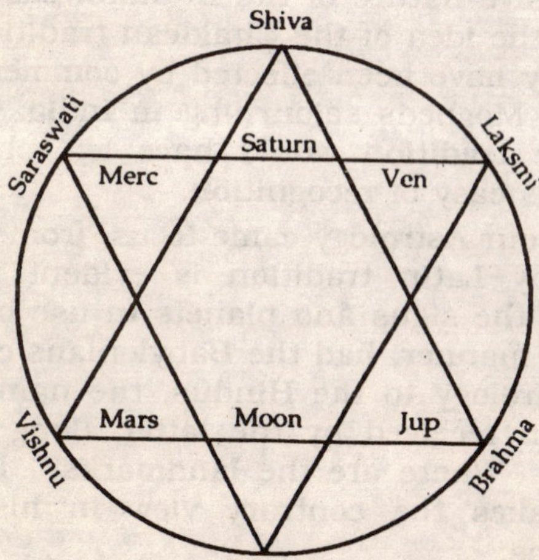

The solar orb in this relation will correspond to Parabrahman. The male trigon (Saturn, Jupiter, Mars) is represented by the right triangle, the female (Moon, Mercury, Venus) by the reverse triangle, the male and female emanations being opposite in position as in nature; for observe, Dhanus and Meena, the signs of Jupiter, are opposed to Mithuna and Kanya, the signs of Mercury; Mesha and Vrischika the signs of Mars are opposed to Thula and Vrishabha, the signs of Venus, etc., the opposition being that due to polarity or equilibrium. The asterisms constituting the Hindu zodiac take their names from the principal stars in each of them. **These stars bear Sanskrit names - not Chaldean.**

The astronomy of the Hindus, like their Astrology, is original with themselves. The asterisms are subdivided into *padas* or quarters, each of which is ruled by one of the planets. The periods of the planets are:

Saturn	19	years
Jupiter	16	years
Mars	7	years
Sun	6	years
Venus	20	years
Mercury	17	years
Moon	10	years
Caput Draconis	18	years (Rahu)
Cauda Draconis	7	years (Ketu)
	120	years

The trine is the basis of Hindu Astrology.

These details are mentioned in support of the statement that there is no known trace of Chaldean tradition. The Chaldeans appear to have divided their zodiac into 28 asterisms and the names of them as received by us are Arabic, showing the channel of tradition.

The insular character of the Hindus, as I have said, is opposed to the idea of a borrowed science. Their terminology is likewise in evidence against the theory of tradition. **But what seems to set the matter beyond all doubt is the fact that the Hindus, who are saturated with astrological beliefs, and whose whole life is regulated by these beliefs, present no single monument or structure, no literary quotation, no theological concept, no social law, no single custom which points to such a tradition. Their architecture, on which all inscriptions are in relief, and not in intaglio, as with the Accacians and Egyptians their ancient language; their classic literature; their theogony; their marriage laws; their methods of life; their regulations in regard to births and deaths— the whole atmosphere of their thought, life, and polity are unique and original with themselves. The religion, science and language of the Hindus, existing uncorruted for milleniums, is exclusively and entirely Hindu in its genesis and evolution.**

Mr. A.G. Trent "(Dr. Richard Garnett. LL.D.) says in regard to Hindu Astrology: "So far as it differs from European Astrology, it appears to differ for the worse. I cannot find any attempt at a theory of Uranus, whose life influence is as demonstrable as that of any other planet. At the same time, the small regard paid to the house seems to me to show that it was not derived from the Arabs, and I am willing to believe it older than Mahomet, while I cannot imagine that it has any such antiquity as the Astrology of Egypt or Chaldea."

This is a very important statement coming from so reputable a source, but I venture to suggest another view of the case, which appears as more worthy of acceptance. The mere fact that the Hindus have not yet adapted Uranus of their system of Astrology (for they are not ignorant of its existence) shows once more the insular reserve of the Brahmin, who stands by the Sastras as the meanest individual among them stands by the Dharma (caste) of his progenitors. In India every thing is hereditary, inviolate, unalterable. No doubt, in the hands of a European, any difference in the system of Astrology taught by us and the Hindus would appear prejudicial to the Hindu system. But put competent Hindu astrologers to the test on their own lines, and I venture to say that they will repeat my experience and produce better result with less labour than we by our methods. At the same time I will point that there are comparatively fewer proficients in India than in Europe. The Hindu astrologers lament the decline of Jyotisha Sastra, we here regret that the masses have never even commenced the study of Astrology. In India everyone knows something of it, in Europe the knowledge of it is restricted to a few who are vey assiduous in their studies. Astrology is not yet nearly at high noon, with us, but it has more than dawned upon those who stand on the hill tops. In the East they are lying languid in the evening of a resplendent day, and only a few watchers of the night retain a real interest in the glimmering stars.

As to "The small regard paid to the houses", I can only say that every Sastra considers the Bhavas as an essential part of *Jyothisha*, and a great stress is laid on the several dignities and deblities of the planets in the houses, irrespective of the signs they occupy. I regret that I have not done justice to the part of the subject in my short exposition of Parasara in the New Mammal. **That Hindu Astrology is immeasurably older than the Mohammedan era is certain from the fact that Mihira wrote in the fifth century, at least 120 years before Mohammed, while he makes reference to and quotes from Sastras evidently written in 2700 B.C about 2300 years before Daniel began the study of the books of prophecy!** Narada is regarded by the Hindus as the sage who preserved the ancient astronomical records to those who survived the deluge; and Manu, who struck the keynote of the nation's polity for the *Kaliyuga* in his famous "Institutes", is held to be one of those sages who bridged over the *anti* and *post* deluvian periods. The "Institutes" of Manu have strict regard to the teachings of Astrology, and the conservative Hindu will never neglect the study of his almanac, because the observance of the "Institutes" requires that he should have due regard to the time and seasons.

While it is true that we have no evidence to know that Chaldean Astrology had its birth in India, it certainly is true that Hindu Astrology cannot be ascribed to a Chaldean source. The horoscopes in the Ramayana not only enable us to fix the date of the great epic, but also constitute internal evidence of its historical verity. Above all they prove the great antiquity of Hindu Astrology, showing its existence in the peninsula fully 2000 years before the period ascribed to the Chaldeans. The statement that "... The Hindus compute horoscopes incorrectly" is quite false. They calculate the Lagnasphutam, or the rising degree with great accuracy, and the planets' places are also properly determined in their *panchangams*. But the failings of the Professor must not be laid to the charge of the science, else an equal indictment will dispose of European science forthwith. **This, I know, the Hindus have records of the influence of every six minutes of the zodiac. European Astrology has not as yet more than barely delineated the nature and influence of the twelve signs.**

As to the many authorities "who allege that Hindu Astrology had its birth in Chaldea", I regret to say that I do not know of one Orientalist who has sufficient knowledge of either Hindu or Chaldean Astrology to enable him to institute a comparative study. The assertion almost makes one doubt their right to be called philologists or Orientalists. In reference to Dr. Richard Garrnett and George Wilde, however, it should be observed that, whereas neither was a reader of Sanskrit, both were competent students and exponents of European modern Astrology. Dr. Garnett entertained great suspicions in regard to the antiquity of Aryan literature in distinction from Prof. Maxmuller, Sir Willian Jones, and others who were disposed to trace all tradition and language to an Aryan source. Mr. Wilde, on the other hand, had conceieved an idea that Chaldea was the birthplace of astronomy and Astrology, and even went so far as to call well-known modern methods by the name of Chaldean Astrology. Sparse references to astronomical facts to be found in the Accadian and Assyrian records were for him evidences of a complex system of Astrology having been current among them. I think it highly probable that such a system existed but we have no evidence of it still less that it had the least influence over the Astrology of the Hindus.

From my general statement of the Orientalists' position in regard to Astrology, it was to be expected that the supposed evidences of a Chaldean or an Egyptian origin of Astrology would resolve themselves into a series of unsupported assertions. An authoritative statment can only emanate from one who has made Astrology a study. One has only to refer to the star texts of the Bible to see their linguistic study does not suffice for correct interpretation of passages of a technical nature. Reference to an article entitled "The Two Gates", which I contributed to the Astrological Journal, *Coming Events*, will show the familiar use of the word, "Gate" as referring to the point of *ingress*. The *Book of Judges* had received scholarly translation centuries before the gates of Gaza were recognised as the sign

Capricorn, or Hebron as the sign Cancer, or yet Samson as the solar body (Shemesh-on) and Delilah as the Moon. In the translation of the *Book of Job* there are many fancied references of stars where none are intended, and the successional rising of the signs under the name of Mazzaroth has troubled many a commentator.

So in reference to the origin of Hindu Astrology, a mere knowledge of Sanskrit does not suffice. The abundant literature of Hindu Astrology requires a technical knowledge for its adequate translation. It is true that the Greeks were in a state of rude barbarism while the Egyptians were pursuing an advanced study of astronomy. It is also true that the modern Parsis in India are followers of Zoroaster, but whereas the Hindus have extensive astronomical literature in the classical Sanskrit, no such record lies to the credit of the Parsis. The statement by the late Mr.George Wilde that "The Indians have some ancient writings of no date" is a very unscholarly remark more particularly when the tablets of Sargon I are set in contrast as if bearing an authentic date. The only means we have of judging in this matter is by the internal evidences.

Had the Hindus borrowed their astronomy from Chaldea or Egypt or Greece, they would have preserved the landmarks—there would be evidences of tradition. For just as we know that the Saxons were vassals of their Norman conquerors from the contrast of such words as cow (sax), beef (norm), deer (sax) vension(norm), sheep (sax), mutton (norm), etc., and just as we have traces of the Latin tradition in language of our day—as, in fact, we localise the Hebrews and know them to have been a nomadic race from the letters of their alphabet, so we know that the Hindus have no astronomical tradition from Greek or Egyptian. In the nameing of the celestial bodies and the asterisms, everything is original, insular, and local. Mr. Wilde himself advanced a statement which goes far to prove. "In none of the old writings is any account to be found of the computation of horscopes by oblique ascension." It has already been shown that the Hindus fix the rising sign and count therefrom.

The Hindus fix the rising sign and count therefrom giving to each succeeding sign (Rasi) dominion over a whole house (Bhava). Bailly states that "the first tables possessed by the Indians only date back to 3102 B.C.". This was the year of the commencement of the Kaliyuga, which opened with the entry of Sun into the constellation Mesha (Aries) in the month of February.

The tables referred to may be the oldest as yet known to us, but it is certain that Varahamihira, writing in the year A.D. 498, remarks upon the coincidence of the vernal equinox with the constellation Aries, and of the summer solstice with the constellation Cancer (Kataka). But in the same passage he states that, "according to former Sastras," the summer solstice once coincided with "the middle of Aslesha" (Leo), and this throws the record back to

3240 B.C. Weber's remark that "it would indeed be a most wonderful play of chance that in all these three countries— Chaldea, China and India — each in a different spot, but in an identical pole or same latitude the observations and calculations of the duration of the longest day should be the same" strikes me as being the most puerile thing ever penned by a professed orientalist. If the countries named are in the same latitude, it would only be strange if observations and calculations as to the length of the day at summer solstice should not be same.

Certainly Chaldea, China, and the Aryan country all have common latitude between the Tropic of Cancer and 30 degrees N., and it was in this territory of India that the ancient records were made. **A careful survey of the passages quoted by Mr. Wilde reveal no evidence whatever that Hindu Astrology had its origin in Chaldea**. They do indeed show the aniquity of astronomical records in all the countries named, but there the matter ends, and the evidences of tradition are nil.

APPENDIX I

Prof. Carl Jung's Letter to Prof. B.V. Raman

Kusnacht-Zch.
September 6th 1947

Dear Prof Raman,

I haven't, yet received THE ASTROLOGICAL MAGAZINE, but I will answer your letter nevertheless.

Since you want to know my opinion about astrology I can tell you that I've been interested in this particular activity of the human mind since more than 30 years. As I am a psychologist, I am chiefly interested in the particular light the horoscope sheds on certain complications in the character. In cases of difficult psychological diagnosis I usually get a horoscope in order to have a further point of view from an entirely different angle. ***I must say that I very often found that the astrological data elucidated certain points which I otherwise would have been unable to understand.*** **From such experiences I formed the opinion that Astrology is of particular interest to the psychologist, since it contains a sort of psychological experience which we call "projected" - this means that we find the psychological facts as it were in the constellations. This originally gave rise to the idea**

that these factors derive from the stars, whereas they are merely in a relation of synchronicity with them. I admit that this is a very curious fact which throws a peculiar light on the structure of the human mind.

What I miss in astrological literature is chiefly the statistical method by which certain fundamental facts could be scientifically established.

Hoping that this answer meets your request. I remain,

Yours sincerely,
(Sd.) C.G. JUNG.

APPENDIX II

THE STARS AND ME

Woodrow Wyatt

Donald Reagan: "Virtually every major move and decision the Reagans made during my time as White House Chief of Staff was cleared in advance with a woman in San Francisco who drew up horoscopes...."

This revelation did not startle me. We take the superstitions of religion as normal and acceptable. They are no more rational than consulting astrologers, a practice older than established religions and which does not conflict with them. Sir Stafford Cripps was a devout Christian who believed in what Attlee disparingly described as the "Mumbo Jumbo" of religion as much as he did in conscientiously modelling his life on the precepts of Christ.

I was the personal assistant on the Cabinet Mission to India. We had been having a sticky time with Congress and Muslim League. Stafford asked at his morning conference if anyone knew of an auspicious day on which to announce the mission's conclusions. Part seriously, part jokingly, I said we should apply to the Bengal Government's official astrologer. Stafford at once commanded Mr. Joyce, the press officer from the India Office, to find out from this astrologer the most auspicious day. This was duly done.

In 1947 the Cabinet and Mountbatten, under pressure, chose August 14 as the start of independence for India and Pakistan, hoping this would not be too late. Mr. Jinnah of the Muslim League was unconcerned. The Hindu Indian leaders were troubled. The astrologers had reported that August 14 was not the best of dates and were ordered to select the most promising moment during it. They came up with exactly midnight. So Pakistan began its independence in the morning and India in the middle of the night. India's subsequent history has been somewhat more successful than Pakistan's.

Apart from setbacks and hiccups which inevitably attend an eight-year presidency, Mr. Reagan has been remarkably successful internally and internationally. Perhaps we should be grateful that seemingly he relies more on advice from astrologers than from political commentators and opponents. As Hamlet observed: "There are more things in heaven and earth, Horatio, Than are dreamt of in your philosophy". That goes for archbishops and popes too.

Confess it or not, the vast majority of mankind believes in what it thinks is supernatural. Some intellectuals (see the *Hidden Power* by Brian Inglis) prefer to call it parapsychology. Arthur Koestler founded a professorship in the subject at Edinburgh University.

"Bomber" Harris consulted Lyndoe, the people's astrologer, on the best times for bombing raids on Germany and presumably was not disappointed by the results. Millions daily read the stars' predictions under their signs of the Zodiac in the newspapers because they feel vaguely that there may be some truth in them. But such predictions are unlikely to reach anywhere near the accuracy of, say, Indian astrologers working on a precise time, date and place of birth of the person concerned.

I went to India in the Army in late 1944. I had a friend, K.M. Panikkar, who was Prime Minister of the princely state of Bikaner. He asked me if I would like the court astrologer, K.P. Sharma to cast my horoscope, emphasising that his accuracy had been sharpened by being put in the local lock-up for a day or so any time he made a serious mistake over the Maharajah's immediate future. This was unfair to Mr. Sharma; frequent applications to an astrologer dilute and muddy the brew.

Mr. Sharma, whom I never met and who knew nothing about me (not that there was anything to know I when was 26), cast my horoscope blind in January 1945 from the actual minute and second of my birth, when I knew, and from the house I was born in. The full text is published as a three-page, appendix to my autobiography, *Confession of an Optimist*.

When I have felt down I have been encouraged by looking at it afresh because Mr. Sharma foresaw most the next-to-come good hits in my life. For example, "The royal planet in the tenth (*viz.*, the Sun) also indicated titles and honours in the latter half of life".

I was knighted when I was 64. I was sent to the Lords when I was 68. How the devil could Mr. Sharma tell that and many other things from my stars. But he did. He made amazingly accurate predictions for my friend Panikkar which puzzled us in 1945 but became clear when, unexpectedly ambassador of independent India in Peking (1948-52), he was able, trusted by both, to persuade the Americans and Chinese Communists to begin the negotiations which ended the Korean war. My horoscope is a main reason why I have always been an optimist.

I cannot explain these matters. But there is something going on out there which is real though we do not understand it. Take care how you laugh at Mr. and Mrs. Reagan - the last laugh may be with them.

(Courtesy : THE TIMES, London).

APPENDIX III

Who Doesn't Consult Astrologers

Stephen Pile

RONALD REAGAN consults an astrologer and the whole of America rises up in derision. Politicians mock, the state totters and cartoonists have a field day.

What hypocrisy. You rarely meet Americans without them saying: "You must be a Gemini." They all read their horoscopes with blind devotion and there is such an astrology boom in the U.S. that you or I could buy a tent, set up in business there and make a healthy living.

No less than three state governors consulted a leading British astrologer for advice about standing in the presidential election. What is more, companies have astrologers on the staff to help with product launches and the second most successful stock market analyst on Wall Street openly makes his predictions on astrological basis.

It is exactly the same in Britain, where a significant number of businessmen, politicians, well-known companies, titled folk and people in the city have an astrologer in the way that others might have a chiropodist.

More Auspicious

Nonetheless, the president felt obliged to deny the report. (In that case, would he care to tell us why he delayed his inauguration as the governor of California from the traditional hour of midday to the decidedly eccentric one of a minute past midnight? Astrologers were queueing up to point out that his chart for the second day was far more auspicious than for the previous one.)

More to the point, why does Ronnie feel that he was to deny it? He would be a fool not to consult an astrologer. In his position it would be tantamount to dereliction of duty. Every body else does, particularly some of the shadier dictactors with whom he seems to be so chummy.

General Pinochet in Chile has a hotline to the stars, General Zia of Pakistan took astrological advice before executing Bhutto, as did Sri Lanka before choosing the exact minute in which it became a republic.

There is documentary evidence that Mossad, the Israeli intelligence service, regularly uses astrologers, most notably in the raid of Entebbe. Sheikh Yamani had one in London and organized OPEC meetings according to her advice. Indira Gandhi had whole gangs of them and the Indian astrological press was full of warnings about the planetary dangers at the time of her assassination.

In world history, of course, Ronnie is the rule rather than the exception. The art of divining the future began around 3000 BC in the Tigris-Euphrates basin because they never knew who was going to invade them next or when the river was going to flood. (There was no divination in Egypt because the desert prevented invasion and the Nile flooded at the same time every year.)

Thereafter, all Roman emperors consulted augurs of astrologers, as did Elizabeth I, Napoleon, Lloyd George, Edward VII, Roosevelt, Churchill, the lot. Only the age of reason wiped astrology out for 300 years until the 20th century decided to give it another half-hearted go.

So why should the President put himself at a disadvantage and ignore this ancient tool, particularly at a time when astrology has intertwined with Jungian psychology to the point where it increasingly counsels you on how to make the most of your individual characteristics?

I last week submitted myself to a tarot reader, a psychic, a clairvoyant in Mansfield who worked from a lock of my hair, a dial-a-crystal-ball reading, a palmist, a medium and several astrologers. Most of them got enough right to keep me interested, but were way off beam on much else.

The one who got everything wrong was the medium who learned from the next world that I am dynamic, organised, quick at decisions and destined to be an editor (in my view this is not a fit job for a grown-up and I would re-train as a vet in preference.)

The Mansfield clairvoyant predicted that I would meet a man called Fred with a flat cap, live in Saudi Arabia, sit near a fountain while having a meal and see a rolled-up pink carpet.

My dial-a-crystal-ball reading brought a flood of information, including the fact that there will be only two more popes before Catholic Church disintegrates. I, meanwhile, am going to be very rich, successful, and a public figure, which is nice because the palmist said I would be strapped for cash and never fulfil my potential.

You can see why astrologers want to dissociate themselves from that sort of waffly occult gang. They stand out in that company for their accuracy and seriousness. *(bold ours)* But even here there is a great range of ability.

My worry is not that Reagan consults an astrologer, but that he should consult a good one. Newspaper reports suggest that he uses Miss Joyce Jillson, who acted in Peyton Place and the Sammy Davis Jr show, wrote a booked called *The Fine Art of Flirting and advertises* her $ 1 introductory service in a horoscope magazine. She may be a first-rate astrologer but I would feel much happier if he was visiting some horribly serious, darksuited person in swish consultation rooms who charges a fortune and is known only by word of mouth.

Real Thing

If you want a good astrologer in Britain, for example, you should contact the faculty of astrological studies in Haywards Heath and ask for its list of consultants, all of whom have completed a five-year training course and signed a code of ethics that prevents them for writing a stars column in the press. Few of those people advertise and some may charge up to £ 100 for a session. However, you will be getting the real thing.

Whatever my reservations about even the most unhelpful of the seers I visited, I accept that they were all compassionate, thoughtful, peace loving and aware that human society is a fragile web in which each of us depends upon the others.

Personally, I would much prefer that Ron listens to an astrologer, psychic or a blind woman with a bucket full of duck entrails than, say, Caspar Weinberger or those document-shredding aides. At last, I feel that Ron is in safe hands.

Courtesy: The Sunday Times and Times of India, 14-5- 1988

APPENDIX IV

BRIGHU NADI READING OF BHAGAWAN RAMANA MAHARISHI'S HOROSCOPE*

Shukra asks:

O Brahman, O great Sage, many persons are born when the constellation Libra is raising, how may I have the detailed knowledge of each individual separately?

Brighu replies:

The birth is in the Tula Lagna(Libra Ascendant) and therein (first house)are, you (Venus or Shukra,) O best amongst Brighus.O son, Mercury (Budha) is in the second house; hence the child will be a yogi. In the third house is the Dragon's Head(Rahu), and the Sun is also there. In the fifth house is Jupiter(Guru) so he will be a knower of Truth. Saturn (Shani) is in the sixth house. In the seventh is Mars(Mangal): hence the child is Yogabrishta (fallen from Yoga). In the ninth house is the Dragon's Tail (Ketu), and the Moon is also there; for this reason he will know the Self in the end.

The correct time of birth (as calculated from sunrise) being :- 48 Ghatis, O Pala, 30 Vipala, 4 Truties. A configuration as this (this Yoga) is

* Furnished by Sri T.N.Venkataraman, President, Sri Ramanasramam, Tiruvannamalai

called"Mukti Sadhaka" (achiever of liberation.) One born in this configuration will see the world as Brahman. He was born on Monday the first superimposed by the second thithi of the Dark half in the month of Marghasheersha, when the Moon was in that Asterism (Nakshatra) which comes after Ardra, viz., Diti (or Punarvasu). He the best among the Brahmins, will be desirous of Liberation (Moksha).. He will be possessed of an elder brother and a younger brother and other possibilities (of Brothers) being destroyed. And I have nothing to say about sisters.

His education will be in accordance with the time and place(he is born in), and his (knowledge) of English will be (just enough) for practical purposes. He will be coming in contact with (study) Philosophy, and though living like an ordinary man, he will be mentally detached. In his palm there is line which will bring him honour and success; at the base of the second (ring) finger, which is actually a Yoga-line, indicative of his desire for Moksha and Omniscience; he will be a knower of truth and he will look upon all equally. He will obtain great fame and respect and a mere sight of him will destroy all sins.

This child (or, from his childhood he) will be pure minded and will aspire to the realisation of Hari. Even though (in his past incarnation) he had made atonements (purification) for his past sins(as will be clear later), he will suffer from severe illness in his childhood; in his thirteenth year his father will go to Heaven (die). His mother will become a widow. The mother will be beloved of the brothers, but this child being disinterested, (in worldly affairs), there will be dissension in the home. Having renounced everything, he will be seer of the self. And again, out of an intense desire to obtain realisation of Brahman, and having left his home, he will practice complete control over the processes of his mind. He of pure heart, having gone to the Holy mountain, will, station himself in a quiet place, and there, his doubts removed, will be intent on the vision of God. Later, many diseases will assail his body; he, however will become pure(free from illness) not only in body, but in soul and mind. He will progress in the practice of Yoga, and absorbed in Yoga he will reach the Samadhi (supramental spiritual consciousness). The cause of everything that happens to all embodied beings is contained in what they have earned or acquired (by their actions) in past births.

Sukra asks:

O Brahman, tell me in the first place what happened in his previous life, by knowledge of which I may have divine vision (explanation of why and wherefore of the present life).

Brighu replies:

O Shukra, in his former life he was a highly intelligent Brahman, who had mastered the lore of the Vedas and was devoted to the worship of God. Intellectual, one who had progressed far along the path of knowledge(Gnyan), he was in the first rank of those learned in the scriptures. Conceited in his learning, he was, however, despised by other learned men. One Pandit, tormented by an insult, cursed him, saying "May you be debased in birth after birth; may you fall from the path of salvation and be born again on this earth." When he heard this terrible and unbearable curse he resorted to reciting the Gayatri Mantra (the mother of the Vedas); and later he became a Sanyasi(an ascetic). After a long time O Shukra he died and guided by destiny, took birth as a Brahmin having knowledge of Brahman and possessing characteristics as have been related before.

Shukra says:

Tell me all the incidents of his life while he remains on earth, beginning with his birth, and also the ceremony of purification, etc.

Brighu replies:

At the moment of his birth a certain old woman of the name of Sulochana (or one who had beautiful eyes) obtained divine vision in which she had a luminous experience of Brahman. O best amongst Brighus, his father will be a lawyer at the Court. From his birth upto his tenth year his father will have respect and standing as a leading lawyer. They will be three brothers, himself being the middle one. His mind will be on learning his lessons, and he will be agile and fond of playing. During those(ten) years he will occasionally have troubles(e.g. minor illness). During his 11th or 12th years he will be devoted to his studies. At this stage an effort (a purificatory penance as prescribed by Brighu) should be made to save the life of his father; but as my words will not be heard no effort will be made. In the thirteenth year his father will go Heaven (die); and his mother having become a widow, will give up all her ornaments.

During his 14th and 15th years, a certain Brahmin will give him spiritual instructions and hearing his words, he will leave his home and resort to Arunachala. Here he will stay, and his doubts having departed, he will gradually acquire knowledge of Brahman. This boy, being a portion of Divinity and because of the actions of his past lives, will desire Spiritual Liberation. At this time a Brahmin, who has taken a vow of silence, comes and takes shelter with him. Again some mischievous boys starts dropping stones upon him. Thereupon renouncing everything (leaving that place) he who has taken the vow of silence takes shelter on Arunachala, maintaining his silence. Up to his 18th year he will observe silence as a means of finding truth. Some times trouble will come to him(e.g. small illness), but he will be protected by merit acquired in the past (by his good deeds). Now, his preminded mother who was very much worried and depressed (by his absence) and desired the return of her son will come to him accompanied by his brother. He, however, being wise and knowing Truth, the mother and brother become disappointed and return home full of anxiety. After that, O Shukra, his knowledge and detachment will increase. Suddenly one day a huge python comes but when he sees this python, the python goes away. His knowledge increases and he becomes a Sidha (a perfect sage).

During his 20th and 21st years : - His elder brother goes to Heaven(dies). During his 22nd, 23rd, and 24th years: his mother again visits him and she, having seen her son, returns home. Also a certain eminent Brahmin comes to see him. He will become a knower of Brahman, and will be known (henceforth, by the name of "Maharshi". Beginning with the 26th year up to the 31st year he becomes known by this name "Maharshi" and is respected by the people around. He—who knows Brahman—the Truth, and whose mind is free gives spiritual instructions(to disciples). During his 35th and 36th year: His brother's wife dies. His mother arrives accompanied by his younger brother. His fame spreads and he is more widely respected: a hermitage(Ashram) like a small village springs up.

Between his 37th and 41st years he becomes indeed a Yogi and his mother goes to heaven. During his 42nd and 44th years there is mortal danger from night prowlers. There is indeed graver danger. The thieves,however, are however unsuccessful. Later, all these thieves though, for committing an offence at some other place, receive the king's punishment as the result of which they perish. From his 45th to 56th year he becomes a King amongst Yogis-the knower of Brahman with a mind unattached. His fame becomes great and he is worshiped by the people to whom he is unattached.

O Shukra, in his 57th year, a certain Solicitor (literally, an adviser in the Court) to whom God is dear, and who is desirous of knowing the qualities of a Yogi will come to hear my words. He (the Solicitor who is also a knower of Brahman, will hear my words first; afterwards, he himself (the Maharshi) will read them, so also will many other people. In the extra month of Bhadrapada the many people staying in the Ashrama, having heard these words, will be wonderstruck

My words should be kept secret and should not be given to the bad, roguish and sinful people ; they should be divulged only to the calm, the devoted, the pure and the firm. In the Kali age, the sinful and wicked people will decry my words and call them false, imagining themselves to be intelligent. Furthermore, in the performance, of the Prayaschitta (purificatory penance) hindrances will arise from day to day; these being the results of sin will say otherwise (i.e., deter from its performance). Therefore, on hearing this, the effort (the ceremony) should be made with the liberal mind and in accordance with the prescribed rites.

Shukra asks :

O great Yogi, if you would be kind to me please tell me whose pooja he should perform and what money in charity he should give so that he may not experience trouble even in dreams and he may become as a child of God.

Brighu replies:

He should make a heap of 400 tolas of gold(the lines from 130 and 141 are omitted since they relate exclusively to the mode of ceremony)

If he does the Prayaschitta ceremony in this manner his knowledge of Brahman will be perfect. By its non-performance there will be mental anxiety and his Yoga will go astray.

His disciples, therefore, should perform the prayaschitta (by doing which) he will becomes lustrous, knower of Brahman and respected of the people, and ultimately a perfect Yogi with infallible will (possessing all Divine powers).

(Line 147 seems a mistake, therefore omitted here).

During his 58th, 59th and 60th years, he shines like a being liberated though dwelling in the body, and has great love for his devotees. He experiences great bliss. he is as though a living image of the Vedas, puissant and ever dutiful.

Now and then ill health arises, but disappears of itself. Pure and holy himself, and therefore beyond the need of acquiring virtue he takes joy in doing religious deeds and works of charity (for the sake of good example).

During his 61st, 62nd,and 63rd years the Light in him increases and burns like fire,and he shines like liberation incarnate.

During his 64th, 65th and 66th years I declare (about) concerning this unattached great Being that he now becomes equal to the highest Brahman (achieves complete unity with Brahman, the highest state of perfection). His face shines with beautiful light, the very sight of which is enough .o give one salvation.

During his 67th, 68th and 69th years this Yogi of Yogis_ this knower of Brahman whose mind is unfettered may have illness which would be cured by the practice of Yoga.

In the 70th, 71st and 72nd years he who has realised truth obtained supre.ne knowledge and achieved complete freedom will dangerously ill towards end, and if finally he is brought back to health by means of Yoga, then alone will happen what I say further.

From the 73rd to the 80th years he will be even as the Supreme Brahman, and will occupy himself in devotion and service to God.

Finally death will approach and in a waking state he will pass into the Supreme trance (Samadhi). If death turns back he will then die in his 83rd year, in the month of Magh on the

12th of bright half in the early part of the night when his body will resolve itself into the five Elements and the Spirit will rest at the feet of Vishnu (Supreme Deity).

If this Yogi does perform the Prayaschitta he will have all the wealth of spiritual power, but by its omission the result will be to the contrary.

Thus I have related the incidents of his life as seen from the first house, which is the most important, and also, though briefly, the other houses, after hearing which nothing more remains to be known.

Thus ends the Horoscope of the Monarch of Yogis in the Sub- Chapter called "Kundali", in the seventh Chapter of the Brighu- Samhita which contains a dialogue between Brighu and Shukra.

ASTROLOGY

AND THE

HOAX

OF

"SCIENTIFIC TEMPER"

Chief Editor

GAYATRI DEVI VASUDEV

MOTILAL BANARSIDASS PUBLISHERS
PRIVATE LIMITED • DELHI

First Edition: 1989
Revised Edition: Delhi, 1998

ISBN: 81-208-1587-4

MOTILAL BANARSIDASS
41 U.A. Bungalow Road, Jawahar Nagar, Delhi 110 007
8 Mahalaxmi Chamber, Warden Road, Mumbai 400 026
120 Royapettah High Road, Mylapore, Chennai 600 004
Sanas Plaza, Subhash Nagar, Pune 411 002
16 St. Mark's Road, Bangalore 560 001
8 Camac Street, Calcutta 700 017
Ashok Rajpath, Patna 800 004
Chowk, Varanasi 221 001

PRINTED IN INDIA
BY JAINENDRA PRAKASH JAIN AT SHRI JAINENDRA PRESS,
A-45 NARAINA INDUSTRIAL AREA, PHASE I, NEW DELHI 110 028
AND PUBLISHED BY NARENDRA PRAKASH JAIN FOR
MOTILAL BANARSIDASS PUBLISHERS PRIVATE LIMITED,
BUNGALOW ROAD, DELHI 110 007